3 0183 03657 6377

D1483524

Residential Landscape Sustainability

Residential Landscape Sustainability

A Checklist Tool

Carl Smith

Andy Clayden

Nigel Dunnett

Department of Landscape
The University of Sheffield
UK

Blackwell Publishing

© 2008 by Carl Smith, Andy Clayden and Nigel Dunnett

Blackwell Publishing editorial offices:
Blackwell Publishing Ltd, 9600 Garsington Road, Oxford OX4 2DQ, UK
Tel: +44 (0)1865 776868
Blackwell Publishing Inc., 350 Main Street, Malden, MA 02148-5020, USA
Tel: +1 781 388 8250
Blackwell Publishing Asia Pty Ltd, 550 Swanston Street, Carlton, Victoria 3053, Australia
Tel: +61 (0)3 8359 1011

First published 2008 by Blackwell Publishing Ltd

ISBN: 978-1-4051-5873-2

Library of Congress Cataloging-in-Publication Data

Clayden, Andy.
Residential landscape sustainability / Carl Smith, Andy Clayden, Nigel Dunnett.
p. cm.
Includes bibliographical references and index.
ISBN-13: 978-1-4051-5873-2 (hardback : alk. paper)
1. Landscape design.   2. Gardens–Environmental aspects.   3. Sustainable horticulture.   4. Building sites–
Planning.   5. Ecological houses.   I. Dunnett, Nigel.   II. Smith, Carl, 1974–   III. Title.
SB472.45.C59 2007
711′.58–dc22
2007011458

A catalogue record for this title is available from the British Library

Set in 11 on 13.5 pt Avenir
by SNP Best-set Typesetter Ltd., Hong Kong
Printed and bound in Singapore
by Markono Print Media Pte Ltd

The publisher's policy is to use permanent paper from mills that operate a sustainable forestry policy, and which has been manufactured from pulp processed using acid-free and elementary chlorine-free practices. Furthermore, the publisher ensures that the text paper and cover board used have met acceptable environmental accreditation standards.

For further information on Blackwell Publishing, visit our website:
www.blackwellpublishing.com

Contents

Acknowledgements

The authors would like to thank the National House-Building Council (NHBC) for funding the research and in particular their Technical Director Christopher Mills for his enthusiasm and advice. We would also like to thank the Building Research Establishment (BRE) for their advice and support concerning *EcoHomes* and the selection of case studies. Finally the development and testing of the Residential Landscape Sustainability Checklist would not have been possible without the considerable input of numerous private house builders, registered social landlords, design professionals and contractors who gave generously of their time in supplying documents and attending interviews: in particular, we would like to acknowledge the contribution of Mike O'Connell, Andrew Upton and Andrew Day. Many thanks also to Bob Bray, Don Munro and David Singleton for their helpful comments concerning the evolving checklist.

Chapter 1

Putting residential development in a sustainable context

Introduction

In December 2006 the UK Chancellor, Gordon Brown, announced in his pre-budget statement that within a decade all new homes should be carbon-neutral. This is a highly laudable ambition given the growing concerns about climate change and the government's drive to create more than 4 million new homes by 2020.

But what about our ambitions for the new landscape within which this housing will be built? Doesn't it also have a role to play in creating a more sustainable future; shouldn't it also be carbon-neutral or, even better, carbon-negative? The landscape has the potential to reduce the energy demands of the building by sheltering it from cold winds in winter or by creating shade in summer. The design of public and private outdoor spaces can also have a significant bearing on how we live, by encouraging us to adopt a more sustainable lifestyle. As will be discussed in Chapter 2, there are many ways in which a landscape designed with sustainability in mind can make an important contribution to the environmental profile of an entire development. It is equally true that we can negate much of the good work that is currently being achieved in sustainable building design by not applying the same rigour to the design of the landscape. We cannot assume that because a landscape is 'green' it is not also energy-demanding, polluting or wasteful of resources, potentially offering very little to the residents and wildlife that inhabit it.

The aim of this book is to provide a resource that will assist housing developers, landscape architects, architects, planners and other professionals involved in residential housing design to create more sustainable residential environments. The book focuses on the development of a residential landscape sustainability checklist, a tool that can be used to score the environmental performance of a residential landscape. The checklist was developed as part of a research study which aimed to evaluate the contribution that the landscape makes to the overall sustainable profile of a new residential development, including the public and private realm. Although the checklist was used to quantify the environmental performance of built developments, we believe that its real value is in helping the designer to reflect on the environmental implications of a scheme throughout the design process, from site planning through to detailed design. The checklist was specifically developed to assess new residential landscapes and therefore includes assessment and guidance that are particularly pertinent to this type of development, for example, the provision of private garden space.

However, much of the information which has been gathered to produce the checklist could equally be applied to a wide range of different types of landscape development, including school grounds, business/retail parks and public parks. For example, the checklist considers the environmental impact of landscape materials and specifically focuses on the contribution that new planting can make to promoting biodiversity. Similarly, although the original research on which this book is based, and the piloting of the landscape checklist, took place in England (and the policy context outlined in this chapter focuses on the UK), much of the guidance can be applied elsewhere. In fact, a good deal of the information compiled within the checklist is derived from international research. The authors have disseminated much of the information contained within this book through teaching and seminar presentations throughout the UK, Europe and North America. The information contained in this book allows designers to deal with global problems through practical, local application of knowledge.

The book is organized into four chapters. The first chapter explores definitions of sustainability, specifically landscape sustainability and how this is now framed within planning and Government guidance. It also introduces and discusses initiatives which have aimed to deliver sustainable residential development, including Urban Villages, Millennium Communities and environmental certification.

Chapter 2 identifies opportunities for improving the sustainable profile of new residential developments through landscape planning, design and management. This chapter is broadly divided into two themes. The first theme looks at ways in which resources can be conserved and pollution and waste minimised. For example, this includes how site planning and appropriate planting design and conservation may reduce energy consumption for domestic heating and cooling by creating winter shelter and summer shading. It also looks at the specification and design of hard and soft materials and how these may impact upon the environment. The second theme looks at the existing habitat of each site and how this may be protected and enhanced in order to contribute to ecological diversity and human well-being. Within this chapter there is an important discussion about the relative merits of using non-native species and their potential role in contributing to biodiversity, especially with regard to disturbed and potentially polluted and damaged urban brownfield sites. The chapter concludes by exploring how sustainable landscape design can contribute to human health and well-being. It looks specifically at garden size and how this may impact on delivering sustainability by, for example, providing adequate space for composting, clothes drying, children's play and possibly even vegetable and fruit gardening.

Chapter 3 begins by reviewing a selection of the assessment tools that have been developed internationally to assess the sustainability of residential developments and identifies their limitations concerning the evaluation of the landscape. This chapter also explains the rationale for adopting the *EcoHomes* assessment tool as the template on which to develop a landscape checklist. *EcoHomes* is the most commonly used tool in the UK for assessing residential sustainability, it is a compulsory assessment for all new housing funded by the Housing Corporation, and it has been instrumental in informing the development of the Government's new Code for Sustainable Homes.

Chapter 4 looks at how the Residential Landscape Sustainability Checklist was piloted and used to assess the sustainability of residential landscapes, for developments that have been promoted as 'sustainable' by some recognised measure. It specifically focuses on two case studies: Greenwich Millennium Village, London, and Childwall, Liverpool. The assessment results for these two developments are discussed in the context of the other sites that were evaluated. The different factors that have either contributed to or discouraged landscape sustainability are then discussed.

The book concludes with a full version of the Residential Landscape Sustainability Checklist. The checklist sets out each of the assessment categories and identifies where credits can be awarded. For each section there is a summary of the literature which has been used to inform the allocation of credits.

Definitions of sustainable development and sustainable landscape

Sustainable development

In 1987 the World Commission on Environment and Development (WCED) published *Our Common Future* (The Bruntland Report). This report brought the concept of sustainable development onto the international agenda for the first time (Sustainable Development, 2000) and defined sustainable development as:

'*development which meets the needs of the present without compromising the ability of future generations to meet their own needs*'.

(WCED, 1987, p 43)

This definition has now been widely accepted, although some authors have sought to add further flesh to it. For example, Barton *et al.* (1995) state that sustainable development is:

'*. . . about maintaining and enhancing the quality of human life . . . while living within the carrying capacity of supporting eco-systems and the resource base. Sustainability is about the maintenance of the health of the biosphere and the husbanding of key resources of air, water, land and minerals. The notion of development in the context of sustainability is broader than economic growth or GNP. It implies improvement to the quality of life, health and nutritional status, equity . . . [and the] perceived quality of the human environment*'.

(Barton *et al.*, 1995, p 8)

In other words, although developments for industry, commerce, retail and housing are vital to a prosperous economy (HM Treasury, 2004; ODPM, 2005a) they are sustainable only if planned, designed, constructed and managed with sensitivity to people and the environment. Farookhi (1998) simply states that sustainable development is about achieving the right balance, a point which is illustrated by Barton (2000) in Figure 1.1 where environmental, economic and social needs come together.

Other authors have also identified the need for balance and integration when defining sustainable development and aspects thereof (see Table 1.1).

Sustainable landscape

Landscape architecture has a fundamental relationship with the environment; it starts with 'place' and each place has its own unique qualities and attributes. The development of the landscape, especially in cases where it has been damaged through previous activities, may enhance the environmental contribution of that place; but it may also diminish it. There is a danger that those who work in the landscape profession will assume that the places they design and build are implicitly 'eco-friendly' (Thompson & Sorvig, 2000). However, designed landscapes frequently overuse energy, water, pesticides and fertilisers and non-renewable materials, and often do more to eliminate biodiversity than to preserve or enhance it.

'*When self-sustaining ecosystems are converted to built landscapes, the hidden costs may include soil loss, degradation of*

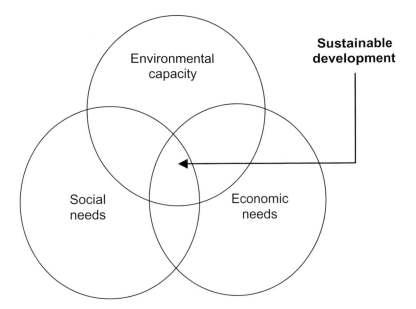

Figure 1.1 Sustainable development fulfils economic needs, but also fulfils social needs and works within limits set by the environment. (Reproduced with permission from Barton, H. (2000) Conflicting perceptions of neighbourhood. In: *Sustainable Communities: The Potential for Eco-Neighbourhoods.* H. Barton (Ed.) London: Earthscan.)

> *'water, introduction of toxic and non-renewable materials, and un-sustainable energy use.'*
>
> (Thompson & Sorvig, 2000, p 1)

We may delude ourselves into thinking that because the 'landscape' of a development includes plants, then by its very nature that landscape must be a force for good in creating sustainable environments. Sadly, this is not always true. Putting aside the argument of whether we should be using native or ornamental species, plant production can require huge amounts of resources in energy for heating and transport, irrigation and fertilisers. If there is a danger that even the vegetation we use is potentially more detrimental to the environment than it is beneficial, it might be argued that:

> *'. . . most products of landscape architecture are simply not sustainable by any definition'.*
>
> (Thayer, 1989, p 102)

In considering the environmental impact of any designed landscape it may be helpful to think about them as a system in which there are inputs, outputs and internal cycling (Dunnett & Clayden, 2000). An unsustainable landscape of the type described above can be viewed as 'greedy' and 'wasteful' with requirements for high resource inputs, minimal internal cycling and large waste releases (Figure 1.2).

Table 1.1 Definitions of sustainable development and aspects thereof. References: *Barton (2000); **Ekins (2000); #Forman (1995); †Elkin et al. (1991); ‡Williams et al. (2000); ††Smith et al. (1998); ‡‡DETR (2000a).

Specific Aspect of Discussion	Definition
Sustainable development	Solutions that successfully marry human welfare and ecological robustness.* Provides a simultaneous increase in the quality of human life and the maintenance of important environmental functions. It is therefore a process involving the improvement of the human condition in a context of environmental sustainability.**
Sustainable environment	An area in which ecological integrity and human needs are concurrently maintained over generations.#
Sustainable cities	User-friendly, resourceful and energy efficient . . . a place for living.† The city functions within its natural carrying capacity, is user-friendly for its occupants and promotes social equity.‡
Sustainable built environments	Provided for through environmental 'interest' rather than 'capital', does not breach critical environmental thresholds, and develops a sense of equity and social justice.††
Sustainable communities	Where human welfare and the environment are reconciled and integrated, rather than traded off against each other.‡‡

A sustainable landscape will aim to minimise the inputs of non-renewable resources and energy, maximise levels of internal recycling and improve the environmental quality of all outputs where possible. This alternative system is presented in Figure 1.3.

Although the focus of this book is how we might improve the environmental sustainability of residential landscapes, it is also important to remember that to achieve the wider goal of sustainable development, this must also be balanced with meeting other sustainable objectives, including social and economic needs. A sustainable landscape is one that balances human needs and the environment.

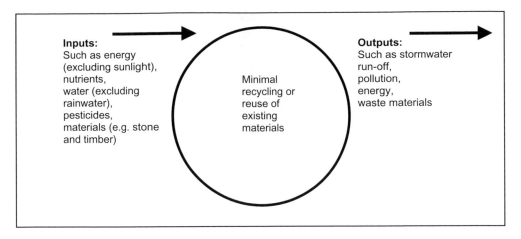

Figure 1.2 A system approach to an unsustainable landscape. (Reproduced with permission from Dunnett, N. & Clayden, A. (2000) Resources: the raw materials of landscape. In: *Landscape and Sustainability*. J.F. Benson & M.H. Roe (Eds) London, Taylor & Francis Ltd.)

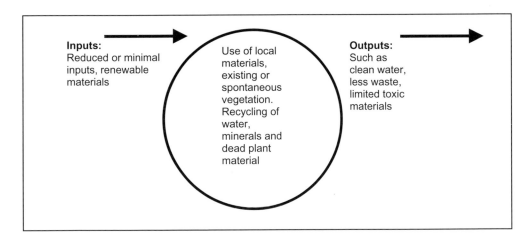

Figure 1.3 A system approach to a sustainable landscape. (Reproduced with permission from Dunnett, N. & Clayden, A. (2000) Resources: the raw materials of landscape. In: *Landscape and Sustainability*. J.F. Benson & M.H. Roe (Eds) London, Taylor & Francis Ltd.)

The social dimension is extremely important. A designed landscape may tick all the right boxes from an environmental perspective but may also appear unkempt or even potentially threatening to the community it serves. We need to find ways of improving the connectivity between people and their environment (Ruff, 1982). Only by improving these connections and our understanding of the importance of the natural processes that are at work are we likely to conserve and protect our local environments, to enjoy using them but, perhaps most importantly, to make the kind of changes in our lifestyles necessary to minimise our own environmental impact. Through design and a growing awareness of the effect that our actions have on the environment, we might find ways of encouraging people, for example, to leave their cars at home and either walk or cycle to work.

Sustainable landscapes are therefore those which:

> '. . . contribute to human well-being and at the same time are in harmony with the natural environment, work with native land-scape conditions, do not deplete or damage other ecosystems, (and) conserve valuable resources such as water, soil, nutrients (and) energy'.

> (CELA, 1988, cited in Thayer, 1994, p 237)

Sustainable development in English planning and development

Any discussion of sustainable development needs to be placed within the context of an evolving set of Government development policies and strategies. For more than a decade, the concept of sustainable development has been taking an ever more central role in planning and development in the UK. Following acts of Parliament in 1999 and 2000, the Scottish Executive, the National Assembly for Wales and the Northern Ireland Office were formed as devolved governments, each responsible for setting individual (but co-ordinated) planning systems with separate White Papers and circulars, and for overseeing the revision of their own planning policy guidance. Since devolution, the UK Government retains these responsibilities for England alone.

The UK Government was one of the first to act on the recommendations of the 1992 United Nations Conference on Environment and Development (the Rio Earth Summit). In 1994 it published its own cross-departmental national strategy, *Sustainable Development: The UK Strategy* (HM Government, 1994), which required local authorities to work with local communities to implement sustainability through Local Agenda 21 strategies (Bhatti, 1996; Patterson & Theobald, 1995). It has been suggested that by the mid-1990s the concept of sustainable development had become the central plank of the UK Government's planning policies (McGhie & Girling, 1995). One of the model components for Local Agenda 21 strategies was the assimilation of these national policies into local authority planning policies (DEFRA, 1998).

In 1999, a new national strategy, *A Better Quality of Life – A Strategy for Sustainable Development for the UK* (HM Government, 1999), was published. The four aims of the strategy suggested a holistic vision of sustainable development similar to those in Table 1.1:

- social progress which recognises the needs of everyone
- effective protection of the environment
- prudent use of natural resources
- maintenance of high and stable levels of economic growth and employment.

The 1999 strategy introduced 147 sustainable development indicators, allowing performance to be reviewed and reported annually (HM Government, 1999). These indicators were published in 1999 (DETR, 1999). Following devolution, the Welsh, Scottish and Northern Irish devolved governments interpreted the UK strategy through their own planning systems.[1] In England, in the same year, there was also the publication of the Urban Task Force report, *Towards an Urban Renaissance* (Urban Task Force, 1999). In response, the Government published its urban White Paper, *Our Towns and Cities: The Future – Delivering an Urban Renaissance*, which, together with its sister rural paper, *Our Countryside: The Future – A Fair Deal for Rural England*, placed sustainable development principles at the heart of Government policies (DEFRA, 2000; DETR, 2000b). At the same time, many of the planning policy guidance notes (PPGs) for England were revised, with a view to further strengthening the position of sustainable development in development plans and within the development control process. For example, the revised *PPG 1: General Policy and Principles* stated that:

> 'A key role of the [English] planning system is to enable the provision of homes and buildings, investment and jobs in a way which is consistent with the principles of sustainable development'.
>
> (DTLR, 2001a, p 1)

In 2003, the Government launched a new sustainable communities plan for England: the White Paper *Sustainable Communities: Building for the Future* (ODPM, 2003a). The plan looked to build on the previous policies within the urban and rural White Papers, by setting out a programme of policies and spending with which to address community problems. Foremost of these was the pressing shortage of affordable housing in the South East and abandonment of housing elsewhere. However, the plan also stressed the need for decent homes and a good-quality local environment in all English regions (ODPM, 2003a).

---

[1] Commitment to sustainable development is a common feature of each of the devolved planning systems in Wales, Scotland and Northern Ireland. In Wales, the assembly states that sustainability lies at the heart of the Welsh planning process (NAW, 2002). *Scottish Planning Policy Note 1: The Planning System* (SPP 1) highlights the Scottish planning system's duty to ensure sustainable development (SE, 2002). Finally, in Northern Ireland, *Planning Policy Statement 1: General Principles* again sets out a commitment to sustainable development through planning (DoE [NI], 1998).

In 2004, the Planning and Compulsory Purchase Act made sustainability appraisals mandatory for development plans and supplementary planning documents in England, Wales and Northern Ireland[2] (ODPM, 2004). This will ensure that sustainable development principles continue to be integrated into English development plans, and other local planning policy documents, irrespective of any commitment previously made by authorities under their Local Agenda 21 strategy.[3]

In January 2005 the Government launched revised over-arching planning guidance for England to replace PPG 1. *Planning Policy Statement 1: Delivering Sustainable Development*, as the title suggests, continues the assimilation of sustainable development into the English planning system.

> *'Sustainable development is the core principle underpinning [English] planning.'*
>
> (ODPM, 2005a)

PPS 1 builds its policies squarely on the four aims of the 1999 UK strategy given above, and emphasises the key role planning must take in the fulfilment of the Government's sustainable communities plan.

In March 2005, in response to the 2002 UN World Summit on Sustainable Development in Johannesburg, the UK Government launched its latest national sustainability strategy, *Securing the Future: Delivering the UK Sustainable Development Strategy* (HM Government, 2005). The policies in the new strategy only apply to England, though the Government has tasked the devolved governments of Wales, Scotland and Northern Ireland with creating their own strategies, to sit within a common framework of shared goals and indicators (HM Government, 2005). The UK strategy again emphasises the importance of placing sustainable development at the heart of the planning system and within all planning policy guidance. The four aims from the 1999 strategy survive into the new document but the suite of UK sustainable development indicators was rationalised from 147 to 68.

The strategies outlined above do not provide detail as to how sustainable development is to be achieved. However, they have been well supported through Government-sponsored guidance and advice for English planners, developers and designers. Table 1.2 describes some of the supporting texts that have been made available over the last ten years by Government and associated agencies.

---

[2] Although having devolved powers in term of setting planning policy, publishing White Papers and circulars, the National Assembly for Wales and the Northern Ireland Office do not have primary legislative powers. Acts of UK Parliament therefore remain the source of primary legislation for these devolved countries (though not Scotland, which does have primary legislative powers).
[3] Although over 400 Local Agenda 21 strategies had been published in the UK by 2000, they are no longer currently pursued by all local authorities (HM Government, 2005).

Table 1.2 Government-sponsored texts supporting sustainable planning policy in England. *The Government's national regeneration agency; **a non-departmental public body sponsored by Government; [†]the Government-sponsored agency for promotion of design quality.

Reference	Source/Sponsor	Title/Description
Barton *et al.* (1995)	Local Government Management Board (produced as part of the Local Agenda 21 Initiative)	*Sustainable Settlements: A Guide for Planners, Designers and Developers.* A comprehensive guide intended to help stakeholders convert the theory of sustainable development into action. Areas covered: architectural design; landscape design; site layout and urban design.
DETR (1998)	Department of the Environment, Transport & the Regions	*Building a Sustainable Future: Homes for an Autonomous Community.* Sets out the basic requirements for a sustainable community, including architectural design and site layout.
Sustainable Development (2000)	Department of the Environment, Transport & the Regions	*Building a Better Quality of Life. A Strategy for More Sustainable Construction.* Identified priorities for action within the construction industry, if the challenge of the 1999 UK sustainability strategy was to be met.
English Partnerships/ Housing Corporation (2000)	English Partnerships* and the Housing Corporation**	*The Urban Design Compendium.* A guide for local authorities, developers and designers on achieving high-quality, more sustainable urban landscape design and building layout in line with the Urban Task Force Report of 1999
DETR/CABE (2000)	Department of the Environment, Transport & the Regions and the Commission for Architecture & the Built Environment[†]	*By Design. Urban Design in the Planning System: Towards Better Practice.* Scope broadly similar to the above document.
DTLR/CABE (2001)	Department for Transport, Local Government & the Regions and the Commission for Architecture & the Built Environment[†]	*Better Places to Live By Design: A Companion Guide to PPG 3.* A guide for local authorities, developers and designers on achieving high-quality, more sustainable residential landscape design and building layout in line with the Urban Task Force Report of 1999 and the revised PPG 3 of 2000.

Table 1.2 *Continued*

Reference	Source/Sponsor	Title/Description
ODPM (2003b)	Office of the Deputy Prime Minister	*Planning for Sustainable Development: Towards Better Practice.* A guide for planners on incorporating sustainable development into local plans, and advice on spatial strategies to deliver sustainable objectives such as reduced car use, nature conservation and energy conservation.
CABE (2005)	Commission for Architecture & the Built Environment	*Creating Successful Neighbourhoods: Lessons and Actions for Housing Market Renewal.* Collates case studies and good practice advice for regeneration of areas of England's North and Midlands which have a recent history of housing abandonment and housing market failure. Includes advice on high design quality and sustainability in housing regeneration.

However, as pointed out by the World Wildlife Fund for Nature (WWF), to be fully effective in encouraging sustainable development, the planning system needs to be complemented by the building regulations, which control the detailed design and construction of buildings and associated services and spaces (WWF, 2004a). In January 2004 a private member's bill, the *Sustainable and Secure Buildings Bill,* was presented to Parliament. The bill aimed to make buildings and associated services and structures more sustainable (and safer), by bringing sustainability issues into the building regulations (WWF, 2004b). The bill received cross-party support, as well as the backing of the Sustainable Buildings Task Group (SBTG), a body formed in 2003 under the aegis of the ODPM (now Communities and Local Government), DEFRA and DTI to advise Government on sustainability in English development (SBTG, 2004). In September 2004, the bill received Royal Assent and became law for England and Wales. The bill gives new powers under the Buildings Act 1984, so that green issues can be addressed through the building regulations.

The key role of housing in sustainable development

Appropriate new housing is crucial to delivering sustainable development in England and the rest of the UK. Of the 147 national indicators introduced as part of the UK Government's 1999 sustainable development strategy, 70 could be linked to housing and community issues (Ekins, 2000; Housing Corporation, 2002a; WWF, 2004c). When this list was revised in 2005 down to 68 indicators, 33 of the new indicators continued to be directly related to housing and community issues. This reinforces the pivotal role that housing plays in achieving a sustainable society. Edwards (2000) highlights the importance that is attached to housing by seeing it as the central element which links together economic development, environment and social welfare (see Figure 1.4). He states that:

> 'No society is balanced and in harmony with nature unless housing is sustainable. [Also] housing is central to perceptions of quality of life [and] is the agent that cements communities'.
>
> (Edwards, 2000, p 12)

Ekins (2000) has also suggested that housing is an activity with deep connections to sustainable development, and listed the following reasons for this connection.

- Housing is a basic human need. Its quality, price and availability are crucially important to quality of life.
- The location, planning, layout and design of housing make an important contribution to community spirit.

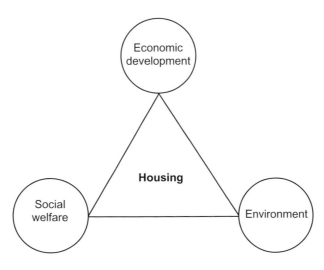

Figure 1.4 The importance of housing in a sustainable society. (Edwards, B. (2000) Sustainable housing: architecture, society and professionalism. In: *Sustainable Housing: Principles and Practice*. B. Edwards & D. Turrent. (Eds) London: T & F, Spon.)

- The siting of houses and the materials from which they (and their environments) are made, and the uses their occupants make of such resources as energy and water, all have major environmental implications.

With regard to the latter point, Table 1.3 provides a summary quantification of some of the environmental impacts of house-building and occupation in the UK as a whole. It gives an indication of the impact which housing has on the environment in terms of both the consumption of finite resources and pollution from domestic waste and energy consumption.

Housing also contributes to impacts of the wider construction industry, described by Howard (2000) as the largest consumer of resources in the UK. A summary of the impacts of the UK construction industry as a whole (where figures could not be found for housing alone) is given in Table 1.4.

Housing is also crucial to the economy of the UK as a whole (HM Treasury, 2004) and England specifically (ODPM, 2005a). As already noted, housing is a key component of quality of life; poor-quality housing causes harm to the physical and mental health of residents and is also understood to have major impacts on educational performance and crime rates (WWF, 2004c). Simply put, our homes have significant environmental, social and economic impacts throughout their lifetime. In recognising this point, the Government has tried to specifically address this through planning guidance. *PPG3: Housing* was revised in 2000 and the creation of sustainable residential

Table 1.3 Summary of environmental impacts associated with UK housing. References: WWF (2004d); Rao *et al.* (2000); Howard (2000).

Impact	Quantification
Timber use	Approx. 20 million m^3 in UK housing construction p/a, over 98% being imported from northern Europe or Canada/USA.
Aggregate use	50 tonnes of aggregate per new home, with recycled materials accounting for only 17% of the current market.
Energy use/CO_2 emissions	Housing in use accounts for 27% of UK's emissions p/a. Also construction of homes (manufacture and transport of materials) accounts for 3% of the UK's total energy consumption.
Domestic refuse	34 million tonnes p/a, with only 12% recycled.

Table 1.4 Summary of environmental impacts associated with UK construction industry. References: WWF (2004c,d); Rao *et al.* (2000); Howard (2000); Smith *et al.* (1998); Skinner (1998).

Impact	Quantification
Raw resources	Figures in million tonnes p/a: aggregates, 160; concrete aggregates, 100; road-stone, 80; iron/steel, 25; cement, 20; masonry, 15. In total approx. 6 tonnes of building materials are used per person, p/a in the UK.
Construction and demolition waste	Approx. 70 million tonnes p/a in UK; estimates vary as to the amount recovered, from one-fifth to one-third.
Energy use/CO_2 emissions	10% of UK energy use associated with the manufacture of all construction materials; 22% of UK CO_2 emissions arise from people travelling between buildings.
Other pollutants	Manufacture of construction materials accounts for 0.7% of volatile organic compounds (VOCs), 2.5% of NO_X and 8% of SO_2 emissions.
Land use	Projections of 12% UK urbanisation by 2016.
Water use	Not quantified, but described as 'wasteful' (WWF, 2004c).

environments was set as one of the key objectives (DETR, 2000c). The link between sustainability and housing was further reinforced by the 2003 sustainable communities plan for England, which stated:

> *'It will be essential for all development, especially new housing developments, to respect the principles of sustainable development and address the potential impacts on the environment alongside social and economic goals'.*

(ODPM, 2003a, p 30)

As well as planning policy, the Government and its agencies have considered aspects of residential sustainability in many of their guidance texts and the Government has included sustainability as one of its ten housing quality indicators – its voluntary assessment tool for English housing quality (DTLR, 2000). The importance of new housing to a sustainable England has been intensified by the sheer numbers of households that the country must accommodate in the relatively near future. Because of societal changes which include growing number of single-person households, rising personal wealth and increasing life expectancy, the Government predicts that around 4 million additional homes will be needed in England by 2021 (DETR, 2000b). The pressure for new housing is especially high in the South East, where around 1 million homes are required by 2016 (HM Government, 2005). However, current rates of house-building are not sufficient to deliver these targets[4] (HM Treasury, 2004; ODPM, 2003a). Rao *et al.* (2000, p 1) have stated that:

> '[Housing] *developers face the often conflicting demands of providing large numbers of new homes whilst maintaining adverse environmental effects'.*

The challenge to English housing developers is, if anything, more complicated: the large numbers of new homes will have to be delivered at an increased rate of construction, whilst also taking account of social well-being and quality of life for residents, as well as environmental effects. The compliance of the house-building sector is crucial to meeting national sustainable development objectives. However, despite the long assimilation of sustainability into planning and development in the UK, even by 2002 there may have been only a limited impact on the way planning is applied to house-building, and there is still a general reticence to embrace sustainability within the UK house-building sector (WWF, 2004c).

In England, house-building is dominated by two types of tenure: private companies and registered social landlords (RSLs) (Table 1.5). The private companies account for approximately 90% of all house-building, with the

Table 1.5 The percentage of permanent households completed in England by tenure since 2000. Based on Government housing statistics drawn from NHBC and English local authority planning statistics (ODPM, 2005b).

Financial Year	Private Companies	Registered Social Landlords	Other
2000/2001	87%	12%	1%
2001/2002	89%	11%	<0.05%
2002/2003	90%	10%	0.1%
2003/2004	90%	10%	0.1%

[4] In 2003 it was reported that house-building has fallen steadily in England from a peak of 350,000 p/a in the late 1960s to below 140,000 p/a in the mid 2000s. Current projections predict that 155,000 additional English households will be required p/a to meet current targets (ODPM, 2003a).

remaining 10% built by RSLs for renting to tenants. Although dwarfed by the number of houses built privately, RSLs still account for around 20,000 new-build households per annum and will play a major role in the achievement of a sustainable future in England (Housing Corporation, 2002a). RSLs consist mainly of housing associations, but also trusts and 'not for profit' companies that are registered with the Housing Corporation, the non-departmental body sponsored by Government to regulate and promote the public housing sector in England (Housing Corporation, 2002b). The corporation also funds most (but not all) public housing development in England (Priaulx, 2004).

Clearly it is the activities within these two tenures which will be the key to delivering a future of more sustainable housing and communities in England. Despite reports of a disappointing response from the general house-building sector to date, one would hope that the ongoing assimilation of sustainable development principles into the English planning system and building regulations will effect an improvement. However, there are development concepts and initiatives which proponents claim have already resulted in more sustainable private and RSL-built housing in England. What is more, these concepts and initiatives look set to play an important part in encouraging sustainable housing in the future and guiding Government policy.

Current concepts and initiatives for delivering sustainable homes in England

Urban Villages and Millennium Communities

In his personal treatise on architecture, *A Vision of Britain*, HRH The Prince of Wales proposed a model of residential communities called 'Urban Villages', which offer an alternative vision of urban development and regeneration (HRH The Prince of Wales, 1989). In 1989, in order to promote this vision, the Prince brought together a small group of like-minded developers, investors, planners and designers to form the Urban Village Group (UVG) (Biddulph et al., 2003). In 1992 the UVG launched the *Urban Villages Report*, which detailed the Urban Village concept, described historical precedents and set out a framework for achieving Urban Village development (Aldous, 1992). The report proved popular and was revised by the renamed Urban Villages Forum (UVF) in 1997 to include case studies of built and ongoing Urban Villages (Aldous, 1997). The key requirements of the Urban Village concept which were set out in the two editions of the report are summarised below (see Huxford, 1998; McArthur, 2000; Tait, 2003; Tait et al., 2001).

17

- Mixed-tenure housing
- Interspersed with local facilities, employment opportunities and open space
- Well designed/high design quality
- Based on walking/reduced car reliance
- High density/compact
- Environmentally benign
- Sense of place
- Community integration and involvement

By comparing these key requirements with the definitions presented in Table 1.1, it would appear that the Urban Village model corresponds well with the aims of sustainable development. In particular, there is much overlap with the definition of sustainable housing provided by Edwards (2000) which also includes high density, mixed use, mixed tenure, public transport, open space for ecology and social interaction, resource conservation and integration of natural habitats with housing. In fact, in the second edition of the *Urban Villages Report*, the UVF stated that:

> *'The twin objectives* [of an Urban Village] *must . . . be to ensure a sustainable global environment; and to provide local environments that are . . . more sustainable'.*
> *'The term "Urban Village". . . is now in common use in any debate on sustainable development'.*

(Aldous, 1997, pp 25, 11)

The Urban Village concept has therefore become linked with the notion of sustainable development, by presenting itself as a way of creating more environmentally and socially sustainable urban communities (Biddulph *et al.*, 2001). What is more, private house builders and RSLs are often the developers responsible for delivering Urban Villages. Of the 14 developers listed in the case studies in the revised *Urban Villages Report* in 1997, 12 were either private housing developers or RSLs (Aldous, 1997). This is not surprising, as although mixed use is one of the ideas underpinning the Urban Village concept, housing is the dominant land use in Urban Villages (Biddulph *et al.*, 2003; Tait *et al.*, 2002).

Although the Urban Village concept has been criticised for being utopian and nostalgic (Biddulph *et al.*, 2003), advocates of Urban Villages have moved from the fringe of the UK planning fraternity (McArthur, 2000) and Urban Villages have become popular (Biddulph, 2000; Tait, 2003). The Government's support for Urban Villages is likely to have been crucial in this. According to Biddulph *et al.* (2003), this support was won initially through intense lobbying from the Urban Village Forum in the mid-1990s. Furthermore, the 1999 Urban Task Force report to Government borrowed heavily from the Urban Village concept (Biddulph, 2000) and the 'urban renaissance' outlined in the subsequent White Paper inevitably provided a fertile environment in which the Urban Village concept could flourish.

Through effective lobbying and a close affiliation with the ideas of the urban renaissance, the Urban Village concept became referenced as a preferable mode of development for urban sites in England in both the 1997 and 2001 revisions of *PPG1: General Policy and Principles* (DoE, 1997; DTLR, 2001). Urban Villages also appeared in Government-endorsed good practice guides on residential design (DTLR/CABE, 2001) and examples appeared within the popular press as models of 'greener living' (Siegle, 2003). However, there is no reference to Urban Villages in PPG1's 2005 replacement. Nevertheless, *PPS1: Delivering Sustainable Development* does describe the delivery of sustainable communities as the key aim of English planning (ODPM, 2005a), and the Government's description of sustainable communities has many similarities with that of Urban Villages (Table 1.6). This is perhaps unsurprising given that the Urban Village Forum (now part of the Prince's Foundation) contributed to the drafting of the Government's sustainable communities plan for England.

Although the term 'Urban Village' may have fallen out of favour in planning policy, Table 1.6 demonstrates that the concept has been perpetuated (though 're-badged') in the Government's current vision for sustainable communities.

In 1997, John Prescott, the then Secretary of State for the Environment, challenged the development industry to create a model for 21st-century urban living (DETR, 2000a). This was the start of the Millennium Villages Programme (now termed Millennium Communities Programme), which is co-ordinated and facilitated by English Partnerships. To date, the programme has resulted in seven schemes throughout England which include: Greenwich, London; Allerton Bywater, West Yorkshire; Milton Keynes; Manchester; King's Lynn; Telford and Hastings. The aim of the programme is to provide mixed-tenure residential development interspersed with community facilities such as shops and schools, which can be seen by others in industry as exemplars of sustainable housing and community development (DETR, 2000a; ODPM, 2003). There are a number of key similarities between Millennium Communities and Urban Villages: both should feature mixed-tenure housing with community facilities; should be built to high density; be walkable and not dominated by cars; should be designed to a high quality with a sense of place; and should be environmentally friendly. Like Urban Villages, Millennium Communities are predominantly residential; the programme's emphasis is on the planning, design and construction of new sustainable homes, and they are being developed by consortia of private house-builders and RSLs (English Partnerships, 2005).

Table 1.6 Points of similarity between the key requirements of an Urban Village and the Government's requirements for a sustainable community. *References: Tait (2003); Tait *et al.* (2001); McArthur (2000); Huxford (1998). [†]Taken from ODPM (2003a, p 4).

Key Requirements of an Urban Village*	Key Requirements of a Sustainable Community[†]
Mixed-tenure housing	Well-integrated mix of decent homes of different types and tenure.
Interspersed with local facilities, employment opportunities and open space	Good public local services, including community facilities and well-designed public green space.
Well designed/high design quality	Places where people want to live and will continue to want to live.
Based on walking/reduced car reliance	Basic amenities provided in the neighbourhood, good public transport and other transport infrastructure within the community and linking to other centres.
High density/compact	Minimise use of land.
Environmentally benign	Minimise use of all resources and a healthy local environment.
Sense of place	Sense of place.
Community integration and involvement	Engagement and participation by local people, especially in the planning, design and long-term stewardship of their community.

English Partnerships currently requires environmental certification through the Building Research Establishment Environmental Assessment Method (BREEAM) (which is discussed more fully below) for all housing built on their land, including all seven of the Millennium Communities. Urban Villages such as Hulme in Manchester and Poundbury in Dorset have also undergone BREEAM certification for housing (Duchy of Cornwall, 1999; Hulme Regeneration Ltd, 1994). However, the use of this certification method has had an impact beyond Urban Villages and Millennium Communities. The following section briefly discusses the evolution and adoption of BREEAM for housing (including *EcoHomes*) by private housing developers and RSLs in England.

BREEAM certified housing

The Building Research Establishment Environmental Assessment Method (BREEAM) developed by the Building Research Establishment (BRE) is one of the more established environmental certification schemes that enables owners or occupants to gain recognition for the building's environmental performance. Initially created to set out environmental objectives for new UK offices in 1990, BREEAM was quickly modified for use with regard to supermarkets and houses (Guest, 1991). In 1995 the BRE replaced *BREEAM for New Homes* with the *Environmental Standard – Homes for a Greener World* (Prior, 1995). However, for various reasons, including the pass/fail nature of the assessments, the *Environmental Standard* was not widely taken up by house builders.

In order to facilitate the next revision of BREEAM for housing, between 1997 and 1998 the BRE's Centre for Sustainable Construction carried out research, whereby a wide range of interest groups from the UK's environmental and construction sectors were asked which areas of sustainability they considered most significant, and their relative importance (Rao *et al.*, 2000). This research was used to devise the current version of BREEAM for housing, *EcoHomes*, which was launched in April 2000. Rather than assessing housing schemes on a pass/fail basis, *EcoHomes* instead applied research to provide weighted category scores, which are then summed to give a single percentage score and an appropriate rating on a scale of 'Pass' to 'Excellent' (Rao *et al.*, 2000). *EcoHomes* claims to certify on the basis of:

> '. . . the environmental performance of a residential development, looking at the environmental performance of the individual homes and of the development as a whole'.
>
> (Rao *et al.*, 2000, p 6)

Reflecting this claimed holistic vision, reviews in the popular press of developments that have achieved a high *EcoHomes* rating have described the certification as demonstrating 'environmental friendliness' for the whole estate, rather than the individual buildings (Weaver, 2003).

From a private housing developer's point of view, one of the key benefits of achieving *EcoHomes* certification, and previously the *Environmental Standard* award and the *BREEAM for New Homes* certificate, is that this allows them to differentiate their developments from other, non-sustainable competitors and thus improve marketability (BRE, 1991, 1995; Rao *et al.*, 2000). Though the marketing benefits of certification are arguably less important in the public sector, the broader benefits of BREEAM for public housing, such as reduced fuel bills for low-income residents, are made explicit in *EcoHomes*, and several RSLs were involved in the steering groups for both *EcoHomes* and the *Environmental Standard* (BRE, 1995; Rao *et al.*, 2000).

In April 2003, the Housing Corporation made it mandatory for all RSL housing schemes it funds to achieve an *EcoHomes* certificate (Housing Corporation, 2002a). Even prior to this, the English public housing sector had widely adopted the various revisions of BREEAM for housing.

Although *EcoHomes* has been widely adopted by RSLs, take-up in the private house-building sector has been much slower (Priaulx, 2004). However, as noted earlier, sustainability appraisal of local plans by English, Welsh and Northern Irish local authorities is now compulsory, and an increasing number of councils are setting *EcoHomes* certification as part of Supplementary Planning Guidance to be applied to all new housing (Priaulx, 2004).

Following the 'Better Buildings Summit' in 2003, the Government set up a Sustainable Buildings Task Group which had the job of identifying cost-effective improvements in the quality and environmental performance of buildings. A report from this committee, entitled *Better Buildings – Better Lives,* amongst other recommendations proposed the establishment of a code for sustainable buildings to be based on, and run in parallel to, BREEAM/*EcoHomes* with a high BREEAM/*EcoHomes* achievement being the entry level (SBTG, 2004). This met with the Government's approval and the code, which is to be introduced on a voluntary basis, is now part of its five-year strategy for sustainable communities in England (ODPM, 2005c).

In December 2006 the Government released the new Code for Sustainable Homes which is set to replace *EcoHomes* for the assessment of new housing. A new version of *EcoHomes, EcoHomes XB,* was also released in 2006 by the BRE and has been developed to enable the assessment of existing housing stock (BRE, 2006). In relation to the Code for Sustainable Homes, there is an ongoing initiative to produce a Regional Sustainability Checklist for Developments. The new regional checklist will take account of the wider landscape implications of development on the environment and will use regional planning and sustainable development policy.

What impact have these initiatives had on delivering sustainable residential communities?

Despite the Government's drive towards sustainable development in England, and the key part that housing will play in this, there has been surprisingly little research into existing examples of English housing that claims to be sustainable. Key questions of how far these schemes deliver on their claims of sustainability, and the reasons for successes and failures, remain largely unanswered. This is particularly surprising given that the Urban Village concept, the Millennium Communities Programme and BREEAM (specifically *EcoHomes*) certification responsible for these schemes continue to be assimilated into the policies and actions of central and local government and their agencies.

Urban Villages and Millennium Communities are predominantly residential developments. However, despite touching on related areas such as open space provision and urban design quality, previous evaluation studies of English Urban Villages and Millennium Communities within the DETR – commissioned *Millenium Vilages and Sustainable Communities Report* (DETR, 2000a) have not provided a comprehensive and detailed critique of the sustainability of the residential landscape provided by the developers.

The BRE's *EcoHomes* claims to be a 'development-based' rather than 'building-based' certification method. However, this is true only to a very limited extent; a more detailed examination of the assessment criteria within *EcoHomes* reveals that they are biased towards building issues. Although *EcoHomes* credits are awarded for the use of relatively benign landscape boundaries and surfacing within the housing curtilage, and provision of semi-private space and safe pedestrian routes, the only landscape-related issue to attract significant attention is site ecology (see Rao *et al.*, 2000) and many important aspects of landscape design, procurement and management continue to be omitted. Nevertheless, this is an improvement on 1995's *Environmental Standard* and 1991's *BREEAM for New Homes*, which only considered site ecology in addition to building issues (see BRE, 1991, 1995). However, all three versions of BREEAM for housing contain an appendix of landscape sustainability issues that the assessed developer may additionally wish to consider; for example, provision of cycle routes, grey water recycling, wind shelter and solar shading by planting, garden compost bins, wildlife corridors, water-permeable landscape and traffic calming (see BRE, 1991, 1995; Rao *et al.*, 2000).

However, none of these issues are currently included in BREEAM's assessment criteria. Therefore, housing certified through BREEAM does not claim to have sustainable landscapes *per se*. Nevertheless, it would be reasonable to suppose that developers who are building certified schemes might be more aware of sustainability than those who are not[5] and that they would recognise and address the potential incongruity of constructing sustainable buildings surrounded by, and set within, unsustainable landscape. However, to date, there has been no research to test this supposition and assess the extent to which the ideas of sustainability have been taken up in landscapes associated with BREEAM certified housing built to be, and promoted as, sustainable. The new Code for Sustainable Homes and its companion assessment tool, the Regional Sustainability Checklist, are very recent introductions and were not in use when the assessment study described in Chapter 4 took place.

The research on which this book is based has provided the most comprehensive assessment of residential landscape sustainability within the UK to

---

[5] As well as marketing benefits, the BRE states that BREEAM for homes is intended to raise environmental awareness amongst developers (BRE, 1991).

date. The findings of this research are summarised in Chapter 4. Suffice it to say at this point that a wide range of landscape performance was noted in the analysed case studies, and that development under the aegis of sustainable concepts and initiatives (Urban Villages, Millennium Communities and BREAM certification) does not by any means guarantee residential landscape sustainability.

As discussed earlier in the chapter, landscape sustainability is a key part of sustainable development. In relation to housing development in particular, the residential landscape often comprises a significant, if not dominant, proportion of a site's area and potentially introduces toxic materials and invasive plants unbound by walls and other structural impediments (Thompson & Sorvig, 2000). The landscape is also an opportunity to make the aspirations of creating a sustainable development visible to the residential community and visitors in ways that may improve their aesthetic and social environment. A building may be thermally efficient and constructed from materials that have low embodied energy and excellent life-cycle profiles, but appear no different from a thermally inefficient and unsustainably constructed building. This is not necessarily a bad thing as, for some consumers and developers, the idea of sustainable design always being associated with 'alternative' or 'different' may be a turn-off. In the landscape, however, sustainable design can come to the surface, be visible, enjoyable and informative. It encourages us to think about the positive contribution that, for example, vegetation can make towards achieving sustainability by reducing heat loss from buildings or increasing habitat diversity. Rainwater becomes a site asset and design opportunity to animate the landscape through swales and ponds rather than being perceived as a nuisance that must be quickly gathered and conveyed beneath the ground to a treatment works.

In short, sustainable design, especially in residential environments where building costs frequently diminish the landscape budget, may become a strong argument which encourages developers to look more favourably on the value of landscape. By making sustainable approaches to design more visible and in a manner which enriches our lives, there is also an opportunity to encourage residents to reflect on their own lifestyle choices. If we can see the value that vegetation has beyond making our environment appear more attractive, we may be inclined to take greater care and protect that which already exists.

If the sustainable contribution of the landscape is to be recognised and valued, then it is essential that it becomes an integral component of any sustainable development certification scheme. Whilst aspects of the landscape remain excluded from an assessment there is a danger that sustainable initiatives which inform the design, specification and management of the building may not be carried into the landscape. It may also be the case that developments which incorporate sustainable approaches which are not included in the assessment criteria are not acknowledged and therefore not credited. The following chapter focuses on identifying the sustainability issues that need to be included within a residential landscape sustainability checklist. Although the literature review focuses on the residential context, many of the principles that are discussed in Chapter 2 could equally be applied to other development situations.

References

Aldous, T. (1997) *Urban Villages. A Concept for Creating Mixed-Use Urban Developments on a Sustainable Scale.* London: Urban Villages Forum.

Aldous, T. (1992) *Urban Villages. A Concept for Creating Mixed-Use Urban Developments on a Sustainable Scale.* London: Urban Villages Group.

Barton, H. (2000) Conflicting perceptions of neighbourhood. In: *Sustainable Communities: The Potential for Eco-Neighbourhoods.* H. Barton (Ed.) London: Earthscan.

Barton, H., Davis, G. & Guise, R. (1995) *Sustainable Settlements: A Guide for Planners, Designers and Developers.* Bristol: University of the West of England and the Local Government Board.

Bhatti, M. (1996) Housing and environmental policy in the UK. *Policy and Politics*, 24(2), pp 159–170.

Biddulph, M. (2000) Villages don't make a city. *Journal of Urban Design*, 15(1), pp 65–82.

Biddulp, M., Franklin, B. & Tait, M. (2001) *What do Urban Villages Contribute to Sustainability?* Unpublished Research Summary. Cardiff: Cardiff University.

Biddulph, M., Franklin, B. & Tait, M. (2003) From concept to completion. A critical analysis of the urban village. *Town Planning Review*, 74(2), pp 165–193.

BRE (1991) *BREEAM/New Homes, Version 3/91. An Environmental Assessment for New Homes.* Garston, Watford: Building Research Establishment.

BRE (1995) *Environmental Standard – Homes for a Greener World.* Garston, Watford: Building Research Establishment.

BRE (2006) *EcoHomes XB: The Environmental Rating for Existing Housing – Assessment Guidance Notes.* Garston, Watford: Building Research Establishment.

CABE (2005) *Creating successful neighbourhoods; Lessons and Actions for Housing Market Renewal.* London: Commission for Architecture & the Built Environment.

Department of the Environment (1997) *Planning Policy Guidance Note 1: General Policy and Principles.* London: DoE.

Department of the Environment (Northern Ireland) (1998) *Planning Policy Statement 1: General Principles.* Belfast: Department of the Environment (Northern Ireland), Planning Services.

Department for Environment, Food & Rural Affairs (1998) *Sustainable Local Communities for the 21st Century. Why and How to Prepare an Effective Local Agenda 21 Strategy.* [online] Available at: www.defra.gov.uk/environment/sustainable/la21/policy/sec4.htm (accessed 6 April 2005).

Department for Environment, Food & Rural Affairs (2000) *Our Countryside: The Future – A Fair Deal for Rural England.* London: DEFRA.

Department of the Environment, Transport & the Regions (1998) *Building a Sustainable Future. Homes for an Autonomous Community.* London: DETR.

Department of the Environment, Transport & the Regions (1999) *Quality of Life Counts.* London: DETR.

Department of the Environment, Transport & the Regions (2000a) *Regeneration Research Summary: Millennium Villages and Sustainable Communities Final Report* (Number 30) London: DETR.

Department of the Environment, Transport & the Regions (2000a) *Regeneration Research Summary: Millennium Villages and Sustainable Communities Final Report* (Number 30) London: DETR.

Department of the Environment, Transport & the Regions (2000b) *Our Towns and Cities: The Future – Delivering an Urban Renaissance.* London: DETR.

Department of the Environment, Transport & the Regions (2000c) *Planning Policy Guidance Note 3: Housing.* London: DETR.

Department for Transport, Local Government & the Regions (2000) *HQI. Housing Quality Indicators (Version 2)* London: DTLR.

Department for Transport, Local Government & the Regions (2001) *Planning Policy Guidance Note 1: General Policy and Principles.* London: DTLR.

Department for Transport, Local Government & the Regions/CABE (2001) *Better Places to Live By Design: A Companion Guide to PPG 3.* London: DTLR.

Duchy of Cornwall (1999) *Poundbury Building Code, Revision B.* London: Duchy of Cornwall.

Dunnett, N. & Clayden, A. (2000) *Resources: the raw materials of landscape.* In: *Landscape and Sustainability.* J.F. Benson & M.H. Roe (Eds) London: Spon.

Edwards, B. (2000) Sustainable housing: architecture, society and professionalism. In: *Sustainable Housing: Principles and Practice.* B. Edwards & D. Turrent (Eds) London: E. & F. Spon.

Ekins, P. (2000) *The Big Picture: Social Housing and Sustainability.* London: The Housing Corporation.

Elkin, T., McLaren, D. & Hillman, M. (1991) *Reviving the City: Towards Sustainable Urban Development.* London: Friends of the Earth.

English Partnerships/Housing Corporation (2000) *The Urban Design Compendium.* London: English Partnerships/Housing Corporation.

English Partnerships (2005) *The Millennium Communities Programme.* (online) Available at: www.englishpartnerships.co.uk (accessed 21 April 2005).

Farookhi, I. (1998) Welcome to delegates. Proceedings of NHBC Annual Conference: Sustainable Housing – Meeting the Challenges. Amersham: National House Building Council, pp 7–9.

Forman, R. (1995) *Land Mosaics: The Ecology of Landscapes and Regions.* Cambridge: Cambridge University Press.

Guest, P. (1991) Fresh BREEAM. *Building,* 256(39) pp 58–59.

HM Government (1994) *Sustainable Development – The UK Strategy.* London: HMSO.

HM Government (1999) *A Better Quality of Life – A Strategy for Sustainable Development for the UK.* London: HMSO.

HM Government (2005) *Securing the Future: Delivering the UK Sustainable Development Strategy.* London: HMSO.

HM Treasury (2004) *Review of Housing Supply. Delivering Stability: Securing Our Future Housing Needs. Final Report – Recommendations.* London: HMSO.

Housing Corporation (2002a) *The Housing Corporation: Sustainable Development.* (online) Available at: www.housingcorp.gov.uk/resources/sustain.htm (accessed 7 October 2002).

Housing Corporation (2002b) *About Us.* (online) Available at: www.housingcorp.gov.uk/aboutus/whoweare.htm (accessed 15 July 2002).

Howard, N. (2000) *Sustainable Construction: The Data.* BRE Report CR258/99. Garston, Watford: Building Research Establishment, Centre for Sustainable Construction.

HRH The Prince of Wales (1989) *A Vision of Britain. A Personal View of Architecture.* London: Doubleday.

Hulme Regeneration Limited (1994) *Rebuilding the City: A Guide to Development in Hulme.* Manchester: Hulme Regeneration Limited.

Huxford, R. (1998) *Urban Villages: An Introduction.* Institute of Civil Engineers Briefing Sheet. London: Institute of Civil Engineers.

McArthur, A. (2000) Rebuilding sustainable communities: assessing Glasgow's Urban Village experiment. *Town Planning Review*, 71(1), pp 51–69.

McGhie, C. & Girling, R. (1995) *Local Attraction. The Design of New Housing in the Countryside.* London: Council for the Protection of Rural England.

National Assembly for Wales (2002) *Planning Policy Wales.* Cardiff: NAW.

Office of the Deputy Prime Minister (2003a) *Sustainable Communities: Building for the Future.* London: ODPM.

Office of the Deputy Prime Minister (2003b) *Planning for Sustainable Development: Towards Better Practice.* Modified version. (online) Available at: www.odpm.gov.uk (accessed 12 March 2004).

Office of the Deputy Prime Minister (2004) *Sustainability Appraisal of Regional Spatial Strategies and Local Development Frameworks: Consultation Paper.* London: ODPM.

Office of the Deputy Prime Minister (2005a) *Planning Policy Statement 1: Delivering Sustainable Development.* London: ODPM.

Office of the Deputy Prime Minister (2005b) *Housing Statistics.* (online) Available at: www.odpm.gov.uk/stellent/groups/odpm_housing/documents/page/odpm_house_604028 (accessed 4 April 2005).

Office of the Deputy Prime Minister (2005c) *Five Year Strategy. Sustainable Communities: Homes for All.* (online) Available at: www.odpm.gov.uk/odpm/fiveyearstrategy /fact_sheets/007.htm (accessed 1 February 2005).

Patterson, A. & Theobald, K.S. (1995) Sustainable development, Agenda 21 and the new local governance in Britain. *Regional Studies*, 29(8), pp 773–778.

Priaulx, M. (2004) EcoHomes. *Building for a Future*, Spring, pp 11–19.

Prior, J. (1995) Homes for a greener world. *Building Services*, 17(10), p 51.

Rao, S., Yates, A., Brownhill, D. & Howard, N. (2000) *EcoHomes: The Environmental Rating for Homes.* Garston, Watford: Building Research Establishment, Centre for Sustainable Construction.

Ruff, A. (1982) An ecological approach to landscape design. In: *An Ecological Approach to Urban Landscape Design.* A. Ruff & Tregay, R (Eds) Department of Town & Country Planning, University of Manchester. Occasional Paper, No. 8. pp 4–12.

Scottish Executive (2002) *Scottish Planning Policy Note 1: The Planning System.* Edinburgh: Scottish Executive.

Siegle, L. (2003) People who live in green houses. In: *OM* colour supplement with *The Observer*, 19 January, pp 50–53.

Skinner, A. (1998) *Focus on water and waste.* Proceedings of NHBC Annual Conference: Sustainable Housing – Meeting the Challenges. Amersham: National House Building Council, pp 16–20.

Smith, M., Whitelegg, J. & Williams, N. (1998) *Greening the Built Environment.* London: Earthscan.

Sustainable Buildings Task Group (2004) *Better Buildings – Better Lives. Sustainable Buildings Task Group Report.* (online) Available at: www.dti.gov.uk/construction/ sustain/EA_Sustainable_Report_41564_2.pdf (accessed 10 January 2004).

Sustainable Development (2000) *Building a Better Quality of Life. A Strategy for More Sustainable Construction.* London: DETR.

Tait, M. (2003) Urban villages as self-sufficient, integrated communities: a case study in London's Docklands. *Urban Design International*, 8, pp 37–52.

Tait, M., Biddulph, M. & Franklin, B. (2001) Urban villages – a mixed up development idea. *Urban Environment Today*, 7 June, p 12.

Tait, M., Biddulph, M. & Franklin, B. (2002) Urban villages – a concept with mixed uses? *Town and Country Planning*, 71(9), pp 229–231.

Thayer, R.L. (1989) The experience of sustainable landscapes. *Landscape Journal*, 8, pp 101–110.

Thayer, R.L. (1994) *Gray World, Green Heart: Technology, Nature and the Sustainable Landscape.* London: Wiley.

Thompson, J.W. & Sorvig, K. (2000) *Sustainable Landscape Construction: A Guide to Green Building Outdoors.* Washington DC: Island Press.

Urban Task Force (1999) *Towards an Urban Renaissance.* London: E. & F.N. Spon.

Weaver, M. (2003) Streets ahead. In: *The Guardian,* 12 February. (online) Available at: society.guardian.co.uk/urbandesign/story/0,11200,893529,00.html (accessed 10 March 2003).

Williams, K., Burton, E. & Jenks, M. (2000) *Introduction.* In: *Achieving Sustainable Urban Form.* K. Williams, E. Burton & M. Jenks (Eds) London: Spon Press.

World Commission on Environment and Development (1987) *Our Common Future.* Oxford: Oxford University Press.

WWF (2004a) *One Million Sustainable Homes. Moving Best Practice from the Fringes to the Mainstream of UK Housing.* (online) Available at: www.wwf.org.uk (accessed 9 November 2004).

WWF (2004b) *Sustainable and Secure Buildings Bill.* (online) Available at: www.wwf. org.uk (accessed 9 November 2004).

WWF (2004c) *Building Towards Sustainability. Performance and Progress among the UK's Leading House Builders.* (online) Available at: www.wwf.org.uk (accessed 9 November 2004).

WWF (2004d) *Facts and Key Issues.* (online) Available at: www.wwf.org.uk/ sustainablehomes/facts.asp (accessed 9 November 2004).

Chapter 2

Opportunities for improving the sustainable profile of new residential developments

Introduction

Chapter 1 provided definitions of sustainable landscape, from which two fundamental themes can be drawn. First, a sustainable landscape is a *system* in which resources are conserved and waste and pollution minimised. In the context of this discussion, 'resources' include physical materials (for example, minerals and water), cultural and ecological assets (biodiversity and landscape quality) and less tangible resources such as energy and chemical nutrients. Second, a sustainable landscape is, at the same time, a *habitat* which protects and enhances a site's ecological function and value to human well-being. The issues reviewed in this chapter are, as much as possible, arranged under these two fundamental themes. Inevitably there are areas of overlap between them; as pointed out by Barton *et al.* (1995, p 14), *'Social and environmental goals are often mutually reinforcing'*. Furthermore, ecological systems are both a resource, to be conserved and protected from pollution at the global level, and a local issue to be dealt with at the site level.

Conservation of resources and minimisation of pollution and waste

Energy consumption and microclimate control

The greenhouse effect and energy consumption in the home

The majority of the UK's energy comes from non-renewable fossil fuels that produce 'greenhouse' gases, such as CO_2 (Howard, 2000; Sustainable Homes, 2003). These gases absorb a large portion of the infra-red radiation emitted from the earth's surface, causing warming of the lower atmosphere – the 'greenhouse effect' (Rao *et al.*, 2000). This could be disastrous in terms of global ecosystems, food production and flooding of settlements (Johnson, 1991). Notwithstanding the 'precautionary principle', which advocates caution irrespective of definitive scientific evidence (Barton, 2000), a key part of the UK's sustainable development strategies (HM Government, 1999, 2005), scientists have recently claimed to have found an unequivocal link between man-made greenhouse gases and global warming (Conner, 2005).

As shown in Table 1.3 in Chapter 1, the energy consumed in operating homes accounts for almost 30% of the UK's annual CO_2 emissions. However, landscape design around buildings can reduce their operational energy and CO_2 by modifying wind and solar radiation (Brown & Gillespie, 1995) and there is greatest potential for savings in relatively small buildings with a large surface area to volume ratio, i.e. most housing (BRE, 1990a,b). According to Brown & Gillespie (1995) the energy consumed in heating a typical temperate house (such as in the UK) can be reduced by 15% through the use of windbreaks. The US Federal Government advises that, on average, annual domestic energy savings of 25% can be made through wind and solar shelter provided by landscape features (US Department of Energy, 1995). This higher figure presumably takes account of reduced domestic air conditioning in hotter parts of North America, which is currently less of an issue in the UK (Rosenheck, 2003). However this may be set to change with rising summer temperatures and a population which is becoming more accustomed to modifying their microclimate to increase their physical comfort. For example, in recent years we have become used to air-conditioning in our places of work and recreation and in the cars we drive. Relatively inexpensive air-conditioning units are also now available to the DIY market.

Providing wind shelter

During the UK's cold season (October to April) the interior temperature of a house is likely to be higher than that outside. This can lead to heat being conducted to the external skin of the home, where it is then removed by external air convection. The colder and/or faster the wind against the house, the more effective this process (Brown & Gillespie, 1995). Landscape design which slows winds around the home can therefore reduce heat loss (especially if used in combination with measures to maximise the solar energy warming the outside of the home). Even a well-insulated house can suffer significant heat losses through air exchange, which also increases in faster, colder winds (Brown & Gillespie, 1995; DTI/AA, 1994; Sustainability Works, 2002). Good insulation and air tightness in building design should be considered in a holistic strategy alongside landscape and site layout measures

(Barton *et al.*, 1995; Courtney, 1998; Edwards, 2000; Sustainability Works, 2002; Woolley & Kimmins, 2000).

South-westerly winds are the prevailing and fastest flowing in the UK's cold season (BRE, 1990a; Dodd, 1989) whilst winds from the north, north west and north east are the coldest (Barton *et al.*, 1995; BRE 1990a). Micro-climatic residential landscape design in the UK should consider all these winds as priorities (Sustainability Works, 2002). Although wind speeds tend to be slower in built-up areas, due to the 'surface roughness' of the ground (BRE, 1990b; Dodd, 1989) such wind will also tend to be more turbulent (BRE, 1990a,c) and will still have a high capacity to carry heat away from a building (Brown & Gillespie, 1995). Landscape boundaries and individual trees and shrubs contribute to the surface roughness of housing areas and help reduce wind speeds (Beazley, 1991; BRE, 1990c). Studies also suggest that vegetation can decrease the turbulence of wind between buildings (Cambridge University, 2001) although solid boundaries can increase turbulence (BRE, 1990c).

The relative importance of landscape features in slowing and calming wind through housing will depend upon the design and arrangement of the buildings on and around the site. If the roughness of a built-up area is uniform and buildings that induce funnelling and ground-level turbulence are avoided, it is possible to create a sheltered environment (BRE, 1990c). However, uniform roughness is only achieved where buildings are spaced no more than 2.5 times their height, and thus it is in spaces larger than this that the effect of landscape features will be able to contribute most (BRE, 1990c).

Microclimatic landscape design may also introduce strategic elements into housing which do more than contribute to surface roughness. Major windbreaks significantly deflect the flow of air and can be used to protect the edges of a development or can be located at regular intervals throughout a scheme (BRE, 1990c). On reaching a windbreak, the air is forced over and around, creating a lee where there is less air passing at any given moment, perceived as reduced wind speed. If the windbreak is permeable then some air will pass through and the reduction in wind speed in the lee will be less dramatic but more extensive (Brown & Gillespie, 1995). It has been suggested that the optimum permeability for windbreaks is 40–50% void space (Barton *et al.*; 1995; Beazley, 1991; BRE, 1990c; Dodd, 1989). Although it has been suggested that the effect of a windbreak can be experienced at a distance up to 20 times the feature's height (Beazley, 1991), the most effective zone in terms of sheltering a home has been suggested as around seven times the height of a shelter belt (Barton *et al.*, 1995.; Brown & Gillespie, 1995; Starbuck, 2000; Welch, 2003).

Tall trees and shrubs, in various combinations, can be used to create windbreaks (Dodd, 1989) with species selection and vertical and plan structure affecting efficiency (BRE, 1990c; Dodd, 1989; Starbuck, 2000; Welch, 2003). An effective windbreak can require significant land take and evergreen climbing plants grown against the north, west and east elevations of a home, creating a layer of still or slow-moving air against the building, may offer a more effective solution where space is restricted (Dodd; 1989; Starbuck, 2000).

Though it is desirable to shelter homes from prevailing south-westerlies in winter, these winds are also prevailing in the summer and as such aid natural ventilation of the home (BRE, 1990c). Clearly it is difficult to combine these two benefits if using windbreaks. A compromise might be to provide dense shelter to the north, whilst also providing more open shelter to the south west that will slow the wind but still allow significant air passage. As an alternative, wall-mounted evergreen climbers on the west elevation of the home will not affect summer wind flow through open windows, doors and vents. Furthermore, through the upturning action of leaves towards the sun, these climbers allow cool air to flow around the outside of the home in the summer. In the winter, these same leaves turn down to the low sun, thus providing the required insulating layer of still air (Johnston & Newton, 1993). Similarly, one of the benefits of a green roof is insulation of the home during the cold season (Armstrong *et al.*, 2000; Johnston & Newton, 1993;Thompson & Sorvig, 2000). Further benefits of vegetated buildings are discussed throughout this chapter. It is worth noting that green roof systems are available which do not require an increase in the build-ing's load-bearing capacity (Dunnett, 2004; Environment Agency, 2003; Thompson & Sorvig, 2000) so that their benefits can be enjoyed without the drawbacks associated with concrete and steel manufacture (which are discussed later in this chapter).

Providing solar access and shade

During the cold season, incoming solar radiation can heat the home directly through windows, and heat external surfaces to reduce the amount of energy lost through conduction (Brown & Gillespie, 1995). Maximising solar gains into the home is particularly significant in reducing heating costs towards the beginning and end of the cold season[1] (BRE, 1990c). Landscape features should be specified and located so that solar gain is not reduced during these periods through overshadowing; the obstruction of direct sunlight is the main challenge to successful passive solar design (Barton *et al.*, 1995). As well as evergreen species, densely planted deciduous trees

---

[1] During the middle of this period, around the winter solstice, the angle of the sun (solar altitude) is so low as to make passive solar access difficult to achieve.

can greatly reduce the solar energy reaching a house, even when bare (BRE, 1990c).

In summer the desired interior temperature and that outside are closer than they are in winter. As a result, convection of heat away from the home does not occur to any degree (Brown & Gillespie, 1995). However, high levels of incident solar radiation can be transmitted directly through windows and cause a temperature gradient through the walls and roof into the house (Brown & Gillespie, 1995). As highlighted by the BRE (1990c), measures to ensure solar access during the UK's heating season should not exclude the provision of summertime shade.

Appropriately selected and located deciduous trees can provide welcome shade whilst providing for solar access in the winter. Openly spaced plant-ings or single specimens with high bare branch transparency (such as the English oak) and/or long defoliation times (i.e. species which drop their leaves early and do not refoliate until relatively late the following year, for example ash) will be most suitable (BRE, 1990c; Brown & Gillespie, 1995). Deciduous climbing plants on south-facing walls provide shade in summer (see Figure 2.2) whilst allowing unimpeded solar access in the winter, whilst green roofs (see Figure 2.1) can also help keep houses cool through inter-cepting solar energy (Armstrong et al., 2000; Johnston & Newton, 1993; Thompson & Sorvig, 2000). Furthermore, green roofs actively cool buildings through the process of evapotranspiration from plants extracting heat energy from the surrounding air. Another point to note is that, applied on a settlement-wide scale, vegetated roofs and walls as well as more general planting can make a contribution to reducing an unwanted 'urban heat island' effect (Johnston & Newton, 1993). Whitford et al. (2001, p 92) describe the urban heat island effect thus:

> 'Energy uptake is promoted during summer days by the increased area of buildings and roads that have a high thermal storage capacity . . . more heat is therefore stored during the day and reradiated at night. In contrast energy loss due to evapotranspi-ration [and photosynthesis] is lowered by the reduction in the area of vegetation.'

Encouraging walking and cycling

Impacts of car use

Energy use and CO_2 emissions associated with housing also stem from resi-dents' car use. As shown in Table 1.3 in Chapter 1, the transportation of people between buildings accounts for 22% of UK CO_2 emissions. What is more, UK energy use and emissions from transport are growing by 4% per

Figure 2.1 The green roofs on this housing development in the German town of Duisberg serve multiple functions: they absorb rainfall, cool the building in summer, link the houses visually with the surrounding landscape, and provide a degree of additional habitat.

annum, mostly owing to increases in personal transport (Rao *et al.*, 2000). Obviously the location of housing with respect to amenities and places of work plays a large role in determining car use (see Barton *et al.* 1995; Rao *et al.*, 2000). However, housing can also be planned and designed to encourage movement on foot or cycle, thus contributing to a less car-dependent society (Barton *et al.*, 1995; DETR, 1998a). Car use has impacts beyond energy use and CO_2 emissions: specifically noise, congestion, air-borne pollutants and road accidents, especially in residential areas (Brownhill & Rao, 2002; Rao *et al.*, 2000).

In order to make a contribution to reduced car reliance, cycleways and footpaths must be safe, convenient for all intended users, legible and con-vivial (Barton *et al.*, 1995; Brownhill & Rao, 2002; CABE, 2002; DTLR/CABE, 2001; English Partnerships/Housing Corporation, 2000; Rao *et al.*, 2000). The benefits of introducing such features into a residential landscape can go beyond the environmental to include health benefits and social cohesion (Barton *et al.*, 1995; DETR, 2000d).

Design of transport routes

If people are to be persuaded to leave their cars at home, the routes for walking and cycling demand particular design attention (DTLR/CABE, 2001). To provide a convenient pedestrian/cycle network, access to amenities, facilities and the existing movement network around the site should be direct, with a lack of abrupt junctions and changes in direction (Barton

Figure 2.2 Vertical greening of the building through the use of climbing plants may soften their visual impact and also help to reduce heat loss from cold winter winds and shade the building in summer.

et al., 1995; English Partnerships/Housing Corporation, 2000). Residential pedestrian/cycle routes are safest where overlooked by houses (English Partnerships/Housing Corporation, 2000) and where not overlooked, they should be kept as short as possible, with the ends intervisible (DoE, 1992). Good lighting is also a key determinant in generating feelings of safety on residential routes (CABE, 2005). Pedestrian and cycle routes should be furnished to provide a positive experience, with signage, litter and dog bins (DETR, 2000d). Pedestrians require surfaces that prevent sliding, whilst cyclists require well-drained pathways without drainage gratings or manhole covers (Barton *et al.*, 1995). The pedestrian/cycle network should generally follow site contours, though guidance on maximum comfortable gradients should also be considered (for example, 1:20 and 1:12 are normal maxima for cyclists and pedestrians respectively) (see Barton *et al.*, 1995; Beer, 1983; DoE, 1992). Similarly, guidance is available on the width of footways and cycle paths (both segregated and shared) depending on the size of the housing development and proximity to amenities such as schools (see DoE, 1992).

When *PPG 3: Housing* was revised in 2000, emphasis was placed on prioritisation of pedestrians over cars (DETR, 2000c). This was a reversal of previous thinking, which had seen the prioritisation of vehicles in most modern housing developments (DTLR/CABE, 2001). To achieve this shift in priorities, the design language used at crossing points must favour pedestrians (Barton *et al.*, 1995; English Partnerships/Housing Corporation, 2000) and traffic should be slowed to less than 20 mph, by limiting the length of unimpeded road to 60 m or 40 m for speeds 'well below 20 mph' (DoE, 1992). The entrance to such areas can be marked by signs and gateway features (DETR, 1998b). Speed humps and ramps can be used to slow traffic but they have drawbacks: they produce noise, vibration, and wear and tear on roads, and cars may speed between them (Barton *et al.*, 1995). Alternatively, the arrangement of buildings, spaces and activities can calm traffic, whilst being less intrusive and far more pleasant for pedestrians and cyclists (DTLR/CABE, 2001; English Partnerships/Housing Corporation, 2000).

Planting can play a key role in providing a pleasant pedestrian and cycle network (Figure 2.3). Plants, at a site-specific scale, have the ability to improve the microclimate with respect to energy use in buildings (and on a broader scale, contribute to reduced urban ambient temperatures). Plants can also be used, perhaps simultaneously, to improve the microclimate experienced by pedestrians and cyclists through shade and shelter (Barton *et al.*, 1995). It has been suggested that planting along roads can also reduce noise pollution (Barton *et al.*, 1995). However, there is little empirical evidence to support this and work which has been undertaken has found that only deep, dense planting belts have any significant effect (Laurie, 1986). Clearly, providing deep planting belts alongside the road network is unlikely to be a viable option for most housing areas, though Bayley (2004) noted that planting may affect the perceived level of noise from a road, through simply screening the source of the noise.

Claims have also been made that sequestration of atmospheric CO_2 by trees and other plants can help offset emissions associated with residential development (see Barton *et al.*, 1995). However, the area of trees required to counteract the carbon emissions of even a few cars may be more than a hectare, and CO_2 sequestration by trees is only temporary; if the wood is burnt or rots down, the CO_2 makes a delayed return to the atmosphere (Dunnett & Clayden, 2000). A positive contribution to carbon balance can only come about through vegetation if it is cropped on a cycle, and used as an alternative to fossil fuels (Dunnett & Clayden, 2000; Rao *et al.*, 2000).

Less contentiously, planting, especially trees, adjacent to roads can improve air quality by filtering noxious exhaust gases such as carbon monoxide and sulphur dioxide, and adsorbing air-borne particulates (Barton et al., 1995; Bayley, 2004; Dunnett & Clayden, 2000; Givoni, 1991 cited by Jorgensen, 2001). Furthermore, visual variety and signs of activity are important to perceived safety and conviviality of the movement network (DTLR/CABE, 2001; English Partnerships/Housing Corporation, 2000), both of which can be enhanced through planting and opportunities for residents' own planting adjacent to footways and cycle paths.

Many of the measures outlined in this subsection can be assimilated into an overall concept for shared streets or 'home zone'. The concept has become well established elsewhere in Europe and the UK Government has recognised it as a possible way forward in creating safer, more pleasant and ultimately less CO_2 and energy-intensive neighbourhoods (DETR, 2000d).

Specification and detailed design of hard landscape materials

Embodied energy and life-cycle assessment (LCA) of hard materials

The preceding sections of this chapter have outlined how landscape design can reduce energy use and CO_2 production in buildings, and can encourage energy-efficient transport modes. However, energy is also consumed in the production and distribution of hard (that is, non-organic) construction materials (Sustainable Development, 2000). In fact, as shown in Table 1.3 in Chapter 1, the energy used to manufacture and transport housing materials accounts for 3% of the UK's total energy consumption. Although this is small compared to that used in the operation of housing, it still results in significant emissions of CO_2 (Rao et al., 2000).

Hard materials used in the landscape make up a significant proportion of the total used in residential development; for example, in the UK, the area of fencing around a garden is often comparable to the external wall area of the associated house (Anderson & Howard, 2000). Clearly, to create a more sustainable environment, landscape designers should be careful in selecting hard materials in terms of their energy costs and (as discussed later in this chapter) in relation to their implications for conserving other resources and reducing pollution and waste impacts (Dunnett & Clayden, 2000).

The amount of energy used to manufacture, transport and incorporate a construction material on site is called 'embodied energy' (Barton et al., 1995; Morel et al., 2001; Sustainable Homes, 2003; Thompson & Sorvig, 2000). Several techniques have been developed in order to calculate embodied energy of materials, though no single approach has been accepted as definitive, and there have been concerns regarding the

Figure 2.3 Hellebaek, Denmark. A 1990s housing scheme where the cars are kept to the outskirts of the residential development and housing is arranged around a central lake. (a) The main pathway and cycle route which leads from the parking areas to the housing. (b) An informal pathway accessible from the front gardens meanders around the lake edge. (c) One of the connecting pathways leading through the housing estate, an informal play space for young children. It is worth noting the bold and confident use of planting to create privacy and screening and the relaxed management of planting around the lake edge, which contribute to the naturalistic feel of the landscape and improve habitat diversity. Many of the pathways are also constructed from a single paving module that complements the design form and has required no cutting or wasteage.

Figure 2.3 *Continued*

accuracy of information provided by some manufacturers (Sustainable Homes, 2003; Thompson & Sorvig, 2000; Woolley *et al.*, 1997). Unsurprisingly, when summaries of embodied energy levels for construction materials are published in the research literature, values for the same material can vary widely (for example, see Morel *et al.*, 2001, p 1123; Sustainable Homes, 2003, p 7; Thompson & Sorvig, 2000, pp 248–249). Nevertheless, the published data corroborate the generalisation made by Sustainable Homes (2003), that naturally occurring materials such as timber, stone and aggregate will tend to have a lower embodied energy than heavily processed metals, plastics, bricks and cement.

However, transport energy can, for some materials, be as high as manufacturing energy (Howard, 2000) and for natural materials with low manufacturing energy but high density and bulk, energy used in transportation can be highly significant. For example, timber used in UK construction is often imported from Canada, and although a container ship is a relatively energy-efficient mode of transportation, the energy cost of shipping a tonne of timber from British Columbia is 1.0 GJ, the same as the manufacturing energy of a tonne of concrete containing very high-energy cement (Woolley et al., 1997). Similarly, naturally occurring aggregates and stone can accrue significant embodied energy by an average of 0.00561 GJ per tonne per mile when transported by road (Woolley et al., 1997).

Clearly, using local materials will reduce the transport component of embodied energy of materials (BRE/DTI, 2003: Howard, 2000; Morel et al., 2001; Woolley et al., 1997). In particular, this is a key aspect to consider when using high-density, bulky materials (Sustainable Homes, 2003). The mode of transportation, as well as distance travelled, is also important. Although their estimates may differ and the units used to express their data vary, several authors have pointed out that the energy required to transport a tonne of construction materials for a given distance by rail or ship is far less than that required to carry a tonne by road for the equivalent distance (Table 2.1).

Furthermore, as noted above, car use has impacts beyond energy use and CO_2 emissions and so it is with freight transport, which can cause dust, noise and air pollution, and vibration and subsidence damage to roads (Howard, 2000). Although transport energy, and indeed embodied energy as a whole, cannot provide the full picture of the environmental profile of materials, maximising the use of local and naturally occurring materials, where possi-

Table 2.1 Transport energy consumption of different transportation modes.

Transport Mode	Transport Energy Consumption			
	Caceres & Richards, 2003	VTPI, 2002	Berge, 2000	Thompson & Sorvig, 2000
Road	2600 KJ/ton/km	0.017 gallons of fuel/ton/mile	1600 KJ/ton/km	4240 Btu/ton/mile
Ship	254 KJ/ton/km	0.002 gallons of fuel/ton/mile	600 KJ/ton/km	445 Btu/ton/mile
Train	291 KJ/ton/km	0.0050 gallons of fuel/ton/mile	600 KJ/ton/km	750 Btu/ton/mile

ble, is a sound principle for a more sustainable residential landscape (Figure 2.4(a)). However, although embodied energy is a useful guide when comparing products and is often used as a proxy for the environmental impact of a material (Anderson & Howard, 2000; Woolley *et al.*, 1997) it is only one area with which a specifier should be concerned (Sustainable Homes, 2003; Woolley *et al.*, 1997).

> *'Many products with minimal energy use in their production can still have considerable impacts on mineral extraction, waste generation and water usage.'*
>
> (Anderson & Howard, 2000, p 5)

A more reliable picture of the environmental profile of a material can be obtained by undertaking a 'life cycle assessment' (or analysis) (LCA) where information is compiled on all the environmental impacts of a material or product from the point of extraction right through to disposal. The LCA approach allows a specifier to identify the impacts of a material beyond embodied energy. For example, a product may have a low embodied energy but the process of extracting raw materials and processing could cause considerable environmental damage and pollution. The LCA of a material or product includes consideration of the stages shown in Table 2.2.

Timber sourcing

Timber is potentially the most sustainable of all construction materials. It can be renewable, of low embodied energy, healthy and, compared to other

Table 2.2 Life-cycle stages and possible environmental issue of hard landscape materials. Adapted from Sustainable Homes (2003, p 12).

Life-Cycle Stage	Examples of Environmental Issues
Pre-production (e.g. mineral extraction)	Water pollution, air pollution, damage to ecology and landscape, social impact, transport, waste
Production/Manufacturing	Water pollution, air pollution, waste
Construction	Water pollution, air pollution, damage to ecology and landscape, transport, waste
In use	Water pollution, local air pollution, traffic generation, health considerations, re-treatment with paints, etc.
End of life	Ecological and landscape implications, water pollution, air pollution from incineration, scope for recycling, demolition waste

Figure 2.4 Friedrichschain, Peninsula Stralau, Berlin. (a) Reclaimed building demolition has been used to construct gabion retaining walls along the edge of this residential block. The development also incorporates sustainable drainage features, including soakaways and swales (b), which have been designed to temporarily store surface runoff before it is gradually released to groundwater or the drainage network.

materials on a weight-for-weight basis, very strong (Berge, 2000; Thompson & Sorvig, 2000). However, only a small proportion of timber production can be described as sustainable, with the majority causing large-scale clear felling, the introduction of fast-growing monoculture and removal of mixed old-growth forests (which cannot be considered renewable in any meaning-ful sense), as well as a range of further environmental and social impacts (Berge, 2000; Woolley et al., 1997).

To be sustainable, timber production must consider the preservation of biological resources of the forest; conserve and manage watershed and soils; recognise local people's rights; and be economically viable (Woolley et al., 1997). Designers can and should stipulate timber which is indepen-dently certified as being from a sustainable source (Woolley et al., 1997). According to the UK's Association of Environmentally Conscious Builders (AECB), in examining the credentials of eco-timber certification schemes, Forests and the European Resource Network (FERN) concluded that only Forestry Stewardship Council (FSC) certification is credible (AECB, 2003).

FSC is an international, independent non-governmental organisation which provides certification to forest owners who require authenticity for their sustainability claims (FSC, 2000). Forests are inspected by FSC-accredited bodies (such as the Soil Association in the UK) against strict environmental, social and economic standards (FSC, 2002). Certification is completed through a chain-of-custody monitoring system, which tracks the procurement chain right up to the point at which the timber or derived product becomes available to the end user. This ensures that only genuinely FSC-certified material is labelled as such.

Timber treatment and detailing

As far as resource conservation is concerned, there is a clear advantage in using robust materials that allow designs to last for as long as possible (Berge, 2000; Woolley et al., 1997). Timber used in buildings can be extremely durable; but what of timber used in the landscape?

Table 2.3 shows that outdoor durability varies between different types of timber, and where and how they are used. Generally speaking, deciduous hardwood species such as oak are more durable than coniferous softwoods such as pine. However, certain softwoods, such as yew, are durable whereas some hardwoods, such as willow, are perishable (Woolley et al., 1997). The demand for timber by the international construction industry means that the use of cheap, fast-growing, perishable softwood has increased (Berge, 2000; Woolley et al., 1997). This has led to a similar increase in the use of timber preservatives, almost unheard-of 60 years ago when durable timbers were more prevalent. In terms of sustainability, timber preservatives are highly controversial products owing to their threat to human health and

Table 2.3 Maximum durability of untreated timber in years in different situations. Adapted from Berge (2000, p 172).

Timber	Always Dry (Indoors)	Outdoors	In Contact with Earth
Oak	800	200	20
Pine	1000	120	8
Spruce	900	75	4
Willow	600	40	–

ecosystems (Thompson & Sorvig, 2000; Woolley et al., 1997) yet landscape design uses a significant amount of treated timber (Thompson & Sorvig, 2000).

Timber preservatives fall into three major categories: tar oils, solvent-borne salts and water-borne salts (Woolley et al., 1997). Respectively, commonly used examples are creosote, pentachlorophenol (PCP) and chromated copper arsenate (CCA) (National Physical Laboratory, 2003;[2] Woolley et al., 1997). Both metal salts and oil products are derived from restricted, non-renewable sources (Berge, 2000) and the production of preservatives requires significant energy inputs (Woolley & Kimmins, 2000). However, the main concern with these substances is their toxicity during production, use and disposal; *all* preservatives are designed to be toxic, some extremely so, as well as persistent (Berge, 2000; Thompson & Sorvig, 2000; Woolley et al., 1997). Preservatives such as creosote, PCP and CCA can have serious impacts on human health, particularly for those involved with the pre-treatment and remedial treatment of timber. Furthermore, creosote continues to release toxins for a considerable time following application and can heavily pollute the groundwater and garden when *in situ* (Berge, 2000), where it is injurious to many forms of plant life (Woolley et al., 1997). Objects treated with PCP remain toxic for years after treatment, and PCP has a high bio-amplification capacity through the food chain (Thompson & Sorvig, 2000). Water-borne heavy metal salt solutions, such as CCA, are also potential sources of contamination *in situ*, as they can leach into soils from exposed external structures and surfaces, and also have high biological amplification capacities (Berge, 2000).

Following advice from an expert committee on toxicity in the early 2000s, the European Commission drew up draft proposals to prohibit the use

[2] The National Laboratory is the UK's national independent standards laboratory, and is responsible for research, development and knowledge transfer in measurement and materials science.

of CCA, based on dangers posed to human health and the impacts when CCA-treated timber is burnt or disposed of (HM Government, 2002). In December 2006 the European Commission published a new directive which introduced restrictions on the use of CCA preservative and CCA-treated timber. The directive specifically prohibited the use of CCA-treated wood in residential or domestic construction (Commission of the European Communities, 2006). These proposals are currently being considered by the European member states. This follows the outright prohibition of CCA-treated timbers in residential landscape works in the USA in 2003 (EPA, 2005). There is no environmentally friendly way to dispose of CCA-treated wood; incineration causes significant air pollution (Thompson & Sorvig, 2000; Woolley et al., 1997) and disposal as solid waste leads to increased pressures on landfill and potential for leachate to soil and groundwater (Thompson & Sorvig, 2000). Similarly, PCP-treated wood may also release dioxins (human hormone disrupters) on incineration (Woolley et al., 1997).

Berge (2000) and Woolley et al. (1997) note that, relatively speaking, the least toxic preservative treatments are water-borne zinc, fluoride, copper and boron salts. However, boron salts are not suitable for landscape applications due to their high leaching potential (Thompson & Sorvig, 2000). Therefore zinc, fluoride and copper salts are likely to be the least toxic and thus relatively the most sustainable preservatives for use in landscape timbers.

Paints and stains can also be used to treat timbers to improve durability (Woolley et al., 1997). Paints are essentially mixtures of solvents, pigments and binders; stains include solvents and pigments only (Berge, 2000). Most paints and stains use one of three types of solvent: vegetable turpentine, distilled from the sap of coniferous trees or pressed from orange peel; 'mineral turpentine' (white spirit), distilled from crude oil; or water (Berge, 2000). Vegetable turpentine is derived from renewable plant sources rather than crude oil, and has reduced environmental impacts in relation to energy consumption, pollution during production and potential nerve damage caused by vaporising mineral turpentine (Berge, 2000). However, plant-based compounds may be toxic and contribute to photochemical smog (Woolley et al., 1997). Although water-based paints and stains are generally safer for users than solvent-based paints, having fewer volatile organic compounds (VOCs), they probably use more toxic petrochemicals and therefore cause more pollution during their production (Woolley et al., 1997).

The pigments used in paints and stains can be organic or inorganic. Organic pigments are less durable than their inorganic counterparts (Berge, 2000) and are therefore less suitable for external use. There are two types of inorganic pigment: mineral pigment and earth pigment (Berge, 2000). Most (but not all) inorganic mineral pigments are now made synthetically and have high associated energy consumption rates and pollution problems, especially cadmium, chrome, zinc, manganese and lead products (Berge, 2000). Mineral pigments are also based on limited or very limited reserves (Berge, 2000). Earth pigments, composed of the decaying products of particular types of stone, can occur ready to use in certain types of earth and have good durability (Berge, 2000).

The final ingredient of paints is the binder. The principal ingredient of 'natural paints' is linseed oil or other vegetable resin oil which acts as a very stable, durable alternative to synthetic resin binders. Historically, linseed oil has been a traditional paint ingredient (Construction Resources, 2002).

If paints and stains are used in a landscape, then natural formulations featuring vegetable-based solvents (or water-based without the use of toxic preservatives and other additives), naturally derived earth or mineral pigments and vegetable-based binders will have the best environmental profile.

The above review has identified some chemical treatments for timber which appear to be less toxic than others. At the very least, a sustainable residential landscape should feature these relatively benign specifications, and use wood that is pre-treated before delivery to site; the risks to human and ecosystem health posed by all treatments can be increased when the application is undertaken *in situ*, especially by untrained members of the public – in other words 'do it yourself' (Anderson & Howard, 2000; Woolley & Kimmins, 2000; Woolley *et al.*, 1997). However, all timber preservatives, paints and stains have some unsustainable characteristics. Ideally, a sustainable residential landscape should remove the need for chemical timber treatments altogether.

One possible approach is to use timber that has received alternative, traditional treatments such as soaking (seasoning) or burning (Berge, 2000; Woolley *et al.*, 1997). Another is to specify naturally durable timber for landscape works, for example oak, depending on availability and cost, which requires no treatment, save for where it is sunk into the ground (Dunnett & Clayden, 2000; Littlewood, 1986; Woolley & Kimmins, 2000; Woolley *et al.*, 1997). Table 2.3 shows the predicted durability of oak to be 20 years, even when untreated and in contact with the ground. This is equivalent to the durability of chemically treated generic timber predicted by the BRE (Anderson & Howard, 2000). However, as pointed out by Woolley *et al.* (1997), if wood is allowed to become wet and cannot dry out, then even preserved timbers will be vulnerable to fungal and/or insect attack. Detailed landscape design which deters moisture uptake is therefore essential to the longevity of exterior timbers and to reducing the possibility of frequent applications of chemical treatments by home owners. Moisture is most readily absorbed at the end of timbers, i.e. along, rather than across the grain. The endgrain must therefore be protected through being covered or cut at an angle to allow drainage and posts should not be set in concrete footings which allow ponding (Berge, 2000; National Physical Laboratory, 2003).

Relatively sustainable plastic and metal

As discussed earlier, in embodied energy terms, minimising the use of highly processed materials where possible makes good sense. What is more, such materials are typically responsible for harmful emissions in production. Unfortunately, some of these materials are currently the most 'fit for purpose' available and cannot easily be replaced. For example, plastic products are easily worked and flexible, and are widely used in landscape construction (Thompson & Sorvig, 2000) and metals used in landscape works are highly durable and their use may be unavoidable where security and vandal resistance are paramount (Woolley & Kimmins, 2000). The following discussion considers relatively sustainable plastics and metals that could be used where necessary in sustainable residential landscape design.

Relative to other plastics, polyvinyl chloride (PVC) plastic has low embodied energy (Woolley & Kimmins, 2000) and is widely used in landscape construction (Thompson & Sorvig, 2000). However, PVC's pollution impacts make it as controversial as timber preservatives (Thompson & Sorvig, 2000). There is some disagreement with regard to the potential for pollution stemming from PVC products in use (Thompson & Sorvig, 2000; Woolley & Kimmins, 2000). However, owing to the use of carcinogenic feeder stock (the vinyl chloride monomer and ethylene dichloride) and the possibility of dioxin release, there is agreement that PVC production poses considerable health risks and the international environmental community has campaigned for a phase-out (Thompson & Sorvig, 2000; Woolley & Kimmins, 2000). As a waste product, PVC contains environmentally dangerous substances which can leach, particularly chlorine compounds and heavy metals (Berge, 2000), which makes landfill a 'less than safe option' (Woolley & Kimmins, 2000, p 64). To compound the problem of disposal, PVC is not easily recycled. Landscape specifiers looking for a more benign option should replace PVC products with other plastics such as high-density polyethylene (HDPE) which have relatively low toxicity in processing and use, and are recyclable (Thompson & Sorvig, 2000). However, HDPE is only relatively benign as, like all plastics, it is derived from the highly polluting petrochemical industry (Thompson & Sorvig, 2000).

Similarly, all metals have high impacts related to the toxic by-products of manufacturing processes, as well as high embodied energy and CO_2 production (Woolley & Kimmins, 2000). For example, the manufacture of cast iron and steel produces large amounts of dioxins, heavy metals and acid mists, and zinc used in galvanizing steel has acid rain and highly toxic waste water as by-products (Thompson & Sorvig, 2000; Woolley & Kimmins, 2000). Furthermore, mining of ores for the most common metals used in construction – iron, copper, zinc and aluminium (bauxite) – leads to deforestation and landscape degradation (Berge, 2000). However, stainless steel is an alloy produced from recycled steel in the UK, rather than from virgin ore, and does not require any protective coatings. This is, relatively speaking, the most benign metal for landscape works (Woolley & Kimmins, 2000).

Relatively sustainable non-metal mineral products

Many of the minerals used in landscape works are non-metals. Whilst some of these can be used in their unprocessed state and have a relatively good environmental profile, for example aggregates and natural stone, other construction products are derived from the processing of non-metal minerals, such as clay fired bricks and cement (and associated concrete and mortar), and are less benign (Anderson & Howard, 2000; Woolley *et al.*, 1997). However, bricks and concrete are widely used as they require little maintenance, appear to have no known hazards once in use, and are very durable. A more sustainable approach is to try to minimise the use of these highly processed materials wherever possible through substitution with more benign, less processed, 'low-tech' materials such as aggregates.

The relatively poor sustainability profiles of bricks, cement and, by association, concrete and cement mortar are a result of high manufacturing energy and toxic pollutants such as fluoride and chlorine produced during processing (Thompson & Sorvig, 2000; Woolley *et al.*, 1997). In contrast, relatively little energy is consumed or pollution produced during the extraction of aggregates (gravel and sand) and natural stone (Woolley *et al.*, 1997). However, all non-metal minerals are high density with potentially significant transport energy implications and are derived from quarried non-renewable sources. The main problems with quarrying are impacts at the point of extraction: noise, dust, and habitat and landscape degradation (DETR, 2000e; Thompson & Sorvig, 2000; Woolley *et al.*, 1997).

Since a legislative amendment in the early 1980s, English mineral workings, which often provide essential employment in rural areas (Sinclair, 1991), are controlled by the planning system, which tries to control adverse impacts (HM Government, 2005). In addition to observance of imposed planning conditions for working practices and restoration, the Government advocates that quarries and associated works operators should use environmental management systems to establish environmentally sound working practices (DETR, 2000e).

When choosing non-metal mineral products, specifiers should therefore check that environmental management systems have been put in place throughout the custody chain, thus providing a measure of environmental commitment over and above responses to planning conditions. There are two principal environmental management systems: ISO 14001 and EMAS (Sustainable Development, 2000). ISO 14001 is published by the International Organisation for Standardisation and offers accreditation based on life-cycle assessment and environmental auditing (ISO14000.org, 2003). The European Eco Management and Audit Scheme (EMAS) requires a verified environmental statement describing life-cycle impacts and a commitment to review and improve performance (Friends of the Earth, 2001). It may be that EMAS provides the more credible system of the two, as it requires public reporting on environmental impact and performance. Unfortunately, by the early 2000s very few firms dealing with quarry products had adopted either of these environmental management systems (Friends of the Earth, 2001).

Lean construction and recovered materials

When specifying hard materials, landscape architects should look not only at their embodied energy and pollution, and impact on ecological and landscape resources, but also at how to use them efficiently, avoiding waste and overspecification whilst detailing materials to last as long as possible. The ethos of 'doing more with less', whilst reducing waste generated during construction and demolition, is termed 'lean construction' (Sustainable Development, 2000). Designers should recognise the relationship between the design forms they are using and how the materials they are specifying relate to these forms. Significant waste can result where, for example, organic design forms are expressed through large modular paving systems which need to then be cut to shape. Where organic forms are being used it may be advisable to express these by either using flexible systems such as loose bound aggregates or smaller modules such as cobbles or sets which can be adjusted to fit the design form (Figure 2.3(c)). Lean construction also anticipates providing the appropriate level specification for each context (Figure 2.5). For example, driveways will require an appropriate specification to support car access but this does not have to be extended to the entire paved surface. Landscape fabrics/geotextile should also be specified between the formation and the base/sub-base in order to reduce the required depth of the granular course by preventing the loss of aggregate into the subgrade.

So far, this section has discussed the relative merits of new landscape materials. However, landscape works also offer considerable scope for the use of alternative recovered materials (Dunnett & Clayden, 2000; Symonds, 1993). First, recovered materials include those which are reclaimed, i.e. potentially waste materials which are instead retained in their original form for further use and constitute the most sustainable material choice of all. Second, there are those that are recycled, i.e. potentially waste materials

Figure 2.5 Galbacken, Copenhagen. Informal, narrow pathways constructed from brick and thin strips of concrete slab permeate this residential development. Once again, planting is allowed to encroach and soften the edge of the pavement. It is also worth noting how close the trees are allowed to grow next to the adjacent buildings.

which are processed to create a new raw material. Recycling helps reduce waste but is generally less preferable to reclamation and is only a sustainable option if the processing involved does not lead to further pollution or require high energy inputs (Thompson & Sorvig, 2000).

Careful selection of recovered materials offers a route for designers to utilise the benefits of a material in a residential landscape, whilst reducing or removing the impacts of their primary manufacture and reducing pressure on landfill (Figure 2.4(a)). For example, the ease of reclaiming metal allows the inclusion of metal structures, whilst avoiding the pollution and resource burden of primary manufacture or recycling (Woolley & Kimmins, 2000). Stone, bricks and blocks are highly durable, and this makes them readily reclaimable in their original form (Woolley & Kimmins, 1997). As well as its other advantages as a construction material, timber is also reclaimable (Woolley et al., 1997). Some treated timber, such as telegraph poles and railway sleepers, can be reused if carefully salvaged (Thompson & Sorvig, 2000). Recycling plastic is a sustainable option, as it requires low energy inputs and the pollution risk is minimal (Woolley & Kimmins, 2000). However, when using recovered materials, the overriding principles of designing to reduce resources and waste (through considering transport energy of recovered materials, and designing for material efficiency, lack of waste and long life) still hold true.

Each year the UK construction industry generates around 70 million tonnes of waste (Rao et al., 2000; Skinner, 1998; Smith et al., 1998; Sustainable Development, 2000;WWF, 2004) which places heavy burdens on scarce landfill sites. A considerable proportion of this, estimated to be around 10 million tonnes, is construction waste, comprising materials delivered to site and thrown away unused (Howard, 2000; Sustainable Development, 2000; WWF, 2004). The remaining waste burden is composed of around 30 million tonnes each of demolition waste and excavated soil (Howard, 2000). There are doubts as to how much of this waste material is actually being recovered. Estimates vary from 20% (Skinner, 1998; WWF, 2004) to 33% (Smith et al., 1998). However, there is general agreement that the vast majority of recovered construction materials in the UK are crushed as aggregates and used for low-grade purposes such as concrete formation, hardcore and fill (Howard, 2000; Skinner, 1998; Smith et al., 1998; WWF, 2004). The more sustainable reuse of materials is currently rare. For example, Howard (2000) reports that only around 3 million tonnes of annual construction and demolition waste are reclaimed, whilst 24 million tonnes of this material are used to form recycled aggregate.

Detailed landscape design can help to facilitate the reuse of materials in the future, by considering 'exit strategies' which make reclamation easier and economically viable. In short, this is about anticipating the likely demolition of a project in years to come. For example, Ordinary Portland Cement (OPC) mortar beds or joints will create difficulties with lifting and cleaning of paviours and bricks while lime mortars are softer and easy to remove (Woolley et al., 1997). Until the early 20th century, all landscape and garden features used lime mortars, until OPC mortar became the industry standard. Lime mortars have further sustainable advantages over OPC mortars, specifically lower embodied energy and the reabsorption on setting of a great deal of the CO_2 released during production (Berge, 2000; Woolley et al.,

1997). Sharp sand may also be used as a substitute for OPC mortar beds, which also aids reuse of hard modular paving. Finally, when detailing timber, screw and bolt fixings, rather than nails, mean that materials can be easily dismantled and reused (Berge, 2000). Further to providing an exit strategy, such approaches also allow features and structures to be repaired during use, without wholesale replacement.

Specification and detailed design of soft landscape materials – vegetation

Life-cycle assessment (LCA) of vegetation

Planting can contribute to landscape sustainability on two levels. First, as a multifunctioning landscape element, vegetation can influence sustainability indicators such as energy use, biodiversity, water management and human health and well-being. These issues are discussed throughout this chapter. Second, the actual specification of plants, their production, transport, incorporation and maintenance can all affect resource inputs and waste and pollution generation associated with a landscape project, and it is these issues that are dealt with in this section.

As noted in Chapter 1, landscape design is often overlooked in the sustainable development debate. Perhaps this is because of the close ties of designed landscapes with horticulture and vegetation – the element that seemingly softens, beautifies and offsets the more obviously environmentally aggressive built elements. It may seem counterintuitive that planting can, in fact, cause harm to the environment:

> 'It is troubling and confusing to think that our [planted] creations can damage the environment. How can a green and growing place hurt the Earth?'
>
> (Thompson & Sorvig, 2000, p 13)

Nevertheless, when an LCA approach is applied to planting, sustainability concerns are apparent and require consideration at all stages (see Table 2.4) (Nienhuis & de Vreede, 1996).

Plant production and nursery practices

The UK's water consumption has risen by 70% over the last 30 years (Rao et al., 2000). Nevertheless, on a national basis, the UK should still be able to meet its water demands sustainably (Howard, 2000). However, in many regions water is abstracted unsustainably and aquifers are being steadily depleted. Unfortunately, climate change modelling predicts that this will be exacerbated by drier summers followed by infrequent but high-intensity rainfall in winter, which runs off rather than percolates into the ground. As

Table 2.4 Life-cycle stages and possible environmental issues of soft landscape materials. Dunnett, N. & Clayden, A. (2000) Resources: the raw materials of landscape. In: *Landscape and Sustainability.* J.F. Benson & M.H. Roe (Eds) London: Spon.

Life-Cycle Stage	Examples of Environmental Issues
Plant production and distribution	Pollution, energy consumption, loss of finite resources and ecosystem function (e.g. horticultural peat), packaging
Site treatment and plant establishment	Energy consumption, ecosystem loss, hydrological effects, air, water and soil pollution
Design in use and long-term functioning	Ecosystem disruption, energy consumption, recycling of organic materials, replacement needs

noted in Table 1.4 in Chapter 1, the construction industry has been described as wasteful in terms of water use and, unfortunately, the horticultural industry is equally profligate; irrigation water is the single greatest resource input into horticultural production after sunlight (Orth, 1996) but Molitor (1998) estimates that at least 30% of this is wasted in European plant production. However, a nursery's water consumption can be reduced through the collection of rainwater from greenhouses and roofs and hard standing areas (Molitor, 1998). Furthermore, irrigation water can be recirculated and, if required, disinfected, in a closed system, thereby reducing both water inputs and outputs (Molitor, 1998; Nienhuis & de Vreede, 1996).

As well as reducing water consumption and waste, closed irrigation systems within greenhouses also reduce the risks of pesticide pollution to the wider environment (Molitor, 1998; Nienhuis & de Vreede, 1996). Pollution of soils, groundwater, surface waters and the air can be caused by the high intensity of horticultural pesticide use, whether under glass or in the field (Dekeyzer, 1996; Molitor, 1998). However, in an approach known as integrated pest management (IPM), biological pest control systems (using beneficial insects, mites and nematodes) combined with optimum hygiene and temperature management can help control pests with much reduced recourse to chemical applications (Dekeyzer, 1996; Dunnett & Hitchmough, 1996; Molitor, 1998). Use of efficient climate controls in IPM can also reduce the amount of energy consumed in greenhouses (Molitor, 1998).

Peat is the dominant raw material for horticultural growing media in Europe (Molitor, 1998). However, the use of horticultural peat is a major threat to the UK's remaining lowland raised peat bogs (Rollins, 2003) of which only 6000 ha remain (Jowett, 2005). Kendle *et al.* (2000) have argued that, on a global scale, the rate of peat accretion far exceeds the demand and therefore it can be considered renewable, and in certain countries is a resource so vast that it can be harvested without concern for habitat fragility. However, this would suggest that peat compost used in the UK is likely to be either from a threatened local source or imported, with a transport energy penalty. Common sources include relatively near nations such as Ireland and Finland, as well as more remote countries such as Germany, Lithuania, Estonia and Latvia (Holmes *et al.*, 2000). It has been suggested that peat-free compost should always be used when sustainable landscape planting is the aim (Dunnett & Hitchmough, 1996). But is this viable?

Unfortunately, peat-free media have suffered from a poor reputation with regard to the quality of associated plant growth (Jowett, 2005). However, in the UK, the Composting Association (TCA), together with the the Waste and Resource Action Programme (WRAP), have now developed Publicly Available Specification 100 (PAS 100) for composted materials. Launched in November 2002 and published by the British Standards Institute, the specification provides minimum requirements for input materials, process of composting and, crucially, the quality of the compost. Media which meet this specification are also entitled to TCA accreditation and can be used as an alternative to peat. Accreditaton provides a quality assurance for the horticultual industry that may have been lacking in the past.

However, total substitution of peat with alternative recycled materials (even those achieving the new standard) is not yet viable for some plants (Jowett, 2005). For example, ericaceous shrubs require lower pH in the growing medium and may not establish in the currently available peat alternatives (Holmes *et al.*, 2000). However, there are viable peat alternatives, such as green compost and forestry by-products, for many of the sectors of commercial horticulture, and where total substitution is not yet viable, there could be reductions in peat use through the use of peat-free dilutants (Holmes *et al.*, 2000). A more pragmatic approach to sustainable planting may therefore be to specify peat-free material where possible (Dunnett & Clayden, 2000) and favour nurseries which have otherwise reduced peat inputs through diluted formulations.

The principal waste ouputs from horticultural production are organic matter, such as prunings and clippings, and packaging, particularly plastic containers (Molitor, 1998). Clearly nurseries can reduce their organic waste outputs through retention and treatment of materials for use as compost or mulch. The environmental consequences of plastics were discussed earlier in this chapter, and the horticultural industry uses a range of these materials in pots and containers, including PVC, polyethylene and polypropylene (Thompson & Sorvig, 2000). Nurseries can reduce the impact of plastic waste and reduce inputs of virgin plastics by adopting reuse policies. They may also use recycled plastic pots and trays (Dunnett & Hitchmough, 1996).

Certification for the use of all or some of these sustainable horticultural approaches is available for UK nurseries. The Dutch MPS, the Floriculture Environmental Project, undertakes 'green' assessment and certification of horticultural growers and this has included a small number of UK firms (Jenkins, 2001). The British Ornamental Pot Producers accreditation scheme (BOPP), which takes environmental credentials into account, has been expanded to growers of hardy nursery stock (Sawyer, 2003). Finally, though intended as a general certification scheme for organic husbandry, a small number of UK nurseries have met the accreditation standards of the Soil Association in the UK (Soil Association, 2002a). This standard covers benign pest control, peat-free composts, water management and recycling of waste (Soil Association, 2002b).

Planting design, implementation and maintenance

This section explores the impact of planting design, implementation and maintenance on resource inputs, and waste and pollution outputs.

Plant palette and planting style

A sustainable approach to landscape planting rests on specifying species and cultivars which are well suited to the site for which they are to be used (Ard, 1999; Dunnett, 1995; Dunnett & Hitchmough, 1996; Ruff, 1982). This will aid plant establishment and healthy growth, and also remove the need for expensive ground preparation, resource inputs of water, fertilisers and pesticides, and long-term build-up of maintenance problems. Appropriate site-specific plant choices require an understanding of the site's pre- and post-development characteristics (climate, soils and drainage) and so an inventory of the plants thriving on the site pre-development can give design clues (Dunnett & Hitchmough, 1996; Nassauer, 1988). Such analysis can be used to refine or modify species lists suggested by regional guidance (Gilbert & Anderson, 1998).

One of the common justifications for focusing on locally native species in sustainable plantings is that they are pre-adapted to the local climate and soil conditions, resulting in better establishment and growth (Kendle & Rose, 2000). However, whilst this might be true for an undisturbed rural site, other sites, particularly in urban areas, may display soil and climatic characteristics greatly modified from the natural situation (Dunnett & Hitchmough, 1996). In such circumstances, some exotic species may be far better adapted than some of their indigenous counterparts (Kendle & Rose, 2000) as indicated by the spontaneous assemblages of natives and non-natives on derelict urban sites, giving rise to ecologically rich 'urban commons' (Gilbert, 1989). In any case, some of the exotic species found on such sites may be regarded as both 'honorary natives' (Kendle & Forbes,

1997) and valued contributors to local identity (Mabey, 1993). Exotic species that are adapted to site can also help regeneration through soil building and reduction of erosion (Williams, 1997). It is important to recognise the potential benefit of non-native vegetation for modified sites, given the Government's ongoing advocacy of 'brownfield development' in English planning policy, including, crucially for this study, guidance for new housing (DEFRA, 2000; DETR, 2000b,c; HM Government, 2005).

The use of non-native plants has been a hotly debated topic for over 100 years and continues to be so today (see Dunnett & Hitchmough, 2004; Spirn, 1998; Thompson & Sorvig, 2000). However, in terms of improved plant establishment and reducing resource burdens on disturbed and modified sites, there is little logical basis for advocating exclusively native species (see Figure 2.7) (Dunnett & Clayden, 2000). In any case, as reported by Gilbert & Anderson (1998), there has been little research into the establishment success of native stock compared to that of exotics, and the results of work that has been done are contradictory (Kendle & Rose, 2000).

Further to selecting plants well suited to the site, the style and detailing of a planting scheme are very important in determining its overall sustainability. Current standard landscape planting styles tend to be based on simple, formal compositions such as closely mown turf, perhaps with emergent specimen trees, and low diversity or monoculture shrub mass (Dunnett & Clayden, 2000; Dunnett & Hitchmough, 2004). However, such compositions are based on remaining static over time and are likely to rely on considerable resource inputs in terms of site preparation, site establishment and maintenance. The relatively low maintenance cost of such plantings is misleading in terms of the resource inputs required: gang-mowing and electrical pruning and strimming are quick, unskilled and cheap, as fuel costs are artificially low; whereas labour charges are high (Thompson & Sorvig, 2000). The actual resource costs of such landscape maintenance cannot be evaluated accurately simply by the monetary cost (Thompson & Sorvig, 2000).

Although any designed landscape which includes vegetation cannot be 'no maintenance', the style of the planting can reduce this burden. The resource input for all plantings is greatest during the initial 'establishment phase', i.e. the time between planting and the fusing of a plant community canopy, and therefore it is advantageous to minimise this period (Hitchmough, 1994). Choosing plants which are fit for the site is essential, but the planting style and habit of individual plant selections can also play a part. Although a monoculture of 'fit for site' shrubs can establish and fuse quickly, such an approach has serious drawbacks in terms of a site's ecological function (as discussed later in this chapter) and potential maintenance requirements. Whilst diversity in planting is generally agreed to provide resistance to pests and disease (Dunnett, 1995; Dunnett & Clayden, 2000), infestations are likely

Figure 2.6 Berliner Strasse, 88 Zehlendorf, Berlin. The scheme, which was completed in 1993, comprises 172 dwellings in houses between two and six stories high. The development includes a day nursery, small allotment gardens (a), community meeting house and public green spaces. It is an excellent example of nature-like planting creating a green oasis within a busy city environment. Rainwater is harvested from the roofs and stored in a large retention pond located in front of the community building and nursery (b). The water is circulated, using wind and solar power, along an informal stream which runs through the heart of the development (c). The planting may appear untidy to some but it is extremely effective in softening the visual impact of the taller buildings and creating semi-private doorstep spaces (d). This bold and confident use of vegetation is taken through to the small private gardens, where lawned areas are small and trees and larger shrubs are used to provide structure and privacy (e).

Figure 2.6 *Continued*

to be more severe in monoculture plantings (Ard, 1999; Dunnett, 1995). Furthermore, uniformity and formality in monoculture or low-diversity plantings lower the composition's visual robustness against even limited levels of disease or infestation, incoming spontaneous vegetation and plant failure, thus potentially increasing the need for agrochemicals.

By way of contrast, it has been suggested that diverse nature-like planting (Figure 2.6) designs, which are not only fit for site but are also dynamic and accommodate self-regeneration and nutrient cycling, will minimise maintenance requirements (Ard, 1999; Dunnett, 1995; Dunnett & Hitchmough, 1996). In designing such a plant community, compatibility of plants with one another, as well as with the site, is crucial. The basis for this compatabilty is to use plants whose physiological niches allow them to survive and thrive together as a community (Thompson, 1997). Once these diverse communities become established, they form a matrix of roots, stems, foliage and flowers which provides protection for its members and resists invasion from outsiders (Thompson, 1997), although such informality is also more able to accommodate the dynamism of plant failures and self-sowing where it does occur (Ard, 1999). Structural as well as species diversity in plantings also has implications for sustainability, specifically biodiversity, and this is discussed later in this chapter.

Figure 2.7 This annual meadow in a housing estate in Sheffield is very popular with local residents. Although it appears to be a wildflower meadow, there are in fact very few native species within the meadow. The whole area is sown each year and although this is not an extremely low-maintenance landscape, it is very cost-effective. As well as being visually exciting, it also supports biodiversity through provision of food sources for birds and insects.

Having established the clear benefits of diverse, naturalistic plantings, it should be noted that small areas of more formal soft landscape treatments may also have their place in residential development. For example, high resource bedding may attract considerable human attachment. Clearly, the aim of the sustainable residential landscape should be to locate and design higher intensity elements where they will achieve greatest visual benefit with minimum extent. Furthermore, although requiring significant maintenance, closely mown turf is ideal for residential areas where sitting out or informal play is to be accommodated (Beer, 1983). However, patches of grass which are too small to accommodate these activities are relatively expensive to maintain (see Hitchmough, 1994), are potentially unsightly and their upkeep is not offset by social benefits (Beer, 1983).

Size of plant material

The size of plants used in a planting design can also affect sustainability. Large plant material involves relatively large resource inputs in the nursery, greater amounts of packaging and greater potential for high transport energy. Furthermore, smaller material will tend to be more adaptable, will establish more easily on site and attain higher rates of growth, catching up with larger material planted at the same time (Dunnett & Clayden, 2000; Hitchmough, 1994). However, smaller trees may be more vulnerable to vandalism. In 'high-risk' circumstances, larger material that increases the initial environmental impact of the design must therefore be weighed against the potentially greater resource implications caused by the compounded impact of replacement and making good works, or even the broad undermining of sustainability through abandonment of the tree planting. An online tree planting guide published by the UK's Tree Council suggests that semi-mature trees may be required where there is risk of vandalism (Tree Council, 2003) and this is echoed by the similar guidance produced by ENFO, the Irish Republic's public information service on environmental matters, which advocates heavy standard trees in such conditions (ENFO, 2003).

Site conditions and preparation

There are construction and implementation activities that can prejudice the establishment and growth of all plants, and hence reduce the sustainability of the scheme through wasted materials and increased resource consumption. Clearly, avoidance of these activities will be beneficial in a sustainable landscape. Common factors include compaction of soils during the earthworks contract to a point where they cannot support plant growth. This is particularly acute if earthworks are undertaken in wet weather (Gilbert, 1989). As noted above, a site's pre-existing soils can provide valuable clues as to the vegetation which will thrive; however, this information may only be useful if there is subsequent conservation of the site's soils during construction (Nassauer, 1988). Furthermore, a construction programme may necessitate out-of-season planting, facilitated by containerised plant stock, which requires large amounts of labour, contractor movement and inputs of plant food and water, as well as the increased embodied energy and pollution of the material due to the containers themselves (Dunnett & Clayden, 2000). As pointed out by Thompson & Sorvig (2000), the quality of a contractor's work can also be crucial to landscape sustainability. With this in mind, the landscape contractor responsible for the planting should ideally be retained to undertake maintenance for a period following completion of the works. In this way the contractor will be responsible for making good any defects that occur in the planting during the defects liability period.

Integration of existing, established planting

Finally, a sustainable approach to planting and design should try to reduce the impact of new plantings through preserving and integrating existing site vegetation wherever possible. In many ways this is analogous to utilising reclaimed hard materials, in that the benefits of the materials are enjoyed whilst the impacts of production are avoided. Measures to conserve and enrich a site's existing vegetation are also the first priorities in ensuring the ecological function of a site (Dunnett, 1995; Dunnett & Hitchmough, 1996), as discussed later in this chapter.

Prohibition of synthetic chemical use for on-site landscape works

The preceding section has introduced design approaches that can significantly reduce the amount of agro-chemicals required to establish and maintain landscape plantings. However, should a sustainable landscape go further and be completely free of agro-chemicals? Pesticides are prohibited in some European cities (Hitchmough, 1994) and in the standards for organic husbandry (HDRA, 2001; Soil Association, 2002c). Avoidance of synthetic pesticides and fertilisers would, at first glance, seem the ideal approach for sustainable residential landscapes. However, a fuller consideration of pollution risks and other issues indicates that this may not be viable or necessary.

Agro-chemicals can provoke considerable public unease, which may be an echo from the period of the 1950s to the 1970s when the use of persistent and bio-accumulating substances was endemic (Hitchmough, 1994). However, modern synthetic fertilisers pose little toxic hazard in the landscape if used correctly (Thompson & Sorvig, 2000) and modern pesticides are tightly regulated (Simons, 2004), designed to target desired species, have reduced human toxicity and, unlike the timber preservatives discussed earlier in this chapter, have low environmental persistence[3] (Hitchmough, 1994; Kendle et al., 2000; Thompson & Sorvig, 2000). A very small percentage of landscape workers can develop chronic allergies to pesticides, but for the community at large there appears to be little risk of chronic toxicity (Hitchmough, 1994). In any case, landscape works tend to use only small amounts of insecticides and fungicides, and the use of herbicides could be as little as 0.1% of that used per hectare, per annum in horticultural production (Kendle et al., 2000) where, as discussed earlier, such intense use can cause pollution problems.

In fact, the greatest risk to human and ecosystem health from the use of chemicals in on-site landscape works stems from misuse, i.e. if they are mixed, not diluted, overused, or not applied and handled in accordance with the manufacturers' instructions (Hitchmough, 1994; Simons, 2004; Thompson & Sorvig, 2000). However, in terms of pollution risk, there seems to be little evidence against responsible use of modern agrochemicals in the landscape.

While it is theoretically possible to replace synthetic pesticides with hand or machine cultivation for a given plant community, this could occur only with a 'phenomenal' increase in time, effort and resources (Hitchmough, 1994; Kendle at al., 2000). Even though pesticides are generally produced from non-renewable resources and have significant embodied energy (Thompson & Sorvig, 2000), the energy costs of controlling weeds through alternative means are likely to be greater (Hitchmough, 1994; Kendle at al., 2000). Additionally, Kendle et al. (2000) report on a tree-planting scheme at the Earth Centre in South Yorkshire, UK, where the original intention to work without chemicals was substituted with judicious use of herbicides, and increased established tree cover was the result. In the long term, on sites where a pre-existing pernicious weed bank exists, pesticides can contribute to the establishment of diverse vegetation that provides food and shelter for a range of wildlife. Furthermore, herbicides may sometimes be required if a more formal area of planting becomes infected with disease or weeds (Kendle et al., 2000) though, as discussed earlier, generally sustainable planting design should try to minimise such areas and maximise plantings which accommodate dynamism, including plant failures and spontaneous seeding.

Synthetic fertilisers, if used correctly, may not have associated pollution risk but they do have a very high manufacturing energy (Kendle et al., 2000; Thompson & Sorvig, 2000). Is there an alternative? The volume of manure required to provide an equivalent amount of readily available nitrogen as

---

[3] The effects of modern pesticides on non-target species are limited to the immediate area of application, and to the period of time between application of the chemical and it breaking down on the soil surface; these effects have been shown to be biologically insignificant (Kendle et al., 2000).

100 kg ammonium nitrate synthetic fertiliser has been estimated as 25 tonnes (Kendle *et al.*, 2000). In energy terms alone, the savings related to a prohibition of man-made fertiliser may be lost on the transport of alternative materials (Kendle *et al.*, 2000).

The total prohibition of synthetic chemicals would not appear to be a viable or necessary indicator of sustainable landscape. In fact, the approach adopted by most landscape professionals – to use chemicals where they have obvious benefits, but to use them responsibly (Kendle *et al.*, 2000) – would seem fundamentally correct. However, in order to remove significant pollution risk in a sustainable landscape project, it is paramount that landscape specifications clearly stipulate that contractors are to be competent and suitably licensed to use the materials specified, and explicitly reference all relevant codes of practice and statutes. This measure, together with those discussed earlier (careful selection of nurseries that reduce their pesticide use through IPM, and planting specification and design which will tend to reduce the need for fertilisers, pesticides and other resources) should significantly enhance the sustainability of residential landscape plantings.

Water management

Reduced domestic water consumption

The sharp increase in the UK's water consumption has resulted in substantial infrastructure works for water supply and transportation, with associated energy, material and landscape resource impacts (Rao *et al.*, 2000). A more sustainable approach is to identify ways of reducing water consumption (Barton *et al.*, 1995; Rao *et al.*, 2000). Water consumed by industries such as construction and horticulture have played a part in the increased demand, but the greatest contributors to water consumption, at least in England and Wales, are electricity generators and domestic users (DEFRA, 2003). However, in resource consumption terms, the water used in electricity production is abstracted from rivers and returned in a short period, with little net loss, and therefore domestic users should be prioritised in efforts to promote a water-efficient society (Howard, 2000).

In the mid-1990s it was estimated that approximately 3% of all domestic water consumption was used for irrigating the garden (Barton *et al.*, 1995). This is equivalent to 3.5 litres per person per day. The specification of plant species which are well suited to the site's soils and climate, and which have a relatively short establishment phase, could make a contribution to reducing water consumed by residents as they nurture plants in their private gardens. Furthermore, water lost from planting areas by soil surface evaporation can be dramatically reduced through the application of a 50 mm depth of bark mulch dressing (Thompson & Sorvig, 2000).

Further to planting design, domestic water consumption can also be reduced through other landscape features. Garden water butts can be connected to the downpipes which transport water from the roof of the house down to the drainage system (CIRIA, 2000). This water can then be used to irrigate the garden or for other 'low-grade' uses instead of potable water from the mains supply. Water butts are a very simple form of water harvesting but other, more sophisticated systems can be used which store rainwater in the rear garden, before pumping it back into the house for toilet flushing (Barton et al., 1995). Yet more complex systems can be used which store grey water from baths, showers and wash basins within tanks beneath the garden which, following treatment with chemical tablets, can be pumped back into the house, combined with harvested rainwater and used for not only WC flushing but also washing machines and external taps for irrigation and car washing (see Figures 2.8 and 2.12). Such a comprehensive grey water recycling system could provide 80% of the daily domestic consumption (Barton et al., 1995).

Management of surface water runoff

As well as helping to reduce mains water consumption, rainwater harvesting from roofs also prevents significant volumes of water from contributing to surface runoff from residential areas. Surface water runoff must be managed if the challenge of sustainable residential development is to be met.

The major effects of development on hydrology occur through the replacement of vegetation with impermeable surfacing and buildings, thereby reducing infiltration of the water into the soil and reducing interception, evaporation and evapotranspiration from vegetative surfaces, thus increasing the surface runoff from the site (Whitford et al., 2001). Together with collecting water for reuse, the most fundamental step in an alternative, sustainable water management solution is to minimise the area of impermeable surface on a site (CIRIA, 2000). By increasing the amount of green space, i.e. lawns, plantings, trees and green roofs, and introducing permeable paved surfaces, the amount of runoff can be reduced. Nevertheless, as noted by the Scottish Environment Protection Agency (SEPA) (2000), in actuality all developments need to be drained to remove excess rainwater.

Traditional drainage systems endeavour to remove rainfall from a site as quickly as possible (CIRIA, 2000; Environment Agency, 2003). However, this approach, based on the conveyance of rainwater runoff directly to a water course via a pipe, can cause a number of environmental impacts.

> 'Unattenuated runoff from developments increases the risk of flooding from the receiving water course, and can damage river habitat. It will also decrease the amount of water soaking into the ground, reducing the water available for abstraction.'
>
> (Environment Agency, 2003, p 3)

Figure 2.8 Hedebegade, Copenhagen. The restoration of this inner-city housing block in 2002 incorporated sustainable design features including waste recycling, solar heating and rainwater harvesting. (a) A collection channel which gathers water from the surrounding roofs and paved surfaces. The water is directed to an infiltration pond (b) where the water is temporarily stored before it is filtered and retained for use in the communal building. The harvested rain is used for flushing toilets and to supply the communal laundry. The courtyard also supports other sustainable activities by providing covered areas for bicycle storage, recycling and composting facilities (c).

Pollution and flooding

The impacts of a traditional surface water drainage system are as follows. First, there are impacts related to pollution. Diffuse pollutants can be washed from urban areas, including dust, oil, litter, hydrocarbons, pathogens, toxic metals and salts, which are then carried into receiving water courses (Environment Agency, 2003; SEPA, 2000). As a consequence of these repeated discharges, silt can blanket the water course habitat, rapidly reducing oxygen levels (Environment Agency, 2003). The Environment Agency (2003) estimates that pollution by urban drainage accounts for 21% of Scotland's most seriously polluted water courses. Pollutants can also be washed into groundwater (Environment Agency, 2003) which is extremely difficult to treat (CIRIA, 2000). In addition, traditional drainage systems are often wrongly connected, causing foul sewers to fail under storm conditions when they are required to carry large volumes of rainwater (Environment Agency, 2003; Rao *et al.*, 2000; SEPA, 2000). This can result in untreated, raw sewage being

Figure 2.8 *Continued*

forced through the system and into river networks, where it may cause considerable environmental damage.

Second, as land is developed, natural drainage patterns are disrupted which can lead to flooding. When rainwater is conveyed in pipes to rivers, the time between the rainfall event and water entering the river is reduced compared to the situation prior to development and thus large volumes of water converge on a water course in a short period of time, causing flooding (DTLR, 2001b; Environment Agency, 2003; SEPA 2000). The delivery of

(c)

Figure 2.8 *Continued*

large quantities of water can also cause erosion within the receiving water course (SEPA, 2000).

Amenity and habitat

The traditional approach to managing drainage has had significant impacts on the potential recreation value of the landscape and its ability to support habitat diversity. Most obvious is the loss of surface water where rivers have been redirected beneath the ground into culverts. River engineering has also included the straightening of natural river channels and modification of the river profile in order to improve rates at which storm water can be moved through the system whilst also reducing bank erosion. This attempt to control what is essentially a dynamic system has resulted in a loss of complexity and richness in terms of both visual amenity and interest and habitat diversity (CIRIA, 2000; Environment Agency, 2003; SEPA, 2000). Furthermore, by putting drainage systems out of sight and by placing them in a 'straitjacket', they lose their potency to articulate the vibrant qualities of the hydrological cycle to the public.

Sustainable urban drainage systems (SuDS)

Designing and implementing drainage systems that do not cause flooding or pollution, and enhance the local environment, must go beyond the traditional approach described above (SEPA, 2000). Techniques that provide drainage whilst reducing the unwanted effects are collectively referred to as sustainable urban drainage systems (SuDS) (Environment Agency, 2003).

> 'Sustainable urban drainage is a concept that includes long term environmental and social factors in decisions about drainage. It takes account of the quantity and quality of runoff, and the amenity value of surface water in the urban environment.'

(CIRIA, 2000, p 1)

Two fundamental principles underpin the SuDS approach. First, SuDS techniques should strive to consider quantity and quality of runoff, as well as amenity in its broadest sense – water resources, community facilities, education, landscape and habitat value (CIRIA, 2000; Ponds Conservation Trust, 2002; Thompson & Sorvig, 2000). Second, a SuDS system should deal with runoff as close as possible to where the rain falls – source control – with additional techniques further from the source considered only if necessary, in a surface water management train (Figure 2.9) (CIRIA, 2000; Environment Agency, 2003).

As noted earlier, the most fundamental approaches to preventing large amounts of runoff are minimising impermeable areas and maximising green space through reducing sealed paved surfaces and maximising green space cover, and/or harvesting rainwater from roofs for reuse (CIRIA, 2000; Whitford et al., 2001). Other preventive methods consider the quality of runoff and include 'good house keeping' such as regular road sweeping, dog litter bins and educating site users (CIRIA, 2000). In order to deal with residual runoff, further source control techniques should be considered. These techniques include the following:

- **Permeable pavements.** These are load-bearing surfaces that allow surface water to pass through to a permeable fill beneath (CIRIA,

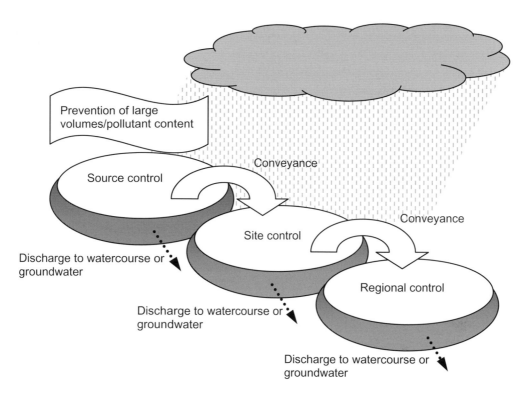

Figure 2.9 The surface water management train: addressing runoff quantity and quality at all stages of the drainage system. (Adapted from The Environment Agency, 2003, *Sustainable Drainage System (SuDS): an Introduction*. Bristol: The Environment Agency. © Environment Agency copyright 2007. All rights reserved.)

2000). The definition of permeable paving embraces many different approaches of varying sophistication, from unbound granular material, such as gravel, through to permeable blocks, porous asphalts and bound gravels. Permeable pavements can be designed to allow either direct infiltration to the underlying subgrade or, where the site's soils are too heavy or fragile or the runoff is highly polluted, the sub-base may be sealed from below and can be used to store the runoff for *managed* discharge to a water course (CIRIA, 2000; Interpave, 2003). Storage and passage of the water through the sub-base allow both attenuation and quality improvement by removing sediment and oil (CIRIA, 2000). Permeable pavements have negligible wildlife value (Ponds Conservation Trust, 2002) but they can be designed to be attractive and are well suited to high-density, urban situations (CIRIA, 2005).

- **Infiltration trenches and soakaways**. These devices drain water directly into the ground by enhancing the natural capacity of the soil to store and drain water (CIRIA, 2000). Infiltration trenches and soakaways are effectively excavations backfilled with crushed stone to create an underground reservoir (Environment Agency, 2003). Removal of pollutants such as trace metals, solids, organic matter, phosphate and nitrate occur within the backfill through adsorption, filtering and microbial decomposition (Environment Agency, 2003).

Where these source control measures are insufficient to deal with the anticipated runoff, then the water may require further downstream management. The first step is to deliver any excess runoff to a conveyance system. These include the following.

- **Swales and filter strips**. These are vegetated surface features that drain water evenly from surfaces; swales are long shallow channels, whereas filter strips are gently sloping areas of ground (CIRIA, 2000). Both mimic natural drainage (Figure 2.4(b)), in that they allow rainwater to run through vegetation, allowing the velocity of the flow to be checked and pollutants filtered (Environment Agency, 2003). Swales can also be used as an infiltration device which, depending on the nature of the soil, can be made more efficient through the use of check dams (CIRIA, 2000). Where the ground is unsuitable for infiltration, the swale acts primarily as a conveyance system to downstream devices. Swales can also be used to accept runoff directly from impermeable surfaces, where there has been no upstream source control; they can be used alongside impermeable roads and footways. Swales and filter strips can be planted to provide both visual amenity and habitat function (CIRIA, 2000).
- **Filter or French drains.** These are similar to the infiltration trenches introduced earlier, in that they are linear excavations backfilled with stone, though in this case their main function is to transfer water in a managed fashion downstream (Environment Agency, 2003). The backfill in the trench again acts as filter, removing sediment, organic matter and oil residue. If, however, sufficient infiltration occurs through the trench wall and bottom into the surrounding soil, the drain effectively acts as an infiltration trench. Like swales, these features can therefore act as source control as well as downstream conveyance.

The final stage in the water management train is passive treatment within basins and wetlands, which receive residual runoff from conveyance systems at either a site scale or a regional scale.

- **Infiltration basins**. These are shallow surface depressions where runoff is stored until it infiltrates through the soil of the basin floor. Infiltration basins can be planted to provide recreation and other sustainability benefits (CIRIA, 2000).

- **Detention basins**. Like infiltration basins, these are free from water under dry flow conditions (CIRIA, 2000). They are designed to hold back storm runoff for a few hours to allow sediment to settle out, before releasing the water at a managed rate (Environment Agency, 2003). These basins can be used to separate out the highly polluted 'first flush' of runoff and are most efficient when used in series with other retention ponds and wetlands.
- **Retention ponds and wetlands**. Retention ponds retain a fluctuating volume of water at all times (CIRIA, 2000; Environment Agency, 2003). A typical retention pond (Figure 2.6(b)) will have around three weeks' retention time, allowing biological breakdown of pollutants. Wetlands are a further enhancement of retention ponds, due to their inclusion of shallow areas planted with aquatic vegetation which further filter the water. Ponds and wetlands can provide habitat function and visual amenity (CIRIA, 2000; Environment Agency, 2003).

The disposal of surface water has long been a material consideration for English local planning authorities when determining planning applications (DTLR, 2001b). *PPG 25: Development and Flood Risk*, published in 2001, supports the use of SuDS to manage surface water runoff and advocates close collaboration between local authorities, developers and statutory consultees and statutory undertakers to encourage their use (DTLR, 2001b). This guidance was closely followed by a revision of Part H of the Building Regulations *Drainage and Waste Disposal*, *Part H Rainwater Drainage*, which prioritised the use of infiltration systems and managed discharge to water courses over traditional solutions (DTLR, 2002). Although there is now legislative provision for the encouragement of SuDS in England, there is no specific legislation in effect which requires that SuDS schemes must be incorporated into new developments (Ponds Conservation Trust, 2002).

The water management strategies identified here are typically applied at the large scale and are seen primarily as engineered features. Many of these features rely on the infiltration and purification functions of natural soils and vegetation. As such, they have potential to support biodiversity and habitat, and may enable diverse vegetation to be introduced within residential development that has amenity, hydrological and biodiversity benefits. The replacement of traditional drainage infrastructure with attractive, vegetated infiltration features such as swales in housing and neighbourhood development has been applied on a relatively large scale in a number of North American cities, notably Chicago, Portland and Seattle (Figure 2.10). Native plant species and plant communities are favoured, creating networks of prairie vegetation in residential subdivisions. A new

Figure 2.10 This infiltration planter in a street in Portland, Oregon, fills up with water following heavy rainfall. The water slowly infiltrates into the ground below. For much of the time, however, the feature is dry. Stormwater management features such as this offer great potential for introducing vegetation into situations where it may not otherwise be considered necessary. Photograph by Tom Liptan.

approach to landscape and garden planting that actively promotes stormwater capture and infiltration is gaining in popularity: so-called 'rain gardens' are attractive features in themselves but also contribute to small- and large-scale water management (Dunnett & Clayden, 2007). Some of the most exciting developments in this field relate to the substitution of vegetation solutions for standard concrete and pipe engineering in close proximity to built development. Portland, Oregon, is a centre of activity in this regard. Street swales collect excess runoff from road surfaces after heavy storms and double as attractive street features or traffic-calming measures (Figure 2.11). Stormwater planters fit within the immediate curtilage of a building and take the runoff (by disconnecting the downpipes) from the roofs of a building and intercept it before it enters the drainage system or soaks away into the ground.

Figure 2.11 This street swale captures some of the water that would normally flow directly into the drains after heavy rain. Moreover, as well as increasing the amount of vegetation, the planted area also acts as a traffic-calming facility.

Enhancement of site ecological function and human well-being

Site ecological function

Preserving and encouraging biodiversity

The conservation of biological diversity, or 'biodiversity', is essential to the achievement of sustainability, and the variety of living species on earth is a key global resource (Jensen *et al.*, 2000; Williams & Cary, 2002). Following the 1992 Rio Earth Summit, in 1994 the UK Government launched the UK Biodiversity Action Plan (UKBAP) (O'Mahony, 2004). The UKBAP contains action plans for the UK's most rapidly declining and endangered habitats and species, and also takes stock of the 'everyday' natural assets which form the nation's diverse wildlife resource (DoE, 1994a). It has been suggested that preservation of the everyday is the key to true nature conservation (Barton *et al.*, 1995) and the basis for national and, in turn, global biodiversity (Grant, 2000). The UKBAP stresses the importance of local action,

(a)

Figure 2.12 Marzahn, Berlin. Developed in the 1990s, Marzahn is a good example of using more innovative approaches to rainwater management whilst also enhancing the aesthetic value of the landscape. The galvanised water barrels (a) are a feature of the garden rather than merely a functional solution. Overspill from the water barrel is directed through a series of open channels to a large central channel which winds its way through the landscape (b). When dry, the channel reveals a poem which has been inlaid into the stonework. The water passes through a series of ponds before it is finally stored in a large underground container. This water is used for irrigating the landscape. Once again, planting plays a pivotal role in the design of this landscape. Native plants dominate in the role of defining space and boundaries. Within this native mix, edible varieties have also been included, bearing fruit and berries (c). The sustainable features within this design contribute to improving the environmental profile of the development but also enhance the residents' pleasure in their private gardens and communal spaces.

Figure 2.12 *Continued*

tailored to local conditions and the values of local people, and under its aegis, local authorities have formulated local biodiversity action plans (LBAPs) (UK Biodiversity Steering Group, 1995).

Landscape ecology concepts that drive biodiversity, such as dynamism, richness, complexity, structure and connectivity of vegetative habitats, can be adapted into an ecological landscape design and management philosophy at site level. Ecological landscape design and management promote complexity and spatial structure in a site's planting, apparent both in plan and in vertical layers; encourage dynamism, succession, nutrient cycling and age structure in planting; consider the shape of habitats and their juxtaposition with each other and other land uses; and encourage connectivity and minimise isolation of habitats. Effective ecological landscape design and management work at a range of scales, where no pattern exists in isolation but is dependent on the smaller patterns which are embedded within it. The ecologically sensitive landscape professional must therefore be mindful of biodiversity at a range of scales: biodiversity is the variation of ecosystems and habitats; the number and species of flora and fauna; and the genetic diversity within species (DoE, 1994a; Jensen *et al.*, 2000).

Key aspects of ecological landscape design and management

This section considers ecological landscape design and management approaches which can be applied by developers and their designers to all types of development, including residential landscapes, thus maximising biodiversity and minimising the threat to local ecology. The principal objectives with regard to site habitat and ecosystem conservation should be to:

- identify and plan for what already exists; a fundamental objective should be the enrichment of existing ecological capital
- restore existing habitats which may be degraded
- identify future potential. Create new habitats where land offers potential opportunities. Restore (and create) appropriate connections between habitats.

Protecting existing ecological capital

As noted earlier, the preservation of existing vegetation on a development site makes good sustainable sense in terms of resource conservation and the retention of ecological capital. An initial survey of a site's pre-development characteristics should guide new planting proposals and also provide a picture of the site's ecological capital in terms of existing habitat features (Dunnett & Hitchmough, 1996; Thompson & Sorvig, 2000). Once an inventory of these features has been made, steps must be taken to integrate them into the design proposal and management plan, and physically protect them during the construction process. Building sites are frequently chaotic environments where there is considerable pressure on available space and access. For example, unless there is appropriate protection, mature established trees can appear to be healthy but may be irreparably damaged when materials are stored on site, causing soil compaction and root damage.

Opportunities for improving diversity and ecological networks

Diversity of habitat on a single site can be maximised through the use of extraneous material arising from the construction phase, such as the use of building rubble and subsoil as planting media, and the use of dead or uprooted vegetation to form habitat features (Ruff, 1982). The inclusion of vegetated SuDS (as introduced earlier) can also diversify the habitats found on a site. Furthermore, by locating different habitats adjacent to one another, transitional 'ecotones' are created which are especially diverse and may be of high value for wildlife (Dunnett, 1995; Gilbert & Anderson, 1998; Ruff, 1982). On the other hand, habitats should be located away from potentially disruptive land uses such as roads and play areas (Collinge, 1996; Jensen *et al.*, 2000). The extent of habitats should be maximised (Barton *et al.* 1995; Goldstein *et al.*, 1983) as should the degree of irregularity and convolution of their edges which is positively correlated with biodiversity and also nutrient, material and organism exchange between a habitat and its neighbour (Collinge, 1996; Dramstad *et al.*, 1996; Dunnett, 1995; Gilbert & Anderson, 1998).

The isolation and resulting vulnerability of habitats can be addressed through landscape connectivity, particularly in the forms of wildlife corridors and 'stepping stones' (Dramstad *et al.*, 1996; Spellerberg & Gaywood, 1993). Connectivity between vegetation patches within and around a site is a key principle of landscape ecology and ecological design. Though much of the research on habitat connectivity has focused on large remnant vegetation patches and biodiversity on a regional scale (for example, see Andrews, 1993; Pirnat, 2000), several authors have reported on the importance of connectivity at the site scale, and the use of fine-scale connecting features such as lines of trees, fences and hedgerows (Barton *et al.* 1995; Dramstad *et al.*, 1996; Goldstein *et al.*, 1983; Johnston & Newton, 1993). Fine linear features may also provide an additional habitat resource in their own right (Spellerberg & Gaywood, 1993). For example, green roofs can form part of an urban 'green network' (Johnston & Newton, 1993) and can also be designed to offer a range of micro-habitats when spontaneous vegetation on crushed waste substrates is used in lieu of standard sedum mats.

In terms of species biodiversity within a habitat, heterogeneity in relation to vertical and age structure (reinforcing the need to retain existing vegetation wherever possible) and number of plant species present are key (Knops *et al.*, 1999 cited by Jensen *et al.*, 2000; Ruff, 1982; Tregay, 1986). For example, Dunnett & Hitchmough (2004) and Hitchmough *et al.* (2004) have suggested that biodiversity in urban green space is driven by the number of plant species and vegetation layers present. Through a study of Sheffield gardens, Thompson (2004) has identified that tree canopy layers are especially important for supporting invertebrate diversity. There is also some evidence that residential street trees can indirectly increase long-term biodiversity of a site, by discouraging residents from laying their front gardens to closely mown turf (Henderson *et al.* 1998). Because shading from the trees prevents the turf from establishing, residents select shade-tolerant shrubs which are much better in terms of habitat diversity. The conclusion therefore is that approaches to planting design which may be naturalistic in style are well placed to not only reduce resource requirements through rapid establishment but also increase a site's biodiversity through its inclusion of a range of species and biomass layers (Dunnett, 1995).

Plant origins: natives, non-natives and provenance

Kendle & Rose (2000) report on the rise of 'native-only' planting policies which exclude introduced and exotic species from landscape schemes, partly because of their presumed inferior biodiversity value. Planting of locally native species can not only drive the biodiversity of an individual site but also contributes to the over-arching biodiversity relating to regional variations between native habitats, floral species and genetic variety within species, whereas exotic species clearly cannot (Dunnett & Clayden, 2000; Dunnett & Hitchmough, 1996). Furthermore, native flora may be better able to support some co-adapted native fauna (Dunnett & Hitchmough, 2004).

When dealing with an undisturbed rural site within a context of established native habitat, the sustainable landscape designer's priorities should be to tie a new development into its context and use common, locally native species to extend and link these surrounding habitats, thus perpetuating regional native variety (Dunnett & Hitchmough, 1996). However, with regard to disturbed and modified urban, and sometimes rural, sites without this sensitive context, the priorities are likely to be less conservation based. That is not to say, of course, that the biodiversity of the site can be ignored. The previously discussed principles of species diversity, variety in plant layer and age structure, and shape and connectivity of habitats still hold true, but without a context of sensitive native habitats to acknowledge, and a modified strata and microclimate providing the growing conditions, mixtures of native and exotic species are likely to be more suitable.

Mixed native/exotic plantings are often better suited to modified site conditions and therefore require less resource input, but they may also have significant ecological value. For example, Hitchmough et al. (2004) and Thompson (2004) report on studies of site biodiversity in London squares and Sheffield gardens respectively, and conclude that it is structural complexity and species variety of mixed plantings, rather than native origins of the species, that are the key to supporting diversity and abundance of wildlife. Despite the UK Royal Society for Nature Conservation's condemnation of exotic plants as 'ecologically useless' (Kendle & Rose, 2000) they actually have much to offer in terms of biodiversity. Non-native plants fill gaps left by the species range and phenology of the UK's natives, and encourage the establishment of other plant and animal populations through extended fruiting and nectar production and provision of shelter (Hitchmough et al., 2004; Johnston & Newton, 1993; Kendle & Forbes,

1997; Kendle & Rose, 2000; Thornton-Wood, 2002; Williams, 1997). Furthermore, non-native plants can carry a high biomass of invertebrates, providing food for predators (Gilbert, 1989). Hitchmough *et al.* (2004) and Kendle & Rose (2000) have summarised that it is entirely appropriate to use local native species whenever possible in sustainable planting proposals, but this is not to say that potentially ecologically valuable, fit-for-site non-natives should be excluded, specifically in less sensitive contexts.

However, there are concerns that exotic plants can become invasive, outcompete their neighbours and thus threaten the biodiversity of a site and its context, and if used near sensitive native habitats, erode the regional variation of native habitats (Kendle & Rose, 2000; Thompson & Sorvig, 2000). Of course, such species should be avoided and those seen as a priority risk have been identified in the DEFRA report *The Non-native Species Review Group Report* (Seddon, 2003). However, very few of the introduced exotics in the UK are aggressive and problematic, and invasiveness and exotic origins are not closely related (Kendle & Rose, 2000; Thornton-Wood, 2002).

With regard to protecting the most detailed level of biodiversity – genetic variety between the same species from different regions – there is concern that native plants should be specified as provenance from the area local to the development site. However, there is little scientific evidence to prove that the genetic make-up of local populations is being altered by the introduction of plants from outside the local area. In any case, some local populations may have become isolated and inbred and have little ability to survive predicted changes in climate, a situation that could be improved by broadening the gene pool (Kendle & Rose, 2000). Again, the emphasis on local provenance should be determined by the context of the site being developed, local provenance material being a key consideration in a sensitive rural context, and the use of general UK provenance being appropriate for less sensitive sites.

Providing for the health and well-being of residents

Private and communal space

Private garden space is highly valued in the UK. In a 2004 survey across the full range of life-stage groups and types of dwellings in England, over three-quarters of respondents preferred to have a private garden space rather than a shared communal space (CABE, 2005). This echoes the findings of an earlier survey by the Scottish Executive in which, generally, residents expressed a preference for private space, where they can be self-expressive, over communal space (SE, 2002). Dunnett & Qasim (2002) reviewed a number of studies on the value of private gardens and noted a range of social benefits in addition to opportunities for self-expression: safe children's play; health, therapeutic and restorative benefits; and neighbourly interaction and community building. According to Maslow's hierarchy of human needs, as presented by Preece (1991, p 107), gardens thus contribute to meeting the full range of human needs, from the basic requirement of security for the family, through to higher needs of friendship, esteem and self-actualisation.

Many of the garden-bound activities which contribute to the well-being of people also have benefits in terms of resource conservation and waste and pollution reduction. One-fifth of UK citizens suffer from food poverty, exacerbated by the out-of-town locations of many cheaper food stores (Hopkins, 2000); but gardens can be highly productive alternative sources of healthy fresh food (Dunnett & Qasim, 2002; Hopkins, 2000). They can also be pleasurable to work in and personal well-being can be generated through direct contact with the landscape (Boyes-McLauchlan, 1990). Further environmental impacts of the food industry are also highly significant: modern agriculture has had a devastating effect on global biodiversity, and with each phase of food production and transportation, considerable amounts of fossil fuel-derived energy are consumed (Hopkins, 2000). Local food production is therefore an essential component of any settlement striving for sustainability (Barton *et al.*, 1995; Hopkins, 2000). Gardens can also provide opportunities for composting (Dunnett & Qasim, 2002) which can enrich the garden soil and contribute to successful plant husbandry, whilst vastly reducing the amount of waste going to landfill (Hopkins, 2000).

Garden planting undertaken by residents not only achieves aesthetic and creative goals but also provides a great deal of diverse, multi-layered plantings which drive invertebrate biodiversity (Owen, 1991; Thompson, 2004; Thornton-Wood, 2002). The garden can also be used by residents to increase tree cover in particular, a crucial factor in a housing area's biodiversity, its production of runoff and CO_2 and, as discussed below, social qualities.

In terms of resident satisfaction, it is not only the provision of a private space that is important, but also its usability and size (CABE, 2005). The basic characteristics of the garden or private space provided by house builders are fundamental to the range of social and environmental benefits that can accrue, and should be carefully considered. It has been shown that friendship/acquaintance with neighbours is a strong influence on the way in which people settle into their new home (Beer, 1983) and helps promote physical and mental health (Gilchrist, 2000). However, Martin (1997) has noted that successful neighbourhood design tends to balance opportunities for neighbourly interaction with opportunities for privacy and withdrawal. For example, although private spaces with low boundaries traditionally facilitate neighbourly interaction (Thwaites, 2001) they may also lead to residents feeling uncomfortable and 'watched' (Beer, 1983). Conversely, tall screening around the whole of the space removes opportunities to make friends over the fence (Beer, 1983). Barton *et al.* (1995) suggest that privacy can be provided immediately adjacent to the home through the use of relatively tall (1.5–1.8 m) screen fencing. Further details to be considered in garden design are the depth of topsoil (in order to provide greatest opportunities for residents' planting, topsoil depths of around one foot should be provided) and appropriate bins and receptacles to encourage composting.

In modern English society, garden size is important, and inadequate space is a common motive for moving home (CABE, 2005). Modern housing (i.e. that built since 2000) is often criticised by the public for providing too little garden space (CABE, 2005). To provide sufficient space for children's play, a minimum garden area standard of 20 m^2 has been suggested (Beer, 1983), although 40 m^2 minimum would be preferable for gardens which need to reconcile play and other activities such as sitting out, clothes drying, storage and composting (Barton *et al.*, 1995). Findings from studies based in Sheffield suggest that gardens of all sizes are capable of supporting a range of wildlife (Thompson, 2004) and those below 50 m^2 can accommodate vegetable growing, bird boxes and ponds (Dunnett & Qasim, 2002). However, gardens measuring less than 50 m^2 may not be conducive to tree planting by residents (Dunnett & Qasim, 2002).

A minimum garden standard of 50 m^2 would therefore appear to provide adequate space for children's play if required (although large families with more than three children may require at least 75 m^2 [Cook, 1968]) as well as sufficient space for residents to contribute to a site's tree cover. This is, however, a slight increase on some current minimum local authority standards for some homes (Table 2.5).

As shown in Table 2.5, the standards currently adopted by Essex County Council allow much reduced private space of just 25 m^2 in some circumstances. The BedZED project in South London has demonstrated that careful building design can provide 25 m^2 of personal space for all units, even for flat dwellers, through the use of roof terraces (zedfactory, 2002) and such features can be detailed to be safe for use by families with children (CABE, 2005). However, where there is relatively small private space provision it is important that it is complemented by adjacent, high-quality communal space. Although the model of small private spaces complemented with intimate shared spaces is well established in some continental European cities (Dunnett & Clayden, 1997), it has little tradition in the UK (Armstrong *et al.*, 2000).

Loss of existing gardens

In the future, overall provision of urban gardens will depend on both the additions made by new dwellings and changes in existing stock of gardens.

Table 2.5 Current local authority garden size standards. References: *Cardiff University, 2002; **Essex County Council, 1997; #Sunderland City Council, 1998; †Brent Borough Council, 2001; ††Newham Borough Council, 2001.

Planning Authority	Garden Size Standards
Sefton, MBC	A depth of at least 10.5 m and an area of at least 70 m^2*
Liverpool City Council	For three-storey houses a depth of at least 11.5 m, 10 m for bungalows*
Essex County Council	50 m^2 for one/two bedroom houses, 100 m^2 for all other houses except in urban areas, where 50 m^2 is appropriate. Gardens of around 25 m^2 can be accommodated if the gardens are immediately adjacent to a well-designed communal open space**
Sunderland City Council	10 m^2 for each bed space in the home#
Brent Borough Council	A minimum of 50 m^2 should be provided for a family home, 20 m^2 for a flat†
Newham Borough Council	45 m^2 for one/two bedroom houses, 55 m^2 for three bedroom houses and 65 m^2 for four bedroom houses††

As house-building adds less than 0.1% to existing housing stock each year (Leishmann *et al.*, 2004), what happens to existing garden provision is of great importance. Over the past decade or more, urban consolidation has moved to the front of the policy agenda. These policies have been seen as a means of making savings on infrastructure costs, reducing demand on edge of city land, reducing travel distances and possibly promoting increased use of public transport (Haughton & Hunter, 2003, p 89), all issues that have resonated in sustainable development discourse. In terms of housing provision, urban consolidation policies which can have an effect on provision and/or access to private garden space typically include:

- infill on non-developed urban land
- residential plot subdivision
- reducing residential plot sizes in land use plans
- allowing medium-density housing in areas previously designated for low-density housing in local plans
- a shift towards two- or three-storey housing.

The effects of urban containment on garden provision were noted in the early 1980s by Hall (1984), who suggested that there was a *prima facie* case for arguing that there was a reduction in the provision of private open space attached to dwellings in large areas of cities and that the problem was concentrated in existing housing areas that were subjected to partial (e.g. conversion to flats) or complete (demolition of housing and rebuilding as flats) redevelopment. This is supported by Evans (1991), who suggests that in the South East land use within urban areas has intensified and urban open space which is not safeguarded has been eliminated.

> 'Houses are extended over their garden space and the ends of gardens sold off . . . we also see the demolition of existing houses built at low density and their replacement by flats or town houses to intensify further the density of urban development.'

By the 1990s, government advice in *This Common Inheritance* contained some qualification of policy, as follows:

> 'Land in urban areas should be used to meet as much as possible of the demand for sites for new housing . . . (but this) should not mean the disappearance of the playing fields and green spaces which every town and city needs'.

> (DoE, 1990)

This point is reiterated in *PPG3: Housing* (DoE, 1992) and followed by the formal policy framework set out in *Sustainable Development: The UK Strategy* (DoE, 1994b) which draws attention to the potential benefits of the 'compact city' whilst also warning of the need to establish the limits to which built-up areas can be developed before loss of amenity is incurred (Lock, 1995, p 173). However, it was not until 2000 that research commissioned by the DETR (2000b) attempted to obtain a national overview of the process of intensification in the UK over the period 1981–1995. A nationwide survey of local planning authorities (LPAs) and in-depth interviews identified pockets of intensification in all regions of England, Scotland and Wales although there were extreme variations in the extent, with most occurring in the south and south-east of England and less in the north. In particular, inner, central and outer London boroughs had experienced the most intensification. The detailed case studies of 12 areas suggest that 19% of development was on land that was classified as private garden, but this figure disguises considerable variation between areas.

It was not until 2004, after a spate of press releases concerned with either residents' opposition to development in gardens or residents selling off parts of their gardens (Jackson, 2003), that MPs became aware of the fact that gardens were included under the definition of 'brownfield' sites. In 2006 Greg Clark, Conservative MP for Tunbridge Wells, introduced a private member's bill to redefine brownfield land with the aim of restricting development on sites of houses and gardens in residential streets (Norwood, 2006).

Communal spaces

Communal spaces cannot provide the benefits related to personal control (Dunnett & Qasim, 2002) and, as discussed above, are not seen by the public as acceptable substitutes for private space. However, it has been suggested that residential communal spaces can accommodate activities such as allotment gardening, recycling and children's play (Barton *et al.*, 1995; Dunnett & Qasim, 2002; Hopkins, 2000) and facilitate social interaction between residents (Frith & Harrison, 2004; Gilchrist, 2000; Williams, 2005). Furthermore, it has been proposed that residents' ability to see and hear others in 'doorstep' public spaces near their home greatly influences their sense of community (Williams, 2005) (see Figure 2.13). It has also been suggested that the inclusion of communal spaces within housing discourages crime and antisocial behaviour (DETR, 2000a; McKay, 1998 cited in CABE Space, 2004). This would appear to contradict the view that public housing providers dislike communal spaces because of the perceived potential for antisocial behaviour (Frith & Harrison, 2004) and concerns that such spaces may lack the security required for safe children's play (CABE, 2005).

However, two recent studies of North American neighbourhoods suggest that communal residential spaces can provide both a sense of community and safe children's play. Joongsub & Kaplan (2004) compared two contrasting neighbourhoods in Maryland and found that residents with doorstep communal spaces, compared with those without, felt a greater sense of community and gave green space a higher ranking in terms of importance to sense of community. In a further study of two contrasting neighbourhoods in California, Williams (2005) found that communal spaces which accommodate a number of uses and enjoy good surveillance experience more social interaction and children's play than large homogenous spaces with poor surveillance. These findings echo the guidance provided by Quayle & Driessen van der Lieck (1997), Barton *et al.* (1995) and Beer (1983): residential communal spaces which have good surveillance, are small and clearly identified with adjacent housing, and are richly designed to provide for a range of activities are preferred by residents and are more likely to foster community sentiment than large, remote and homogenous areas.

Current government advice for planners and design professionals again emphasises the need for surveillance, sense of ownership and diversity of activities in public space, if crime and antisocial behaviour are to be discouraged (ODPM, 2004). Furthermore, fundamental concerns relating to security, particularly in relation to children's play, and provision of appropriate maintenance within communal spaces need to be addressed before a shared space can be effective (CABE, 2005).

With regard to children's play, Beer (1983) suggests that doorstep communal spaces are key given the propensity for children of all ages (up to

Figure 2.13 Baekgarden, Copenhagen. Developed in the late 1960s, Baekgarden is a fascinating residential development where the protection and provision of shared communal space are at the heart of the design. (a) Street scene where road alignments have been used to restrict the speed of traffic through this residential area. The housing is arranged into rectangular blocks of perhaps a dozen properties which all face onto a central communal space. (b) The view from the street into this car-free 'communal garden' which includes children's toys and play equipment. This space is easily supervised from the house or small front gardens attached to each property. Each courtyard also has its own communal building which can be used for meetings, parties or to accommodate guests. A walkway beneath the canopy of the communal building provides the entrance into what feels like a very private space. The rear gardens to each of the properties are also comparatively small, but open out onto large areas of informal parkland where older children might play more active games.

the age of 15) to play in shared space near the home. Gatherings of young people in communal spaces near the home can be seen as threatening, but this is often unjust (Gilchrist, 2000). Nevertheless, play equipment may cause conflict and is best avoided, whilst low-key play opportunities offered by a variety of surfacing, boundaries, level changes and planting can provide stimulating experiential places for very young children and allow older children, parents and the elderly to socialise (Beer, 1983). In many respects, such a space is similar to 'Local Areas for Play' (LAP). The National Playing Fields Association (NPFA) has described a LAP as a small, low-key games area, which does not include pieces of play equipment and which is intimately embedded within housing (NPFA, 2001). These spaces provide opportunities for informal play and interaction by children in a safe, well-overlooked, appropriately designed space near where they live. The spaces should have good access, be well enclosed and overlooked, and have colourful, textural and scented planting and seating.

Potential social benefits of trees

The coverage of trees within residential areas, independent of other types of vegetation, also has implications for the health and well-being of the residents. The sociological and community benefits of residential trees have been summarised as: increased opportunities for play; pleasant noises such as creaking branches and birdsong; helping the formation of cognitive mental maps; and the symbolic presence of nature (Smardon, 1988). Research in America would also appear to suggest that increased tree cover within shared residential open spaces can contribute to the creativity of children's play and also their contact with adults (Taylor *et al.*, 1998). There is also evidence that the visual quality of residential streets increases with the number and size of trees (Schroeder & Cannon, 1987) and that although living with trees is not without its annoyances, for example leaf litter and honeydew, the perceived benefits were generally seen to outweigh any negatives (Schroeder & Ruffolo, 1996). These studies suggest that trees are strongly valued in American residential developments, for their social and psychological as well as their functional and ecological attributes (Hitchmough & Bonugli, 1997).

There appears to have been little comparable research in the UK, but work by Hitchmough & Bonugli (1997) analysed the attitudes towards street trees in four treeless streets in Ayr, Scotland. Unlike the American studies, in general there was little support for street tree planting, especially in the less affluent streets. However, these residents are likely to lack experience of living with street trees and therefore their presumptions rather than actual experiences may be the basis for their attitudes. The most common reason for not supporting tree planting was anticipated problems with vandalism and associated perceived waste of council tax revenue, though anticipated leaf litter was also offered as a source of annoyance. However, actually not liking trees was not a significant reason for not wanting them in the streets. This study suggests that tree planting by house builders may be most successful; that is, the environmental, social and psychological benefits of trees can be experienced with reduced risk of annoyance when trees are located away from obvious areas of conflict, such as adjacent to driveways, are overlooked by residents and are specified at a size which is sufficiently robust for their context.

Ways of improving the acceptance of sustainable vegetation in the residential landscape

The health benefits of contact with nature, including promotion of well-being, reduced stress and decreased recovery times from illness, have been reported by several authors (for example, Moore, 1982; Rhode & Kendle, 1994; Ulrich, 1984; Ulrich *et al.*, 1991). The sensory and community benefits of trees in particular have been discussed above, but vegetation more generally can help create a sense of community and safety in urban settings (Kuo *et al.*, 1998) and encourage community gathering and interaction in residential areas (Coley *et al.*, 1997).

However, it is reasonable to assume that these benefits will only be associated with vegetation that the public feel comfortable with (Jorgensen, 2001). It has been suggested that the lay public have a preference for planting design which is simple and which typically has relatively low ecological value (Nassauer, 1995; Parsons, 1995; Thayer, 1989) and that only people with an interest in ecology will appreciate richer, perhaps more untidy, habitat-focused treatments (Nassauer, 1993; Schulhof, 1989). Several possible reasons for this bias have been suggested, including genetically programmed preferences for the savannah-like landscapes of our East African origins (Orians, 1986) and learnt aesthetic responses to logic and order (Johnson, 1997). However, a number of further studies have suggested that more diverse vegetation types that symbolise 'naturalness' and biodiversity can be enjoyed by the public (for example, Jorgensen, 2003; Kaplan *et al.*, 1989; Van den Berg *et al.*, 1998).

Different people react differently to the natural world (Rhode & Kendle, 1994) and the relationship between landscape preference and ecological quality is unclear (Williams & Cary, 2002). However, what can be drawn from the existing preference studies is that more naturalistic and diverse vegetation can be made more acceptable through a degree of design intervention and management control. One such approach is the use of 'design cues', which are visible indicators that show a landscape to be intentional and cared for (Nassauer, 1988). Though care, perception of which is a primary determinant of landscape attractiveness (Nassauer, 1988), is usually associated with keeping landscapes neat and tidy, signage and interpretation can communicate the care being shown to 'messy' plantings by explaining the ecological function of the vegetation, and that the look of the planting is intentional and not due to neglect (Nassauer, 1988).

Design cues are important devices in widening the public's perception of what cared-for landscapes look like. It has been suggested by Nassauer (1988, 1993) that this may be particularly important in residential landscapes, where neatness remains the predominant indicator of care. According to Nassauer (1988) the aesthetic of care can be expanded beyond mere neatness. The literature introduces a number of 'design cues' and other design and management interventions that can demonstrate care for, and broaden the aesthetic appeal of, ecologically informed planting, and which could be used to integrate planting of habitat value into a residential setting:

- Rather than remove unsightly elements such as dead trees and hide potentially offensive management activities such as clearing, involve and inform the public about the benefits through newsletters, signage and interpretation (Gobster, 1994; Rhode & Kendle, 1994).
- Neatly mown strips or neat post-and-rail fencing around woodland edges and alongside paths through woodland (Gobster, 1994).
- Neatly mown strips and areas of turf alongside meadows (Jorgensen, 2001; Morrison, 1975; Nassauer, 1993).
- Use traditional planting design rules of colour composition, massing and structure, and attractive foliage to accentuate the appeal of both exotic and native species, particularly near paths and other focal areas (Henderson et al., 1998; Nassauer, 1993; Schulhof, 1989).
- Juxtapose naturalistic plantings with more formal planting treatments such as a limited number of clipped hedges and shrubs (Henderson et al., 1998).

As noted by Schulhof (1989), such measures have an implicit element of stylisation and compromise ecological accuracy to suit public taste. Gobster (1994) has also described these 'compromised' habitats as garden-like and symbolic of an ecosystem, rather than fully functioning, but notes that they still have high species diversity and conservation value. Furthermore, as pointed out by Dunnett & Hitchmough (2004), public acceptance of more ecologically rich vegetation, particularly near the home, is crucial to its success.

References

AECB (Association of Environmentally Conscious Builders) (2003) *The Big Timber Debate.* (online) Available at: www.aecb.net (accessed 1 June 2003).

Anderson, J. & Howard, N. (2000) *The Green Guide to Housing Specification. An Environmental Profiling System for Building Materials and Components Used in Housing.* Garston, Watford: Building Research Establishment, Centre for Sustainable Construction.

Andrews, J. (1993) The reality and management of wildlife corridors. *British Wildlife*, 5(1), pp 1–7.

Ard, J. (IPM Associates Inc.) (1999) *Fundamentals of a Low Maintenance, Integrated Pest Management Approach to Landscape Design.* (online) Available at: www. enf.org/~ipma/des-cnsd.html (accessed 19 May 2004).

Armstrong, H., Brown, H. & Turner, T. (2000) Landscape planning and city form. In: *Landscape and Sustainability.* J.F. Benson & M.H. Roe (Eds) London: Spon Press.

Barton, H. (2000) Conflicting perceptions of neighbourhood. In: *Sustainable Communities: The Potential for Eco-Neighbourhoods.* H. Barton (Ed.) London: Earthscan.

Barton, H., Davis, G. & Guise, R. (1995) *Sustainable Settlements: A Guide for Planners, Designers and Developers.* Bristol: University of the West of England and the Local Government Board.

Bayley, S. (2004) Oh yes, I can get quite demented in defence of trees. In: *The Independent on Sunday*, 20 June, p 5.

Beazley, E. (1991) *Sun*, shade and shelter near buildings: the forgotten art of planning with microclimate in mind, part IV. *Landscape Design*, February, pp 46–50.

Beer, A.R. (1983) *The Landscape Architect and Housing Areas.* University of Sheffield, Department of Landscape. Paper LA 11.

Berge, B. (2000) *Ecology of Building Materials.* London: Architectural Press.

Boyes-McLauchlan, M. (1990) Edible landscapes. *Landscape Design*, October, pp 53–54.

BRE (1990a) *Climate and Site Development. Part 1: General Climate of the UK.* Digest 350. February. Garston, Watford: Building Research Establishment.

BRE (1990b) *Climate and Site Development. Part 2: Influence of Microclimate.* Digest 350. March. Garston, Watford: Building Research Establishment.

BRE (1990c) *Climate and Site Development. Part 3: Improving Microclimate Through Design.* Digest 350. April. Garston, Watford: Building Research Establishment.

BRE/DTI (2003) *Construction Site Transport. The Next Big Thing.* Garston, Watford: Building Research Establishment.

Brent Borough Council (2001) *Design Guide for New Development. SPG 17.* [online] Available at: www.brent.gov.uk/planning.nsf (accessed 27 November 2002).

Brown, R.D. & Gillespie, T.J. (1995) *Microclimatic Landscape Design: Creating Thermal Comfort and Energy Efficiency.* Chichester: John Wiley & Sons.

Brownhill, D. & Rao, S. (2002) *A Sustainability Checklist for Developments. A Common Framework for Developers and Local Authorities.* Garston, Watford: Building Research Establishment, Centre for Sustainable Construction.

CABE (2002) *Paving the Way: How We Achieve Clean, Safe and Attractive Streets.* London: Commission for Architecture and the Built Environment.

CABE (2005) *What Home Buyers Want: Attitudes and Decision Making Among Consumers.* London: Commission for Architecture and the Built Environment.

CABE Space (2004) *The Value of Public Space.* London: Commission for Architecture and the Built Environment.

Caceres, J. & Richards, D. (The David Suzuki Foundation) (2003) *Greenhouse Gas Reduction Opportunities for the Freight Transporter Sector.* (online) Available at www.davidsuzuki.org (accessed 8 October 2003).

Cambridge University (2001) *Environmental Engineering: Microclimate.* (online) Available at: www.building.arct.cam.ac.uk/sidgwick/engineering/microclimate.html (accessed 23 October 2003).

Cardiff University (2002) *Built Environment Lecture 6. Amenity: Overlooking, Access to Light, Privacy, Outdoor Space.* [online] Available at: www.cf.ac.uk/cplan/downloads/built_env6.pdf (accessed 26 November 2002).

CIRIA (2000) *Sustainable Urban Drainage Systems. A Design Manual for England and Wales.* CIRIA publication C522. London: Construction Industry Research and Information Association.

CIRIA (2005) *Benefits of Constructed Pervious Surfaces.* (online) Available at: www.ciria.org/suds/637_benefits.htm (accessed 25 January 2005).

Coley, R.L., Kuo, F.E. & Sullivan, W.C. (1997) Where does community grow? The social context created by nature in urban public housing. *Environment and Behaviour*, 29(4), pp 468–494.

Collinge, S.K. (1996) Ecological consequences of habitat fragmentation: implications for landscape architecture and planning. *Landscape and Urban Planning*, 36, pp 59–77.

Commission of the European Communities (2006) *Directive 2006/139/EC amending Council Directive 76/769/EEC as regards restrictions on the marketing and use of arsenic compounds for the purpose of adapting its annex on technical progress.* Official Journal of the European Union, Luxemburg.

Conner, S. (2005) The final proof: global warming is a man-made disaster. In: *The Independent*, 19 February, pp 1, 6, 7 & 36.

Construction Resources (2002) *Britain's First Ecological Builders' Merchant and Building Centre.* (online) Available at: www.constructionresources.com (accessed 1 October 2002).

Cook, J. (1968) Gardens on housing estates: a survey of user attitudes and behaviour on seven layouts. *Town Planning Review*, 39, pp 217–234.

Courtney, R. (1998) *The Challenge – A Framework for Response.* Proceedings of NHBC Annual Conference: Sustainable Housing – Meeting the Challenges. Amersham: National House Building Council, pp 10–15.

Dekeyzer, M. (1996) *Factors Influencing the Adoption of Biological Control Technologies in Floriculture Under Glass.* Proceedings of XIII International Symposium on Horticultural Economics. R.G. Brumfield (Ed). pp 67–74.

Department of the Environment (1990) *This Common Inheritance. Britain's Environmental Strategy.* London: HMSO.

Department of the Environment (1992) *Planning Policy Guidance 3: Housing.* London: HMSO.

Department of the Environment (1994a) *Biodiversity: the UK Action Plan.* London: DoE.

Department of the Environment (1994b) *Sustainable Development: The UK Strategy.* London: DoE.

Department for Environment, Food & Rural Affairs (2000) *Our Countryside: The Future – A Fair Deal for Rural England.* London: DEFRA.

Department for Environment, Food & Rural Affairs (2003) *The Environment in Your Pocket 2003.* London: DEFRA.

Department of the Environment, Transport & the Regions (1998a) *Building a Sustainable Future: Homes for an Autonomous Community.* London: DETR.

Department of the Environment, Transport & the Regions (1998b) *Places, Streets and Movement: A Companion Guide to Design Bulletin 32 Residential Roads and Footpaths.* London: DETR.

Department of the Environment, Transport & the Regions (2000a) *Regeneration Research Summary: Millennium Villages and Sustainable Communities Final Report* (Number 30). London: DETR.

Department of the Environment, Transport & the Regions (2000b) *Urban Intensification: Impacts and Acceptability.* Oxford: Oxford Brookes University.

Department of the Environment, Transport & the Regions (2000c) *Planning Policy Guidance Note 3: Housing.* London: DETR.

Department of the Environment, Transport & the Regions (2000d) *Encouraging Walking: Advice to Local Authorities.* London: DETR.

Department of the Environment, Transport & the Regions (2000e) *Mineral Planning Guidance Note 11: Controlling and Mitigating the Environment Effects of Mineral Extraction in England, Consultation Paper.* (online) Available at: www.planning.odpm.gov.uk/consult/mpg11/ draft/01.htm (accessed 16 June 2003).

Department of Trade & Industry/Architectural Association (1994) *Solar Energy and Housing Design: Volume 1, Principles, Objectives and Guidelines.* London: Architectural Association.

Department for Transport, Local Government & the Regions (2001a) *Planning Policy Guidance Note 1: General Policy and Principles.* London: DTLR.

Department for Transport, Local Government & the Regions (2001b) *Planning Policy Guidance Note 25: Development and Flood Risk.* London: DTLR.

Department for Transport, Local Government & the Regions (2002) *Approved Document H: Drainage and Waste Disposal. Part H3 Rainwater Drainage.* (online) Available at: www.odpm.gov.uk/stellant/groups/odpm_breg_600283-05.hcsp#1600_100195 (accessed 16 June 2005).

Department for Transport, Local Government & the Regions/CABE (2001) *Better Places to Live By Design: A Companion Guide to PPG 3.* London: DTLR.

Dodd, J. (1989) Greenspace 4: Tempering cold winds. *Architects' Journal,* 189(2), pp 61–65.

Dramstad, W.E., Olson, J.D. & Forman, R.T.T. (1996) *Landscape Ecology Principles in Landscape Architecture and Land-Use Planning.* Washington DC: Harvard

University Graduate School of Design/Island Press/American Society of Landscape Architects.

Dunnett, N. (1995) Patterns in nature: inspiration for an ecological landscape design philosophy. In: *Landscape Ecology: Theory and Application.* Proceedings of the Fourth International Association for Landscape Ecology (UK) Conference, pp 78–85.

Dunnett, N. (2004) Rooftop futures. *Garden Design Journal*, October, pp 30–34.

Dunnett, N. & Clayden, A. (1997) Courtyards for living. *Landscape Design*, October, pp 38–39.

Dunnett, N. & Clayden, A. (2000) Resources: the raw materials of landscape. In: *Landscape and Sustainability.* J.F. Benson & M.H. Roe (Eds) London: Spon.

Dunnett. N. & Clayden, A. (2007) *Rain Gardens.* Portland, Oregon: Timber Press.

Dunnett, N. & Hitchmough, J. (1996) Excitement and energy. *Landscape Design*, June, pp 43–46.

Dunnett, N. & Hitchmough, J. (2004) More than nature. *Landscape Design*, April, pp 28–30.

Dunnett, N. & Qasim, M. (2002) *Private Gardens, Urban Density and City Form.* Unpublished conference paper. Department of Landscape, University of Sheffield.

Edwards, B. (2000) Design guidelines for sustainable housing. In: *Sustainable Housing: Principles and Practice.* B. Edwards & D. Turrent (Eds) London: E. & F. N. Spon.

ENFO (2003) *Tree Planting.* (online) Available at: www.enfo.ie/leaflets/as12.htm (accessed 29 September 2003).

English Partnerships/Housing Corporation (2000) *The Urban Design Compendium.* London: English Partnerships/ Housing Corporation.

Environment Agency (2003) *Sustainable Drainage Systems (SuDS): an Introduction.* Bristol: Environment Agency.

EPA (US Environment Protection Agency) (2005) Chromated copper arsenate (CCA). (online) Available at: www.epa.gov/oppad001/reregistration/cca/ (accessed 21 April 2005).

Essex County Council (1997) *The Essex Design Guide.* Chelmsford: Essex County Council and Essex Planning Officers Association.

Evans, A. (1991) 'Rabbit hutches on postage stamps': planning, development and political economy. *Urban Studies*, 28(6), 853–870.

Friends of the Earth (2001) *Raw Deal. The QPA's Response to the Case for an Aggregate Tax. Consultation Response.* (online) Available at: www.foe.co.uk/ resource/consultation_responses /raw_deal.html (accessed 16 June 2003).

Frith, M. & Harrison, S. (2004) Decent homes, decent spaces. In: *Decent Homes, Decent Spaces: Improving the Green Spaces for Social Housing.* M. Frith & S. Harrison (Eds) London: Neighbourhoods Green, pp 1–5.

FSC (2000) *FSC Principles & Criteria for Forest Stewardship. Document 1.2 Revised February 2000.* Powys: Forest Stewardship Council UK Working Group.

FSC (2002) *Forest Stewardship Council UK Working Group. Annual Report, March 2000–February 2002.* Powys: Forest Stewardship Council UK Working Group.

Gilbert, O. (1989) *The Ecology of Urban Habitats.* London: Chapman & Hall.

Gilbert, O. & Anderson, P. (1998) *Habitat Creation and Repair*. Oxford: Oxford University Press.

Gilchrist, A. (2000) Design for living: the challenge of sustainable communities. In: *Sustainable Communities: The Potential for Eco-Neighbourhoods*. H. Barton (Ed.) London: Earthscan.

Gobster, P.H. (1994) The urban savanna. reuniting ecological preference and function. *Restoration Management Notes*,12(1), pp 64–71.

Goldstein, E.L., Meir, G. & DeGraff, R.M. (1983) Wildlife and greenspace planning in medium scale residential developments. *Urban Ecology*, 7, pp 201–214.

Grant, A. (2000) Building and landscape. In: *Sustainable Housing: Principles and Practice*. B. Edwards & D. Turrent (Eds) London: E. & F.N. Spon.

Hall, A. (1984) Some green thoughts on the garden. *Town and Country Planning*, 54(2), 186–187.

Haughton, G. & Hunter, C. (2003) *Sustainable Cities*. London: Taylor & Francis.

HDRA (Henry Doubleday Research Association) (2001) *What is the Henry Doubleday Research Association (HDRA)?* (online) Available at: www.hdra.org.uk/about.htm (accessed 30 October 2001).

Henderson, S.P.B., Perkins, N.H. & Nelischer, M. (1998) Residential lawn alternatives: a study of their distribution, form and structure. *Landscape and Urban Planning*, 42, pp 135–145.

Hitchmough, J.D. (1994) *Urban Landscape Management*. Sydney: Sydney Inkata Press.

Hitchmough, J.D. & Bonugli, A.M. (1997) Attitudes of residents of a medium sized town in South West Scotland to street trees. *Landscape Research*, 22(3), pp 327–337.

Hitchmough, J.D., Dunnett, N. & Jorgensen, A. (2004) Enriching urban spaces. *Green Places*, April, pp 30–32.

HM Government (1999) *A Better Quality of Life: A Strategy for Sustainable Development for the UK*. London: HMSO.

HM Government (2002) *Chromate Copper Arsenate-treated Wood. Parliamentry questions, 19 September 2002*. (online) Available at: www.parliament.the-stationery-office.co.uk/pa   /cm200102/cmhansrd/vo020919/text/20919w63.htm (accessed 2 December 2003).

HM Government (2005) *Securing the Future: Delivering the UK Sustainable Development Strategy*. London: HMSO.

Holmes, S., Lightfoot-Brown, S. & Bragg, N. (2000) *Peat Alternatives. A Review of Performance, Future Availability and Sustainability for Commercial Plant Production in the UK*. (online) Available at: www.adas.co.uk/horticulture/GOVREPORTS/PTALTREV.htm (accessed 29 November 2001).

Hopkins, R. (2000) The food producing neighbourhood. In: *Sustainable Communities: The Potential for Eco-Neighbourhoods*. H. Barton (Ed.) London: Earthscan.

Howard, N. (2000) *Sustainable Construction: The Data*. BRE Report CR258/99. Garston, Watford: Building Research Establishment, Centre for Sustainable Construction.

Interpave (2003) *Permeable Pavements. Guide to the Design, Construction and Maintenance Of Concrete Block Permeable Pavements.* Leicester: Interpave, the Precast Concrete Paving and Kerb Association.

Jackson, P. (2003) Overview: the battle to save our green spaces. *The Independent Online Edition.* (online) Available at: http://money.independent.co.uk/property/homes/article92578.ece (accessed 15 January 2004).

Jenkins, A. (2001) Proving green credentials pays dividends. *Horticulture Week*, November 15, p 11.

Jensen, M.B., Persson, B., Guldager, S., Reeh, U. & Nilsson, K. (2000) Green structure and sustainability – developing a tool for local planning. *Landscape and Urban Planning*, 52, pp 117–133.

Johnson, C. (1991) *Green Dictionary.* London: Optima.

Johnson, M. (1997) Ecology and the urban aesthetic. In: *Ecological Design and Planning.* G.F. Thompson & F.R. Steiner (Eds) New York: John Wiley and Sons.

Johnston, J. & Newton, J. (1993) *Building Green: A Guide to Using Plants on Roofs, Walls and Pavements.* London: London Ecology Unit.

Joongsub, K. & Kaplan, R. (2004) Physical and psychological factors in sense of community: new urbanist Kentlands and nearby Orchard Village. *Environment and Behaviour*, 36(3), pp 313–340.

Jorgensen, A. (2001) *Why is it Important to Encourage Nature and Wildlife Near the Home?* University of Sheffield, Department of Landscape (online) Available at: www.map21ltd.com/ overvecht/papers/natben.htm (accessed 12 March 2002).

Jorgensen, A. (2003) *Living in The Urban Wild Woods – A Case Study of the Ecological Woodland Approach to Landscape Planning and Design at Birchwood, Warrington New Town.* Unpublished PhD thesis, Sheffield University, Department of Landscape.

Jowett, C. (2005) For peat's sake. *Landscape Design*, February, pp 10–14.

Kaplan, R., Kaplan, S. & Brown, T. (1989) Environmental preference: a comparison of four domains of predictors. *Environment and Behaviour*, 21, pp 509–530.

Kendle, A.D. & Forbes, S. (1997) *Urban Nature Conservation.* London: E. & F.N. Spon.

Kendle, A.D. & Rose, J.E. (2000) The aliens have landed! What are the justifications for 'native only' policies in landscape plantings? *Landscape and Urban Planning*, 47, pp 19–31.

Kendle, A.D., Rose, J.E. & Oikawa, J. (2000) Sustainable landscape management. In: *Landscape and Sustainability.* J.F. Benson & M.H. Roe (Eds) London: Spon Press.

Kuo, F.E., Bacaicoa, M. & Sullivan, W.C. (1998) Transforming inner-city landscapes. Trees, sense of safety and preference. *Environment and Behaviour*, 30(1), pp 28–59.

Laurie, M. (1986) *An Introduction to Landscape Architecture*, 2nd edn. Englewood Cliffs, NJ: Prentice-Hall.

Leishmann, C., Aspinall, P., Munro, M. & Warren, F. (2004) *Preference, Quality and Choice in New-Build Housing.* York: Joseph Rowntree Foundation.

Littlewood, M. (1986) *Landscape Detailing.* 2nd edn. London: Architectural Press.

Lock, D. (1995) Room for more within city limits. *Town and Country Planning*, 64, pp 173–176.

Mabey, R. (1993) Nature and change: the two faces of naturalisation. In: *Local Distinctiveness: Place, Particularity and Identity.* S. Clifford & A. King (Eds) London: Common Ground, pp 21–27.

Martin, M. (1997) Back-alley as community landscape. *Landscape Journal*, Spring, pp 138–181.

Molitor, H.D. (1998) Environmentally sound production in horticulture – the European way. *Journal of the Japanese Society of Horticultural Science*, 67(6), pp 1224–1228.

Moore, E.O. (1982) A prison environment's effect on health care service demands. *Journal of Environmental Systems*, 11(1), pp 17–34.

Morel, J.C., Mesbah, A., Oggero, M. & Walker, P. (2001) Building houses with local materials: means to drastically reduce the environmental impact of construction. *Building & Environment*, 36, pp 1119–1126.

Morrison, D.G. (1975) Restoring the mid-western landscape. *Landscape Architecture*, 65, pp 398–403.

Nassauer, J.I. (1988) The aesthetics of horticulture: neatness as a form of care. *HortScience*, 23(6), pp 973–977.

Nassauer, J.I. (1993) The ecological function and the perception of suburban residential landscapes. In: *Managing Urban and High-Use Recreational Settings.* P.H. Gobster (Ed) St Paul, Minnesota: USDA Forestry Service, North Central Forest Experiment Station, pp 55–65.

Nassauer, J.I. (1995) Messy ecosystems, orderly frames. *Landscape Journal*, 14(2), pp 161–170.

National Physical Laboratory (2003) *Corrosion of Metals by Wood.* (online) Available at: www.npl.co.uk/npl/cmmt/ncs/docs/corrosion_of_metals_by_wood_ pdf (accessed 3 March 2003).

National Playing Fields Association (2001) *The Six Acre Standard. Minimum Standards for Outdoor Playing Space.* London: NPFA.

Newham Borough Council (2001) *Residential Planning Guidelines.* Newham: Newham Borough Council, Environment Department.

Nienhuis, J.K. & de Vreede, P.J.A. (1996) *Utility of the Environmental Life Cycle Assessment Method in Horticulture.* Proceedings of XIII International Symposium on Horticultural Economics. R.G. Brumfield (Ed) pp 531–538.

Norwood, G. (2006) *Suburban garden or brownfield site?* (online) Available at: Timesonline.co.uk (accessed 26 March 2006).

Office of the Deputy Prime Minister (2004) *Sustainability Appraisal of Regional Spatial Strategies and Local Development Frameworks: Consultation Paper.* London: ODPM.

O'Mahony, F. (2004) Globally planned, locally implemented. *The Garden*, May, pp 352–353.

Orians, G.H. (1986) An ecological and evolutionary approach to landscape aesthetics. In: *Landscape Meanings and Values.* E.C. Penning-Roswell & D. Lowenthal (Eds) London: Allen & Unwin.

Orth, U.R. (1996) *Multiple Criteria Analysis for Decisions Affecting the Environment: An Approach Applied to the Natural Resource Water.* Proceedings of XIII International Symposium on Horticultural Economics. R.G. Brumfield (Ed) pp 343–350.

Owen, J. (1991) *The Ecology of a Garden.* Cambridge: Cambridge University Press.

Parsons, R. (1995) Conflict between ecological sustainability and environmental aesthetics: conundrum, canard or curiosity? *Landscape and Urban Planning*, 32, pp 227–244.

Pirnat, J. (2000) Conservation and management of forest patches and corridors in suburban landscapes. *Landscape and Urban Planning*, 52, pp 135–143.

Ponds Conservation Trust: Policy and Research (2002) *Integrating Sustainable Urban Drainage Systems (SuDS) into Inner City Regeneration Schemes in Sheffield.* Oxford: Ponds Conservation Trust: Policy and Research, Oxford Brookes University.

Preece, R.A. (1991) *Designs on the Landscape.* London: Belhaven Press.

Quayle, M. & Driessen van der Lieck, T.C. (1997) Growing community: a case for hybrid landscapes. *Landscape and Urban Planning*, 39, pp 99–107.

Rao, S., Yates, A., Brownhill, D. & Howard, N. (2000) *EcoHomes: The Environmental Rating for Homes.* Garston, Watford: Building Research Establishment, Centre for Sustainable Construction.

Rhode, C.L.E. & Kendle, A.D. (1994) *Human Well-Being, Natural Landscapes and Wildlife in Urban Areas. A Review.* English Nature Science Report No 22. Reading: English Nature.

Rollins, J. (2003) Precious peat. *Natural World*, Spring, pp 35–37.

Rosenheck, D. (2003) Stay cool, and heat up the planet: the answer to the summer's heatwave? *New Statesman*, 16(772), p 18.

Ruff, A. (1982) An ecological approach to landscape design. In: *An Ecological Approach to Urban Landscape Design.* A. Ruff & Tregay, R. (Eds) Department of Town & Country Planning, University of Manchester. Occasional Paper, No. 8. pp 4–12.

Sawyer, G. (2003) EU standards to cover all growers. *Horticulture Week*, February 6, p 6.

Schroeder, H.W. & Cannon, W.N. (1987) Visual quality of residential streets: both street and yard trees make a difference. *Journal of Arboriculture*, 13(10), pp 236–238.

Schroeder, H.W. & Ruffolo, S.R. (1996) Householder evaluations of street trees in a Chicago suburb. *Journal of Arboriculture*, 22(1), pp 35–43.

Schulhof, R. (1989) Public perceptions of native vegetation. *Restoration and Management Notes*, 7(2), pp 69–72.

Scottish Executive (2002) *Scottish Planning Policy Note 1: The Planning System.* Edinburgh: Scottish Executive.

Seddon, E. (2003) Report aims to help win war against alien plants. *Horticulture Week*, April 3, p 4.

SEPA (2000) *Sustainable Urban Drainage Systems: Setting the Scene in Scotland.* Stirling: Scottish Environment Protection Agency, Sustainable Urban Drainage Scottish Working Party.

Simons, P. (2004) Can you dig it? In: *Chemical World.* Colour supplement with *The Guardian,* May 22, pp 20–21.

Sinclair, D. (1991) *Shades of Green; Myth and Muddle in the Countryside.* London: Paladin.

Skinner, A. (1998) *Focus on water and waste.* Proceedings of NHBC Annual Conference: Sustainable Housing – Meeting the Challenges. Amersham: National House Building Council, pp 16–20.

Smardon, R.C. (1988) Perception and aesthetics of the urban environment: review of the role of vegetation. *Landscape and Urban Planning,* 15, pp 85–106.

Smith, M., Whitelegg, J. & Williams, N. (1998) *Greening the Built Environment.* London: Earthscan.

Soil Association (2002a) *UK Organic Producers, Listed by County and Last Name.* Bristol: Soil Association.

Soil Association (2002b) *Soil Association standards for Organic Farming and Production. Revision 14, 2002/2003.* Bristol: Soil Association.

Soil Association (2002c) *Soil Association Standards for Organic Farming and Production. Part 2, General Standards for Organic Husbandry.* 14th revision. Bristol: Soil Association.

Spellerberg, I. & Gaywood, M. (1993) Linear landscape features. *Landscape Design,* September, pp 19–21.

Spirn, A.W. (1998) *The Language of Landscape.* New Haven: Yale University Press.

Starbuck, C. (2000) *Landscape Plantings for Energy Savings.* Columbia: University of Missouri.

Sustainable Development (2000) *Building a Better Quality of Life. A Strategy for More Sustainable Construction.* London: DETR.

Sustainable Homes (2003) *Embodied Energy in Residential Property Development: A Guide for Registered Social Landlords.* (on line) Available at: www.sustainable-homes.co.uk/pdf/ Embeng.pdf (accessed 15 October 2003).

Sustainability Works (2002) *Sustainability Works. The Complete Development Tool for Sustainable Housing.* (online) Available at: www.sustainabilityworks.org.uk (accessed 7 October 2002).

Sunderland City Council (1998) *Unitary Development Plan, Adopted Plan, 1998. Supplementary Planning Guidance. Development Control Guidelines.* (online) Available at: www.sunderland.gov.uk/Public/Editable/Themes/Environment/ UDP/SUPPGUID.DOC (accessed 27 November 2002).

Symonds, G. (1993) Re-used landscapes. *Landscape Design,* April, pp 37–40.

Taylor, A.F., Wiley, A. & Kuo, F.E. (1998) Growing up in the inner city: green spaces as places to grow. *Environment and Behaviour,* 30(1), pp 3–27.

Thayer, R.L. (1989) The experience of sustainable landscapes. *Landscape Journal,* 8, pp 101–110.

Thompson, K. (2004) BUGS in the borders. *The Garden,* May, pp 346–349.

Thompson, P. (1997) *The Self Sustaining Garden.* London: B.T. Batsford Ltd.

Thompson, J.W. & Sorvig, K. (2000) *Sustainable Landscape Construction: A Guide to Green Building Outdoors.* Washington DC: Island Press.

Thornton-Wood, S. (2002) Gardening for the future. *The Garden,* November, pp 844–848.

Thwaites, K. (2001) Experiential landscape place: an exploration of space and experience in neighbourhood landscape architecture. *Landscape Research*, 26(3), pp 245–255.

Tree Council (2003) *Tree Planting Guide*. (online) Available at: www.treecouncil.org.uk/info/packng2.html (accessed 29 September 2003).

Tregay, R. (1986) Design and ecology in the management of nature-like plantations. In: *Ecology and Design in Landscape*. A. Bradshaw, D. Goode & E. Thorpe (Eds) Oxford: Blackwell Scientific Publications.

UK Biodiversity Steering Group (1995) *Biodiversity: The UK Steering Group Report. Volume 1: Meeting the Rio Challenge*. London: HMSO.

Ulrich, R.S. (1984) View from a window may influence recovery from surgery. *Science*, 224, pp 420–421.

Ulrich, R.S., Simons, R.F., Losito, B.D., Fiorito, E., Miles, M.A. & Zelson, M. (1991) Stress recovery during exposure to natural and urban environments. *Journal of Environmental Psychology*, 11, pp 201–230.

US Department of Energy (1995) *Landscaping for Energy Efficiency*. Washington DC: US Department of Energy.

Victoria Transport Policy Institute (2002) *Freight Transport Management. Increasing Commercial Vehicle Transport Efficiency*. (online) Available at: www.vtpi.org/tdm/tdm16.html (accessed 8 October 2003).

Van den Berg, A.E., Vlek, C.A.J. & Coeterier, J.F. (1998) Group differences in the aesthetic evaluation of nature development plans: A multilevel approach. *Journal of Environmental Psychology*, 18, pp 141–157.

Welch, W.C. (University of Texas, Texas Agricultural Extension Service) (2003) *Landscaping for Energy Conservation*. (online) Available at: www.aggie-horticulture.tamu.edu/extension/homelandscape/energy/energy.html (accessed 16 October 2003).

Whitford, V., Ennos, A.R. & Handley, J.F. (2001) 'City form and natural processes' – indicators for the ecological performance of urban areas and their application to Merseyside, UK. *Landscape and Urban Planning*, 57, pp 91–103.

Williams, C.E. (1997) Potential valuable ecological functions of non-indigenous plants. In: *Assessment and Management of Plant Invasions*. J.O. Luken & J.W. Thieret (Eds) New York: Springer.

Williams, J. (2005) Designing neighbourhoods for social interaction: the case for cohousing. *Journal of Urban Design*, 10(2), pp 195–227.

Williams, K. & Cary, J. (2002) Landscape preferences, ecological quality, and biodiversity protection. *Environment and Behaviour*, 34(2) pp 257–274.

Woolley, T. & Kimmins, S. (2000) *Green Building Handbook, Volume 2*. London: E. & F.N. Spon.

Woolley, T., Kimmins, S., Harrison, P. & Harrison, R. (1997) *Green Building Handbook*. London: E. & F.N. Spon.

WWF (2004) *Building Towards Sustainability. Performance and Progress among the UK's Leading House Builders*. (online) Available at: www.wwf.org.uk (accessed 9 November 2004).

zedfactory (2002) *Sustainability KPIs @ BedZED*. (online) Available at: www.zedfactory.com/bedzed/kpi.html (accessed 1 August 2002).

Chapter 3

Creating a residential landscape sustainability checklist

Introduction

The original purpose of the landscape checklist was to create a research tool that would enable a comprehensive assessment of the contribution that the residential landscape made towards delivering sustainability. Having established, in Chapter 2, how the design and specification of the landscape might support sustainability, it was important to review the existing assessment tools to identify the extent to which these issues were already being addressed. This chapter begins by reviewing the checklist tools that were available in 2002–2004, when the landscape checklist was being piloted. The chapter then goes on to discuss the rationale for developing the landscape checklist using the *EcoHomes* template developed by the BRE. This is followed by a discussion for each of the assessment categories, for example, materials, water, transport, etc., and how these have been expanded upon with respect to the assessment of the landscape.

A review of sustainable checklist tools for residential development

As presented in the introductory chapter in Table 1.2, the UK Government and its agencies have been responsible for a number of guidance texts on aspects of sustainable development. Of these, *Sustainable Settlements: A Guide for Planners, Designers and Developers* (Barton *et al.*, 1995), published by the Local Government Management Board, offers the most comprehensive guide to sustainable landscape design. Another guidance tool, *Sustainability Works* sponsored by the Housing Corporation (Sustainable Works, 2002), is similarly comprehensive. However, these guides do not consider the breadth of issues that have been discussed in the previous chapter. For example, the sustainability implications of landscape materials, an issue central to the achievement of sustainable designed landscapes, are barely considered. Although the information they contain is informally arranged into a checklist format, there is no mechanism for assigning a score or rating to assessed schemes, so as to aid their comparison against one another and, more importantly, against a recognised benchmark.

Chapter 1 also introduced two further tools which can be used to assess and rate the sustainability of housing schemes. First, there is the DETR-commissioned *Millennium Villages and Sustainable Communities Report*, which utilised a bespoke checklist. Landscape issues were, however, barely considered and, what is more, the checklist methodology suggested that the assessment benchmarks should be devised on a site-by-site basis by the developer in collaboration with the local planning authority at the outset of each scheme (DETR, 2000). The case sites were rated against a benchmarking system of: exemplary; better than average; worse than average; mixed; and average. This is a flawed approach, especially if it were to be used to rate landscape design where 'average' may be, at best, very difficult to define; for example, how do you go about giving such a rating for ecological value? The *Millennium Villages and Sustainable Communities Report* itself makes the admission that using 'average' values as benchmarks leads to questions as to what is to be agreed as the base data for comparison (DETR, 2000). Second, there are the various revisions of BREEAM for houses and specifically *EcoHomes*, which allows a scheme to be rated according to a 'pass' to 'excellent' benchmarking system, a system devised in collaboration with the UK's construction and environmental sectors. However, as already noted, the assessment criteria of *EcoHomes* are still largely focused on building, rather than landscape, issues.

None of the guides or checklists introduced in Chapter 1 were considered to be suitable for assessing the environmental performance of the landscape. Landscape issues were not fully considered and/or no benchmarking system was used, or was inappropriate. Other countries have produced sustainability assessment tools for residential development which use a scoring or rating system (Boonstra, 2001; Pitts, 2004; Todd *et al.*, 2001). A selection of these are reviewed here and are summarized in Table 3.1. From the information provided in Table 3.1, it is clear that many of the landscape sustainability issues described in Chapter 2 have not been considered in most of the broadly recognised residential sustainability assessment tools. Only biodiversity/site ecology has been consistently included – a common characteristic with the various revisions of BREEAM for housing in the UK, including the current incarnation, *EcoHomes*.

As none of the tools outlined above were considered suitable for wholesale adoption for the study, the focus was therefore on adapting a tool for

Table 3.1 A summary of sustainable assessment tools for use on residential development. References: Centre of Environmental Technology (1999); Chatagnon *et al.* (1998); Cole & Larsson (2002); Pettersen (2000); Todd *et al.* (2001); US Green Building Council (2002); Vale *et al.* (2001).

Tool/Country of Origin	Landscape Criteria	Benchmarking System
HK – BEAM/ Hong Kong (China)	<ul><li>Convenient foot/cycle path network</li><li>Outdoor clothes drying</li><li>Recycled materials in external surfacing</li><li>Porous paving</li><li>Planting suited to site conditions</li><li>Rainwater harvesting</li><li>Improved ecological function of site</li></ul>	Performance is gauged in local relation to regulations. Overall ratings: satisfactory, good, very good, excellent.
EcoEffect/ Sweden	<ul><li>Site biodiversity</li></ul>	Performance against each criterion is gauged against average impact per capita in Sweden.
EcoProfile /Norway	<ul><li>Release of pollutants to surface water and into the ground</li><li>Management of surface water</li><li>Site and surrounding biodiversity</li></ul>	Performance against each criterion compared to a nationally derived figure, and rated on scale of 1 to 3, where 1 is relatively the least environmental impact and 3 the greatest.
Escale/France	<ul><li>Local pollution of air, water and soil</li><li>Integration with movement networks</li><li>Site ecology</li><li>Landscape integration</li></ul>	Performance against each criterion compared to typical practice or, where appropriate, statutory requirement. These are set as reference values of 0, and each criterion is awarded a mark of −1 to +5 based on how it compares (with +5 being best practice and −1 worse practice).

Table 3.1 *Continued*

Tool/Country of Origin	Landscape Criteria	Benchmarking System
GBC2002/ International	• Ecological productivity • Rainwater harvesting • Provision of shade and amenity in the landscape • Porous paving	Performance against each criterion compared to typical practice, local codes or national standards. Each criterion is then scored from −2 to +5 depending on performance relative to these standards (with −2 being unsatisfactory and +5 being outstanding performance).
NABERS/ Australia	• Permeable paving • Beneficial plants for wildlife/food provision • On-site composting facilities	Performance against each criterion is compared to nationally derived figures, and awarded 0–5 'stars'. The score under each of the broad category headings is based on the average 'star count' for all the criteria it covers. The final overall score is calculated by adding all the 'heading stars' together.
LEED/ USA	• Reduced site disturbance • Storm water management • Shade for buildings • Water-efficient planting	Projects earn points towards certification by meeting or exceeding each credit's technical requirements (nationally derived). Points are added up to derive the final score, and this relates to four levels of certification.

use in landscape assessment, and for use against English case sites. The common problem with the tools presented in Table 3.1 was their reliance on either average or typical performance levels, or nationally or locally derived standards as benchmarks. The drawback of using 'average' performances has already been noted, and clearly nationally or locally derived standards would have to be translated into an English context.

Since the original review of the assessment tools in 2003, there have been further developments. For example, the US Green Building Council, which is responsible for the Leadership in Energy and Environmental Design (LEED), introduced in August 2005 a pilot LEED for Homes (US Green Building Council, 2005). LEED for Homes includes mandatory requirement for a landscape design under the sustainable site category and also includes optional credits for use of plant mulches, rainwater harvesting and shading of landscapes. The allocation of credits also reflects the huge variation of climatic zones within the United States, with different credit weightings relating to dry, normal and wet zones.

Given that adaptation of an existing tool was necessary, and given the English focus of the original NHBC-funded study, the clear way forward was to use the UK BRE's *EcoHomes* as the template for the landscape assessment checklist. This allowed the issues covered by the landscape tool's criteria to be arranged under weighted categories, which have been devised in collaboration with the UK's environmental and construction sectors. As the *EcoHomes* category weightings, as well as the benchmarking system, were devised in this way and are increasingly well used and recognised in the UK, *EcoHomes* cannot be easily dismissed as irrelevant by those working in the UK construction industry. A further indication of the credibility of *EcoHomes* is its use by local authorities and the Housing Corporation. Finally, as some of the case sites used in the study derived their sustainable credentials from an *EcoHomes* assessment, there was the additional benefit of comparing their existing profiles with those derived from the landscape-focused study.

Since the development and testing of the landscape checklist, it is important to acknowledge the recent introduction of the Code for Sustainable Homes and its companion assessment tool, the Regional Sustainability Checklist for Developments. The Code for Sustainable Homes was developed by the Government in consultation with the BRE and the Construction Industry Research and Information Association (CIRIA) and through wider public consultation. Compliance with the Code is currently voluntary although the Government has indicated that it may in future become mandatory.

The Code for Sustainable Homes is based on *EcoHomes* but is different in a number of important ways. The Code introduces minimum standards for energy and water, at each level of the Code, and minimum entry level standards for materials, surface water runoff and waste. The Code does not include a transport category but does introduce new or restructured categories which include surface water runoff, waste and management. The Code has dropped the system of assigning different weightings to each category in preference to a simpler approach where the allocation of points reflects the relative importance of a particular issue. The Code is closely aligned to the Building Regulations, although the minimum standards for compliance have been set higher than these.

The Regional Sustainability Checklist for Developments is a complementary checklist to the Code for Sustainable Homes. The checklist uses regional planning and sustainable development policy and integrates this into a straightforward tool for developers and planners (WWF, 2006). It is a significant development in promoting landscape sustainability and includes categories which specifically focus on climate change and energy, transport and movement, ecology, community, place-making, resources, business and buildings.

A detailed description of the template BRE *EcoHomes* method

Using a landscape checklist based on *EcoHomes* allowed the calculation of a single overall percentage score for assessed schemes, which could then be related to a recognised system of ratings from 'pass' to 'excellent'. In the *EcoHomes* method, the overall percentage score is calculated by first deriving the individual percentage scores achieved in each of seven assessment categories. Each of these 'category scores' are then subjected to a weighting factor to take account of their relative importance. The weighting factors were developed through BRE's consultation with the UK environmental and construction sectors. The weighted 'category scores' are then summed to give a single score out of a possible maximum of 100 – the overall percentage score – and the appropriate rating can then be assigned. This process is illustrated in Figure 3.1.

The BRE has provided a generic description of the level of sustainable design commitment that would result in each *EcoHomes* rating (Table 3.2).

Table 3.2 *EcoHomes* ratings and their meanings. Rao *et al.* (2000) and reproduced with permission from *EcoHomes*.

Overall Percentage Score	Rating	Level of Sustainable Design Commitment (from *EcoHomes*)
36–48%	Pass	Most developments should be able to achieve this with minor design/specification changes at minimal additional cost.
49–59%	Good	The developer has been able to demonstrate good practice in most areas.
60–69%	Very Good	Developments which push forward the boundaries of performance.
>70%	Excellent	Developments which demonstrate exemplary performance across the full range of issues.

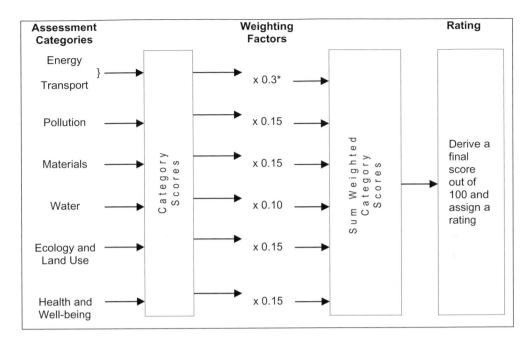

Figure 3.1 The process of calculating an *EcoHomes* rating (adapted from Rao *et al.*, 2000). *The category scores for the Energy and Transport Categories, both of which deal fundamentally with the reduction of fossil fuel consumption by new homes when 'in use', are aggregated prior to the application of the weighting factor. (Reproduced with permission from *EcoHomes*.)

The weighting hierarchy of assessment categories in the *EcoHomes* method, as derived through the BRE's consultation process, is based on a given scope for each category. If the scope of the assessment categories is altered, then their weighting hierarchy is invalidated. If the landscape assessment checklist was to provide credible ratings that could be compared with *EcoHomes* benchmarks and existing ratings, it was necessary that this hierarchy of category weightings was retained. It was therefore important that in adapting the *EcoHomes* method to focus on landscape issues, the proposed assessment criteria did not alter the fundamental scope of each category. The scope of the seven *EcoHomes* assessment categories, identified in the BRE's guidance, is summarised below.

- **Energy**. Design which minimises operational energy inputs and emissions of CO_2 to the atmosphere arising from the operation of a home and its services.
- **Transport**. Design which encourages reduced personal car use and contributes to a pedestrian- and cycle-friendly neighbourhood.

- **Pollution**. Design which severs pollution linkages[1] to the environment, when *in situ* and during the manufacture of materials (excluding CO_2).
- **Materials**. Design which considers the environmental implications of materials selection over a development's lifetime.[2]
- **Water**. Design which includes devices that encourage reduced water consumption on site.[3]
- **Ecology and Land Use**. Design which increases the ecological value of the site.
- **Health and Well-being**. Design which increases the quality of life of residents.

Using the scope of the categories as defined above, it was possible to arrange sustainable landscape criteria, as derived from the literature review presented in Chapter 2, under their appropriate category.

Whilst many of the landscape criteria related to issues that had not been included in *EcoHomes*, some were an adjustment, clarification or amplification of existing criteria. The following section briefly outlines the issues considered in each of the landscape checklist's categories and, where appropriate, explains the reasons behind changes to existing *EcoHomes* criteria.

Adapting the *EcoHomes* method for landscape assessments

The Energy Category

The landscape checklist principally focuses on the use of landscape features to modify winds and incident solar radiation around the home, thus reducing the energy expended and CO_2 produced through domestic heating and cooling. In order to identify the potential relevance of microclimatic landscape design for a given site, the assessment considered the size, location and arrangement of buildings on and around the site. This determined where landscape features could be used to ameliorate prevailing and chill winds. Furthermore, by using shadow-length calculations, it was possible to identify areas where coniferous trees and high walls should be avoided in order to

---

[1] According to the Environmental Protection Act (1990), a pollution linkage can be defined as: a source of pollution; a pathway; and a receptor of the pollution that will suffer damage as a result.
[2] This includes materials with the potential to cause relatively low pollution to the environment compared to other alternatives, while the use of more innovative materials with no polluting impact was considered in the Pollution Category.
[3] According the *EcoHomes* methodology, this does not include the use of water-efficient materials, which is considered in the Materials Category.

allow sunlight to reach otherwise unimpeded southern elevations in the winter months, and where deciduous vegetation would provide welcome summer shade. These calculations considered the height of the obstruction, the topography and latitude of the site, and the solar altitude during the early and latter parts of the heating season (for winter shadow lengths) and either side of the summer solstice (for summer shadow lengths).

There appears to be no quantification of the energy savings relating to different approaches to microclimatic landscape design in the UK. However, because the percentage of British homes with air-conditioning units is negligible (Rosenheck, 2003) it was assumed that a landscape designed to reduce winter fuel consumption alone would have a greater effect than one designed to only consider summer shading and ventilation. The landscape checklist was therefore formatted so that more credit was available for reducing the use of winter heating systems alone than for reducing the use of summer cooling systems alone (though obviously a landscape designed to do both would score the best).

Residential landscapes, unlike housing units, are dependent on the nature of the site and its context in determining the character and constituent elements. Although sustainable houses can be expected to incorporate similar components, sustainable residential landscape will be different from one site to the next. For example, the use of windbreak planting could rightly be considered important on an exposed site. However, a housing development with existing mature vegetation beyond its site boundary may not need to include such planting. Unlike *EcoHomes*, it was therefore necessary for the landscape checklist to include an option for answering 'Not Applicable'. The Government's Housing Quality Indicator tool allows 'Not Applicable' to be entered against an inappropriate assessment criteria and the score associated with that criterion is then removed from the total out of which the scheme is marked. This avoids distortion of the scores by penalising schemes for not doing something that is inappropriate in that case (DTLR, 2000). The Regional Sustainability Checklist for Developments has adopted a similar approach and includes an option for developers to record that it is not possible to deliver on a particular issue. This approach enables the developer and local planning authority to agree that a particular minimum standard is not achievable.

Where a development might also fail to gain credit against a certain criterion due to the omission of a landscape element, this might then invalidate subsequent criteria. For example, where deciduous trees were not used to provide summer shade, this invalidates the subsequent question of whether tree species that maximise solar gain had been used. Rather than penalising a development twice, once for omitting the trees and then again for not using certain species, it was decided that there should be the option to enter 'Not Applicable' against the second invalidated criterion, removing the associated score from the total and thereby avoiding the assessment becoming punitive or unfair.

For reducing the use of tumble dryers, the landscape checklist also awarded credit for the inclusion of a secure external drying space, unlike *EcoHomes* which credits both external and internal drying spaces. Innovative buildings which include large, glazed 'sun rooms' may allow for efficient internal drying of clothes, but clearly there are usually advantages in a secure external drying space (internal drying spaces compete for space with other activities, can cause increased levels of condensation within the home and, more importantly, may encourage the use of internal heating systems). Points are available for a drying space within the Code for Sustainable Homes, although it does not stipulate if this should be external.

The Transport Category

It is acknowledged that a housing scheme's location in respect of walking distance to amenities influences sustainable performance (see Barton *et al.*, 1995; Rao *et al.*, 2000). However, social housing developers often have a limited choice of where they develop, and smaller social sites can precede amenities and improved infrastructure provision in regenerating areas. A location-based criterion would therefore seem prejudicial to the rating of some sites. Such considerations were also considered to fall outside the checklist's focus on landscape design. Therefore, unlike *EcoHomes*, the Transport Category in the landscape checklist did not consider the location of the site in relation to amenities. Rather, the landscape assessment focused on the design of the movement networks within the scheme's site boundary. Compliance with design standards for footpaths, cyclepaths and roads was considered, as was the use of planting to improve the environmental and visual qualities of the routes. The Code for Sustainable Homes awards points for the inclusion of cycle storage under the Energy Category (which is credited in *EcoHomes* under Transport) but makes no provision for the design of safe cycle routes. The assessment of transport and movement will instead be covered under the complementary Regional Sustainability Checklist for Developments.

The Pollution Category

Here the landscape assessment considered the use of chemical-free nurseries and timber production, and the use of detailing to improve the durability of timbers, reducing the need for future chemical applications. The use of reclaimed or recycled materials in lieu of virgin alternatives derived from a polluting manufacturing process was also credited, as was the use of relevant codes of practice with regard to the use of pesticides and other chemicals on site.

The Pollution Category of *EcoHomes* recognises the value of reducing rainwater runoff from housing areas in terms of pollution and other environmental damage. The criterion used by *EcoHomes* is the reduction of peak surface runoff volumes from hard surfaces and roofs by 50% through the use of SuDS. The Code for Sustainable Homes has now introduced a new category which specifically focuses on surface water runoff. Whilst the use of SuDS systems was also included in the landscape assessment, calculations of peak runoff volumes for assessed sites were beyond the landscape assessment methodology. However, as noted in Chapter 2, work by Whitford *et al.* (2001) demonstrated that increased areas of green space within a residential development results in reduced runoff coefficients (the ratio of runoff to incident precipitation). Table 3.3 demonstrates how the percentage area of green space, measured in the four residential areas in this cited study, was used as the basis for classifying performance in the landscape checklist.[4]

Table 3.3 The use of the relationships between runoff and percentage green space observed by Whitford *et al.* (2001) to create landscape checklist criteria for 'embedded green space'.

Residential Area from Study by Whitford et al. (2001)	Relative Runoff	% Green Space in Residential Area (Whitford et al., 2001)	Interpretation in Landscape Checklist, Pollution Category
1	Low	47%	More than 50% of housing area is 'embedded green space' for maximum credits.
2	Medium	38%	30–50% of housing area is 'embedded green space' for half credits.
3 and 4	High	12–30%	Less than 30% of housing area is 'embedded green space' for no credits.

[4] The study by Whitford *et al.* (2001) focused on one geographical area, Liverpool, England, and therefore does not make any allowance for significant variations in soil conditions that might affect the efficiency of natural infiltration.

The landscape checklist made a clear distinction between the 'embedded green spaces' that are located within the built-up areas of housing and areas of green space that exist outside the built fabric and effectively form a separate land-use area. At the scale of a single housing site, these two types of green space contribute to sustainability in different ways. First, there are the 'embedded green spaces' which include the planted or grassed areas of gardens and doorstep communal areas, verges, medians, green roofs and green drainage features. It is the combined area of these features that affects reduced runoff generation in a housing scheme by intercepting rainfall and overland flow. Second, there are the large unsealed green spaces that might be provided by developers alongside housing areas. Though these spaces are unrelated to intercepting rainfall and runoff within an assessed housing area itself, through occupying space that might otherwise be sealed, they reduce the potential runoff generated by a wider neighbourhood. They also provide a useful route for groundwater and aquifer replenishment, as well as offering further potential ecological and recreation benefits, and as such are also credited in the landscape checklist. These areas might include neighbourhood parks and sports pitches.

The Materials Category

The Materials Category of *EcoHomes* considers the environmental implications of materials used in design. As noted in Chapter 2, several organisations have derived life-cycle assessment (LCA) methodologies in order to compare the environmental performance of different building materials and components from the point of extraction or manufacture, through to decommissioning and reuse or disposal. The Materials Category of *EcoHomes* provides credit where, by area, 80% or more of the landscape surfacing and hard landscape boundaries achieves a relatively high 'A rating' against the BRE's own LCA for building components presented in the *Green Guide to Housing Specification* (Anderson & Howard, 2000). This criterion was adopted directly into the landscape checklist. However, there are limitations to the BRE's LCA method, which were dealt with in the landscape checklist.

First, the BRE considers 'landscaping' to be driveways, paths and planting, but not highway. However, the *Green Guide* ratings show that the most ubiquitous road surfacing specifications such as asphalt are relatively poor environmental performers (Anderson & Howard, 2000). By omitting infrastructure areas from its definition of landscape areas, the current BRE methodology allows *EcoHomes* credits to be gained for landscape materials, irrespective of the wide use of environmentally harmful materials in the external works. Therefore the landscape assessment also considered the highway areas for assessment. The assessment of landscape materials is now included in the 'Resources Category' of the Regional Sustainability Checklist for Developments, which promotes the use of reclaimed aggregates in the construction of roads and pavements.

Second, as noted in Chapter 2, the environmental profiles of landscape materials presented within the *Green Guide* focus on the relative merits of common specifications and are fairly generic. They do not consider more innovative specifications and details which might result in improved environmental profiles. For example, a 'stone and mortar wall' receives a moderate profile compared to other common boundary treatments. However, there are clearly further issues that could be considered in building a more sustainable stone and mortar wall: what if the stone was reclaimed or sourced from a local quarry that has undertaken environmental certification for working practices, and used with a pure lime mortar? These are examples of the layers of detail that were used to provide further assessment criteria in the landscape checklist over and above whether or not the specification receives a good profile in the BRE's *Green Guide*.

In summary, the landscape assessment adopted the following approach. A landscape's inclusion of 80% or more, by area, of materials and specifications with a good BRE profile earned the development credit within the Materials Category; however, the assessed landscape could then go on to accrue additional credits in the Materials Category (and the Pollution Category where appropriate) through:

- making detailed specification decisions which would improve a good BRE profile still further, for example use of naturally durable, well-detailed, non-treated timber fencing instead of a pre-treated timber fence
- replacing materials with a relatively poor BRE profile with reclaimed or recycled alternatives
- improving the profile of all materials by using manufacturers and suppliers who undertake good environmental practices
- detailing materials to aid reuse and minimise maintenance and wastage
- reducing the embodied energy and transport pollution of all materials through considering local sourcing.

In reference to the final point, there were four major obstacles to devising universal criteria to benchmark the use of local materials in the landscape assessment. First, there is no workable definition of a 'local material'; at the innovative BedZED housing scheme in London, much of the building materials were sourced from within 35 miles of the site (zedfactory, 2002) but would this have been possible for a development in a more remote area? Perhaps because of the site-specific nature of what practically constitutes 'local', there appeared to be no template benchmarks that the landscape checklist could adopt. Whilst noting the benefits of local materials, *Eco-Homes* does not include it as an assessment criterion (Rao *et al.*, 2000). Second, Howard (2000) has highlighted the fact that development pressures and abundance of local minerals are not equally distributed throughout the UK; South-East England has particularly heavy pressures on its mineral resources, and as a result demands for certain materials can only be met by extended travel distances. Third, if reclaimed materials are specified, the effective definition of 'local' in terms of energy use can be extended; the absence of production energy from the overall embodied energy calculation for the material effectively 'buys' additional transport energy. The BRE has suggested that, for example, reclaimed bricks, aggregates and steel would have to be transported 250, 150 and 2500 miles respectively before they acquired the embodied energy equivalent of their virgin counterparts manu-factured at the site's doorstep (Brownhill & Rao, 2002). Finally, a definition of 'local' can vary depending upon the mode of transport employed; the literature review presented in Chapter 2 showed that the energy required to carry a tonne of construction materials by rail or ship is far less than that required to carry a tonne by road for the equivalent distance. Therefore, rather than prescribe a distance from site as 'local', the landscape assess-ment instead asked the open question, *'To what extent has the source of the materials been considered, with a view to lowering embodied energy and reducing pollution?'*. This allows each site to be judged according to its individual circumstances.

The Water Category

In *EcoHomes*, the Water Category focuses on the use of efficient bathroom fittings and external water harvesting in order to reduce mains water con-sumption; it does not consider the water demand resulting from the produc-tion, implementation and maintenance of materials, which are considered in its Materials Category, nor does it consider the management of rainwater on the site, which is considered in its Pollution Category. The need for pre-serving the scope of each assessment category dictated that the landscape assessment did likewise and therefore there were few criteria related to landscape works which were suited to the narrow scope of the checklist's Water Category. The use of rainwater harvesting devices within the external works was adopted directly from *EcoHomes* and the use of bark mulch dressings which reduce the evaporation of water from planting beds was also credited. Irrigation of plants accounts for significant amounts of resi-dential water use and although this can be reduced by the use of mulches, the need to specify plants that are suited to site conditions and therefore require less water and other inputs to establish and thrive is a key factor in reducing irrigation demands (and pesticide use). This was recognised through the credit allowance for site-specific planting in the Materials Category of the landscape checklist, which was equivalent to the value it would have been if the issue had been included in its Water or Pollution Category.

The Ecology and Land Use Category

The areas considered within this category of *EcoHomes* (and which appear to be replicated in the Code for Sustainable Homes) are: the development of sites with a low ecological value (or the containment of development within a part of a site which is of low value); and the protection of existing ecological features during construction and their enhancement in accordance with recommendations from an ecological consultant. Furthermore, the 'change of ecological value' for the site is scored, based on a comparison of a 'species hectare' index for the site before and after development. Though acknowledged as an important issue, assessing schemes on the basis of ecological value of the site prior to development would again seem prejudicial to the rating of social housing, with limited choice of where they can develop. Therefore this was not included within the landscape assessment. However, the protection of valuable existing site features, as well as the creation and enhancement of habitat on site through design and management, were considered in detail.

The numerical species index was not used as a criterion in the landscape assessment. The index, based on the product of habitat area and the average number of species per hectare within that habitat, is generic and does not take account of important issues that affect the actual habitat value of a vegetated area. As discussed in Chapter 2, in terms of maximising habitat potential (providing habitat for a large number, and a diverse range, of species) the key factors for success are not just the size of a planted area but also its shape; location relative to neighbouring habitat and competing anthropogenic land uses; diversity between and within planting areas in terms of species, age and structure; and connectivity between green features. The Ecology and Land Use Category of the landscape assessment was therefore based on descriptive site analysis that considered these issues.

The Health and Well-Being Category

This category considered the provision of private and communal doorstep spaces and the size and contents of these spaces. The literature review in

Chapter 2 identified the important contribution to health and well-being that can be made by landscapes which encourage direct involvement through growing and harvesting food; landscapes which include significant tree cover; and landscapes that encourage communal interaction but also provide privacy as required. All of these issues were included within the landscape checklist's criteria.

The approach to the provision of private external space in the Health and Well-Being Category of *EcoHomes* is that each dwelling should have access to an 'at least partially private external space' which can be a balcony, roof garden or communal space (Rao *et al.*, 2000). The Code for Sustainable Homes makes similar provision within the Health and Well-Being Category and also stipulates that the space, which can be 'partly private', should also be accessible to disabled people. Whilst taking a similarly broad approach to the definition of external space, the landscape checklist, mindful of the limitations of non-private space identified by the literature review, only allows credit where totally private space had been provided for all units, even where this was through the clear subdivision of an open space with shared access.

Despite being identified in the literature review as an influence on the environmental and social sustainability of housing, neither *EcoHomes* nor the Code for Sustainable Homes considers the size of the private gardens provided, nor the provision of clearly defined communal doorstep spaces. The private garden size criteria in the landscape assessment were devised with reference to the research literature and took into account the space required to accommodate children's play, tree planting and other sustainable features. The resulting standard of $50\,m^2$ may be an increase in the minimum provision suggested by many local authorities (particularly for dense urban areas) but given the positive relationship between garden size and the occurrence of sustainable garden features reported in the literature, housing which is claiming to be more sustainable should be expected to provide significant numbers of households with private garden space above this standard. However, the checklist also makes provision for more innovative housing layouts that provide smaller private gardens backing onto enclosed communal space. In such layouts, the loss of private garden space is compensated by the provision of the communal space, which can be used to accommodate sustainable activities and features such as composting and recycling, and secure children's play. It was therefore appropriate that the landscape checklist, like the current revision of the *Essex Design Guide*,[5] made allowance for such layouts through a relaxed minimum rear garden

---

[5] The *Essex Design Guide* is broadly recognised as the best known and most influential county design guide (McGhie & Girling, 1995).

space standard of 25 m^2 where a recognisable doorstep space was provided immediately adjacent (Essex County Council, 1997).

Given the UK Government's continuing advocacy of higher densities in new English housing, a stipulated maximum garden size might therefore also seem appropriate for the landscape assessment. However, given the need to accommodate larger houses in larger gardens, and the need to maintain minimum distances between houses, it was not possible to devise a universally applicable maximum garden size.

Though the literature review identified that percentage tree cover has implications for a number of health and well-being issues, benchmarks against which these benefits could be directly compared do not appear to have been quantified. However, in addition to providing a means to devise criteria for green space cover, the work by Whitford *et al.* (2001), cited previously, also quantifies tree cover in residential areas described as ranging from tree deficient to verdant. The landscape assessment compares the tree cover facilitated by the developer, with the figures observed in this cited study (Table 3.4).

The canopy area of new trees planted by the developer would be calculated using the spread of the species ten years after planting, according to a reputable UK nursery. This would avoid underestimating their contribution by using planted canopy size but also avoided the use of a period such as 25 years after planting, which would not account for their contribution for a significant period of the lifetime of the housing and its residents. The canopies predicted by the nursery were modified to take account of the

Table 3.4 The use of descriptions of tree cover in different types of residential areas by Whitford *et al.* (2001) to create checklist criteria for 'percentage tree cover'.

Residential Area from Study by Whitford et al. (2001)	Description (after Whitford et al., 2001)	% Tree Cover	Interpretation in Landscape Checklist, Health & Well-Being Category
1	Green residential area with tree cover	10%	5–10% tree cover is medium, half credits.
2	Green residential area with high tree cover	14%	More than 10% tree cover is high, full credits.
3 and 4	Residential areas with insignificant tree cover	0.3–1%	Less than 5% tree cover is low, no credits.

restricting effects of urban conditions; on average, trees within built development reach only 60% of the spread predicted by the nursery (Hodge, 1991).

Adjusting the *EcoHomes* weighting factors

In accordance with the scope of the category defined by the *EcoHomes* method, only two landscape assessment criteria appropriate for the Water Category were identified in the literature review: the use of water butts or other means to harvest rainwater, and the use of bark mulches to decrease rates of water loss from planting areas. As a result, the credit returns for including these elements were exaggerated. In order to minimise any distortion of the percentage scores, the *EcoHomes* weighting factors were slightly adjusted for the landscape assessment checklist, whilst the hierarchy of the category weightings was kept intact.[6] The weighting of the Water Category was reduced from 0.1 to 0.05, and the remaining weightings were all raised by 0.01 so that the total score remained out of 100 (Table 3.5).

Setting compliance standards

For some issues it was appropriate to award credit against some of the assessment criteria on a yes/no basis, for example, *'Were water butts pro-*

Table 3.5 *EcoHomes* and adjusted landscape checklist category weightings.

Assessment Categories	*EcoHomes* Category Weightings	Adjusted Landscape Checklist Category Weightings
Energy transport	0.3	0.31
Pollution	0.15	0.16
Materials	0.15	0.16
Water	0.10	0.05
Ecology and land use	0.15	0.16
Health and well-being	0.15	0.16

[6] In retrospect, the adjustment of the weighting factors was shown to have no effect on the outcome of the assessments in terms of the ratings assigned.

vided for all units?'. However, for many sustainability issues, the BRE has suggested that 100% compliance with a standard may be an impossible target for developers and may undermine the credibility of an assessment method in the eyes of the construction industry (Brownhill & Rao, 2002). As a result, the BREEAM suite of assessment tools, including *EcoHomes*, has adopted, where appropriate, an approach which awards some credit for 'good practice', where 60% of an element meets the standard required, and full credit for 'best practice' where 80% meets the standard (Brownhill & Rao, 2002; Rao *et al.*, 2000). Although this approach may suggest a compromise of sustainable ethics, it was important that the assessment method was seen to be fair and pragmatic in its demands. Furthermore, as highlighted by Dunnett & Hitchmough (1996, p 44) in reference to sustainable planting:

> *'There are some elements which people want to have in urban landscapes that can never be highly sustainable... provided that the overall move is increasingly towards sustainability, a degree of flexibility can be built into the detail of any given site.'*

This suggests that sustainable but pragmatic landscape design might look to minimise the unsustainable and maximise the sustainable, rather than involving the total substitution of unsustainable elements. This supports the case for using, in some cases, 60% and 80% compliance rather than 100% when assessing developers who are claiming to provide more sustainable properties. This approach was therefore adopted within the landscape assessment checklist, unless different levels of compliance relevant to landscape works were suggested by the BRE or previous research.[7]

Judging visual qualities

Some of the landscape checklist's criteria require an assessment of the visual qualities of landscape areas. Assessing whether or not children's play has been integrated into a communal space or whether the design of spaces and routes was appropriate or convivial requires judgement, rather than measurement. It was therefore important that these types of assessment criteria were phrased so that they were not merely subjective but based on objective on-site observations. For example, an assessment against the criterion *'Has a recognisable communal space been provided?'* depends on a

---

[7] The BRE suggests credit benchmarks of 30%, 60% and 75% for use of FSC-certified timber (Rao *et al.*, 2000) and credit benchmarks for 10% and 20% are used for the volume of reclaimed materials, owing to their limited availability (Brownhill & Rao, 2002).

consideration of whether the space is recognisable as a communal resource, rather than simply an unbuilt area labelled as communal space on a drawing. In this case the assessment should consider whether appropriate levels of functionality and visual attributes have been met, including visual variety, enclosure, definition and furnishing. This approach avoids a purely subjective assessment, whereas asking *'Has an attractive communal space been provided?'* would result in an assessment based on the assessor's taste, acting as a proxy for the views of the residents – clearly an undesirable methodological position.

General limitations of the checklist assessment approach

Where possible, care has been taken to ensure that the credits available reflect the impact of design decisions on sustainable performance. For example, more credits are awarded for using pollution-free specifications than alternatives with some polluting potential; thus specification of durable, untreated timber is better rewarded than using an 'environmentally friendly' timber preservative. However, the difference between the credits available for these actions is not based on empirical evidence; the fact that preservative-free timber gained 'x' times more credit than the use of relatively benign preservatives does not mean that the former has been quantified as being 'x times better' than the latter, it simply means that one option was considered to be better than the other and that the checklist should reflect this. Here, at least, the literature had suggested that one course of action was better than another. In other areas there was a total lack of comparative data that could be used to weight credit allocations for different actions. For example, what are the relative savings in CO_2 emissions brought about through microclimatic landscape design compared to the use of locally sourced landscape materials or the provision of an outdoor drying space? The picture was further complicated by the lack of common quantitative units for comparing different environmental impacts. For example, though more embodied energy and CO_2 emissions might be saved by using reclaimed stone than by using reclaimed aggregate, what about the safeguarding of different types of habitats endangered by reclaiming these materials? Can such variables even be quantified?

In future, it might be possible to rank some of the qualitative criteria relating to social sustainability if data relating to resident preferences studies were used to inform a weighting system. The numerical scoring can therefore claim only to be indicative at this stage. Nevertheless, the checklist was piloted to ensure that the ratings were reliable and representative. However, there is clearly scope to build upon the work presented here, through the collection and use of empirical data to inform credit allocations.

During the aforementioned NHBC-funded research that drove the creation of the checklist, the attitudes of developers, designers and contractors involved in 'sustainable housing' were analysed. In many instances, and perhaps unsurprisingly, these bodies and indiviuduals were seen to have been reactive in their outlook, as opposed to proactive and determined to be holistic in their attempt to 'build green'. They had simply used the *Eco-Homes* assessment undertaken on their sites as a 'shopping list' of items, with the final rating seen as an end in itself rather than as part of a wider move towards sustainability. This is perhaps the most fundamental flaw in the checklist/guide approach: although it can impart information, it does not necessarily ensure that those involved will transfer this knowledge from site to site. It may be difficult for *EcoHomes*, the landscape checklist presented here and other similar checklist tools to make a lasting breakthrough into mainstream construction practice unless genuine concerns for people and the environment underpin the industry.

References

Anderson, J. & Howard, N. (2000) *The Green Guide to Housing Specification. An Environmental Profiling System for Building Materials and Components Used in Housing.* Garston, Watford: Building Research Establishment, Centre for Sustainable Construction.

Barton, H., Davis, G. & Guise, R. (1995) *Sustainable Settlements: A Guide for Planners, Designers and Developers.* Bristol: University of the West of England and the Local Government Board.

Boonstra, C. (2001) Green building challenge and sustainable building 2000. *Building Research & Information*, 29(5), pp 321–323.

Brownhill, D. & Rao, S. (2002) *A Sustainability Checklist for Developments. A Common Framework for Developers and Local Authorities.* Garston, Watford: Building Research Establishment, Centre for Sustainable Construction.

Centre of Environmental Technology (1999) *HK-BEAM (Residential): An Environmental Assessment for New Residential Buildings.* Kowloon, Hong Kong: Centre of Environmental Technology Ltd.

Chatagnon, N., Nible, S. & Achard, G. (1998) *ESCALE: A Method of Assessing a Building's Environmental Performance at the Design Stage.* Proceedings of Green Building Challenge '98. Vancouver, BC. October 26–28.

Cole, R. & Larsson, N. (2002) *GB Tool User Manual.* Ottawa: Natural Resources Canada/International Initiative for a Sustainable Built Environment.

Department of the Environment, Transport & the Regions (2000) *Regeneration Research Summary: Millennium Villages and Sustainable Communities Final Report* (Number 30) London: DETR.

Department for Transport, Local Government & the Regions (2000) *HQI. Housing Quality Indicators (Version 2)* London: DTLR.

Dunnett, N. & Hitchmough, J. (1996) Excitement and energy. *Landscape Design*, June, pp 43–46.

Essex County Council (1997) *The Essex Design Guide*. Chelmsford: Essex County Council and Essex Planning Officers Association.

Hodge, S.J. (1991) *Urban Trees: A Survey of Street Trees in England*. Forestry Commission Bulletin 99. London: HMSO.

Howard, N. (2000) *Sustainable Construction – the Data*. BRE Report CR258/99. Garston, Watford: Building Research Establishment, Centre for Sustainable Construction.

McGhie, C. & Girling, R. (1995) *Local Attraction. The Design of New Housing in the Countryside*. London: Council for the Protection of Rural England.

Pettersen, T.D. (2000) *EcoProfile, Reference Document*. Oslo: GRIP Centre.

Pitts, A.C. (2004) *Planning and Design Strategies for Sustainability and Profit*. Oxford: Architectural Press.

Rao, S., Yates, A., Brownhill, D. & Howard, N. (2000) *EcoHomes: The Environmental Rating for Homes*. Garston, Watford: Building Research Establishment, Centre for Sustainable Construction.

Rosenheck, D. (2003) Stay cool, and heat up the planet: the answer to the summer's heatwave? *New Statesman*, 16(772), p 18.

Sustainable Works (2002) *Sustainable Works. The Complete Development Tool for Sustainable Housing.* (online) Available at: www.sustainabilityworks.org.uk (accessed 7 October 2002).

Todd, J.A., Crawley, D., Geissler, S. & Lindsey, G. (2001) Comparative assessment of environmental performance tools and the role of the Green Building Challenge. *Building Research and Information*, 29(5), pp 324–335.

US Green Building Council (2002) *LEED (Leadership in Energy and Environmental Design) Green Building Rating System, For New Construction and Major Renovations, Version 2.1.* (online) Available at: www.usgbc.org/Docs/LEEDdocs/LEED_RS_v2-1.pdf"}http://www.usgbc.org/Docs/LEEDdocs/LEED_RS_v2-1.pdf (accessed 7 December 2002).

US Green Building Council (2005) *LEED for Homes. Rating System For Pilot Demonstration of LEED for Homes Program, Version 1.72.* (online) Available at: www.usgbc.org/ShowFile.aspx?DocumentID=855 (accessed 10 January 2007).

Vale, R., Vale, B. & Fay, R. (2001) *The National Australian Buildings Environmental Rating System (NABERS) Final Draft Version*. Canberra: Environment Australia.

Whitford, V., Ennos, A.R. & Handley, J.F. (2001) 'City form and natural processes' – indicators for the ecological performance of urban areas and their application to Merseyside, UK. *Landscape and Urban Planning*, 57, pp 91–103.

WWF (2006) *A Regional Sustainability Checklist for Developments.* (online) Available at: www.wwf.org.uk/filelibrary/pdf/regsust_checklist.pdf (accessed 15 January 2007).

Zedfactory (2002) *Sustainability KPIs @ BedZED.* (online) Available at: www.zedfactory.com/bedzed/kpi.html (accessed 1 August 2002).

Chapter 4

Case studies: applying the Residential Landscape Sustainability Checklist

Introduction

This chapter looks at how the Residential Landscape Sustainability Checklist was piloted and used to assess the sustainability of residential landscapes. It specifically focuses on two case studies: Greenwich Millennium Village, London, and Childwall, Liverpool. These were selected because they demonstrate the most comprehensive approach to the sustainable landscape design of all the evaluated schemes. It is also worth noting that both of these developments were joint winners of the inaugural House Builders Federation and WWF Sustainable Homes Award in 2004.

The checklist was piloted and evaluated in two phases. The first phase used an outline version of the checklist to assess 19 housing developments built throughout England. All these schemes were selected on the basis that they made some claim to sustainability as a result of certification and/or through association with an initiative which embraces sustainability. The most common form of certification was the BRE Environmental Standard Award or *EcoHomes* which had been used to certificate 15 of the 19 developments. The chosen sites were also selected to include different housing densities, tenures (including private developers and Registered Social Landlords or RSLs), and various physical and social contexts. Each of these projects was evaluated from landscape drawings (as supplied by the developer) and site visits. The second phase used an extended 'detailed checklist' to reassess six of the projects from the original study. The detailed checklist incorporated additional criteria in the Pollution, Materials and Ecology and Land Use categories. The assessment of these criteria required access to the original design documents which gave detailed specification of materials and the timing and approaches to the landscape works. Both Childwall and Greenwich Millennium Village were included in the second phase of the study.

The two case studies, Greenwich Millennium Village and Childwall, are discussed within the context of the 19 pilot studies and six detailed assessments. There is a brief overview of the two case studies which is then followed by a more detailed analysis of how they performed against each of the categories in the checklist. The chapter concludes by discussing the key factors that were identified by designers and developers as being responsible for encouraging and discouraging landscape sustainability.

Greenwich Millennium Village, London

Greenwich Millennium Village is located within a 121-hectare regeneration area in the east of London. The area was originally heavily industrialised until the last major works closed down in 1985. In 1997 the site was purchased by English Partnerships who commissioned a team of internationally renowned consultants to create a masterplan for the area's regeneration. In regenerating the site, English Partnerships were extremely keen that sustainability should be a central tenet of the proposals.

The masterplan proposed that the derelict site undergo remediation and a redevelopment of 1600 new homes, workspaces, shopping and recreational facilities. At the heart of the masterplan was a sustainable community of a further 1377 homes of mixed tenure with an integrated 'Ecology Park', as well as a nearby commercial centre, school and health centre. English Partnerships undertook the demolition and site remediation works in 1997. Greenwich Millennium Village has been developed as a joint venture between Countryside Properties Plc and Taylor Woodrow Developments Ltd in association with English Partnerships.

The site masterplan for the sustainable community was to uphold and refine the sustainability theme of the broader area plan with English Partnerships setting stringent environmental targets, including reduced energy consumption, embodied energy, water demand and construction waste (Figure 4.1). The masterplan illustrates the use of intimate groupings of 'perimeter blocks' of 30–50 housing units formed around communal spaces. One of these blocks was selected as being representative of the whole housing scheme in terms of design ethos, unit density and landscape treatment (Figure 4.2). The detailed landscape design for this area was undertaken by a single landscape practice, Rummey Design Associates, whose remit included detailed hard and soft design for all external areas.

Construction began in 1999 and the first residents moved in a year later. The development was accredited with an *EcoHomes* rating of 'excellent'

Figure 4.1 Site masterplan: location of the study site, 'ecology park' and adjacent services and amenities. (Reproduced with permission from Countryside Properties plc and Taylor Woodrow Developments Ltd in association with English Partnerships.)

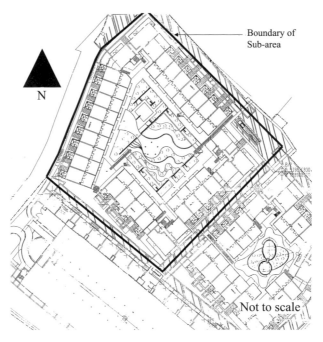

Figure 4.2 Layout of the representative housing block with related gardens and communal spaces. (Reproduced with permission from Countryside Properties plc and Taylor Woodrow Developments Ltd in association with English Partnerships.)

Figure 4.3 View from within the ecology park at Greenwich Millennium Village looking towards the residential housing blocks.

and 'very good' against the detailed landscape checklist. The scheme performed well against the checklist in its creation of the habitat-rich Ecology Park; richly designed communal spaces for the enjoyment of residents; the prioritisation of pedestrians and cyclists; the use of recycled demolition waste as a construction material; and the careful consideration of microclimate design (Figure 4.3).

Childwall, Liverpool

The neighbourhood of Childwall is situated in a suburban district to the east of Liverpool city centre. The scheme that has been reviewed is much smaller than Greenwich Millennium Village and consists of 22 units, part of a larger 157-unit redevelopment of new homes which were to replace the demolition of the 1960s tower blocks.

The redevelopment, which began in 1998, was financed by the Liverpool Housing Action Trust, who stipulated prior to the redevelopment that the scheme should comply with *EcoHomes* certification. Phase 2a of the development was completed in 2002 and was undertaken by Anchor Trust, a Registered Social Landlord. A Liverpool-based landscape practice, BCA Landscape, was appointed to design and detail all external hard and soft works. Childwall also received a 'very good' assessment from the landscape checklist. Childwall was particularly effective in its incorporation of diverse, multifunctioning planting, in both private gardens and an integral communal space (Figure 4.4). The communal space also included features to encour-

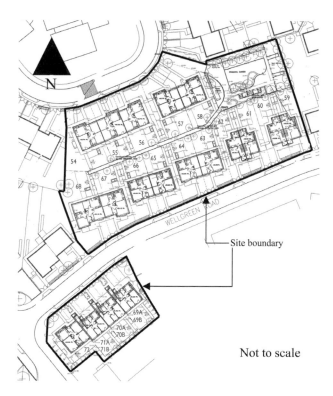

Figure 4.4 Phase 2a of the development which was assessed using the landscape checklist. The plan shows the arrangement of housing and private gardens and the communal doorstep space including allotments, orchard and 'fruit' patch which is located in the top right-hand corner of the site.

age sustainable lifestyles, for instance recycling and composting bins. The hard materials were all either reclaimed or locally sourced, and there was frequent use of detailing to aid the potential future reuse of materials. The landscape architects also made a concerted effort to identify early in the design process any materials that could be reclaimed from the tower blocks that were due for demolition. The project was part of a larger regeneration scheme for the Childwall neighbourhood, which also included a section 106 agreement aimed to improve the quality of public open space through planting and play facilities.

Evaluation of the case studies against the Residential Landscape Sustainability Checklist

The evaluation of the case studies looks at each category of the landscape checklist in turn and identifies where credits were awarded. This review draws on the results from the outline checklist (which was used to evaluate 19 residential developments) and the six detailed case studies where additional criteria under the categories for pollution, materials, ecology and health and well-being were considered.

The Energy Category

Microclimatic landscape design

The retention and enhancement of existing vegetation are an important influence on available credits for Energy Category performance. All the pilot sites gained some credit through the retention of pre-existing tree belts, tree lines or hedgerows lying between the prevailing and/or the chill winter winds and the housing. The only scheme to achieve an 'excellent' rating was the Greenwich Millennium Village, which featured strategic mounding and shelterbelt planting (as well as stepped building profiles) to mitigate the strong north-east winds from along the adjacent river and the prevailing south-westerly winds (Figure 4.5). This was augmented with smaller-scale tree planting within the body of the housing, which also provided summer shade. The houses themselves were arranged into a tight urban fabric of perimeter blocks, facing onto shared courtyards. Although the trees were set wide enough apart (in relation to the height of surrounding buildings) to allow residual winds to drop towards the ground layer, they were planted with lines of multi-stem birch and featured semi-permeable boundary treatments, thus slowing and calming any winds while avoiding the introduction of turbulence.

Figure 4.5 Greenwich Millennium Village. The image shows the use of earth bunds and under-planted belts of moderately dense, quick-growing birch, running along the south-west boundary. This will slow and calm prevailing winds approaching the site, whilst also allowing sufficient air passage for ventilation.

Childwall did not feature retained vegetation or new planting in order to modify the winds, nor were solid boundary features that introduce turbulence into air flows avoided. Summer shade was also not considered for more than 60% of the units.

The Transport Category

Layout and design of pedestrian and cycle routes

The layout of adjacent buildings, lighting provision and the design and management of hard and soft surfacing and boundary treatments were considered in the assessment. These factors determine the degree of surveillance, the frequency of hiding places and blind corners, and the comfort and conviviality of routes. In housing areas, a key influence on whether or not the latter has been achieved, and that can be assessed objectively, is the degree to which the route edges allows expressions of activity, habitation and personalisation.

Generally speaking, each of the pilot sites performed well against the functional criteria; routes were well overlooked, well lit, sufficiently wide and appropriately detailed in terms of gradients, surfacing and kerbs. However, in terms of providing shade, visual screening and a sink for air-borne pollutants, the contribution of planting to the success of the pedestrian and cycle routes was generally poor. Typically where planting was included it made a negligible contribution to microclimate. The use of planting to soften and enliven routes was variable across the range of pilot sites and within the different developments.

Greenwich Millennium Village achieved the highest score under this assessment. The site had a tight built fabric arranged into perimeter blocks, terraces and mews courtyards which were frequently punctuated by through routes, thus achieving a high level of permeability. This led to coherent and convenient access to open spaces and other services within and around the scheme. The design also improved the conviviality of some of these routes through planting (Figure 4.6).

Traffic calming

All the sites within the study (with the exception of one) had incorporated traffic-calming measures to encourage a mean target speed of 20 mph, and thus earned credit. However, the methods employed varied and included speed humps (which may necessitate continuous braking and accelerating and may produce noise, vibration and wear and increased car emissions). Greenwich Millennium Village and Childwall used frequent changes in direction along the access road network; bends, corners and chicanes were located to ensure that there were no straight lengths of road of more than 40 m. Avoidance of problematic calming devices, which may cause vehicles to accelerate and decelerate, earned additional credit. One of the study sites had successfully used 'home zone' principles to create a shared surface for pedestrians and vehicles, where traffic speeds were controlled by changes in the surface materials and strategic placement of parking.

The Pollution Category

Reduced use of timber treatments

The first two criteria in this category focus on the detailing of permanent timber landscape elements. Credit is lost for the use of paints and stains in lieu of 'untreated' timber. Though the paints and stains used on the sites may be relatively 'environmentally friendly', all have some unsustainable characteristics. It was not possible to differentiate between a more benign treatment and a less benign one during the outline pilot study, when the sites were assessed using the landscape drawings and survey. The outline assessment could evaluate how the timber was detailed to avoid excessive exposure to moisture, therefore increasing the durability of the feature without recourse to frequent on-site chemical treatments.

Generally, the timber elements observed in the assessed landscapes were standard features such as fencing, which almost certainly require little

Figure 4.6 Greenwich Millennium Village. The use of planting along the movement network varies between areas. The route without planting (a) lacks the visual interest and conviviality of the routes that have been planted (b).

bespoke detailing. The failings of these elements against the assessment criteria were therefore due to simple specification decisions, rather than complicated design flaws. A common failing of the timber detailing observed was the omission of a capping rail from the garden fence. At Childwall, fencing was detailed in such a way that it kept the base clear of the soil and a capping rail was used to protect the endgrains from moisture (Figure 4.7). An alternative approach would be to include a gravel board at the base of the detail which can easily be replaced if and when it becomes rotten, without causing damage to the rest of the structure.

The detailed assessment was able to identify whether preservatives had been used in the landscape timbers, and what type. It confirmed that the

Figure 4.7 Childwall. The fencing has been detailed to keep the base of the fence clear of the soil, and with a capping rail to protect the endgrains of the fencing boards from moisture; this may allow the fence to avoid further chemical treatment and extend its life.

timber fencing at Childwall had been impregnated with preservative. Greenwich Millennium Village had used naturally durable, untreated cedar for decking within the communal doorstep spaces; the remaining landscape timbers were non-durable softwoods such as pine and spruce which had been pre-treated with paint, stain or preservative, or a combination of these. All the six sites that were evaluated using the detailed landscape checklist failed against this criterion.

Reducing site runoff through green space provision

The remaining criteria in the Pollution Category dealt with landscape design approaches that consider better management of rainwater in housing schemes, thus reducing pollution through runoff. The assessment makes the assumption that runoff rates can be reduced by increasing the proportion of green space, which will also improve rainwater permeability. One would assume that where housing density increased, the proportion of green space would decrease as more space was taken up by development. However, a number of schemes which had relatively high housing densities, for example 45 and 59 units per hectare, also achieved surprisingly high proportions of embedded green space in excess of 40% total cover. This was achieved by building flats in combination with 'soft' communal doorstep spaces. In contrast, some developments with housing densities as low as 15 units per hectare, which included large private gardens, were only able to achieve similar proportions of embedded green space. This was attributed to the loss of green communal open spaces and 'soft' frontages. The non-private spaces between the lower density houses were filled with extensive shared driveways, parking areas and garages.

In addition to the embedded green space within the housing at the larger sites, the developers had in each case also been responsible for the creation of large areas of open space outside the built-up area. This was particularly true for Greenwich Millennium Village which included the 'Ecology Park'. These areas introduced unsealed spaces which might otherwise be dominated by hard areas and therefore helped to reduce the runoff created by the wider neighbourhood.

Use of reclaimed metal, concrete and bricks and recycled plastic

The use of reclaimed metals, concrete and bricks avoids the production of toxins, as well as conserving energy, non-renewable ores and non-metal minerals, and reducing pressure on landfill. However, their use in the six landscapes which undertook the detailed assessment was extremely rare. Childwall was the only site to be awarded credits for using reclaimed concrete block paviours, slabs and also bricks that were sourced from a brick work's pre-consumer waste stream (they were due to be discarded due to imperfections in colour). The landscape architects on this project had also carried out a detailed survey of the tower blocks that were due for demolition and identified the metalwork panels from the balconies for possible inclusion in the design. Unfortunately, this was not permitted by the Health and Safety Executive, who were concerned about the safety of workers involved in the demolition. None of the sites used reclaimed metals or recycled plastics.

On-site control of chemical applications

In order to help minimise the risk of pollution, it is necessary that those engaged in the application of pesticides and other chemicals on site do so in an appropriate manner. The criterion used to assess this was the inclusion of explicit references to relevant regulations and codes of practice within the landscape implementation and maintenance specifications. Four of the six sites that were evaluated using the detailed checklist, including Greenwich Millennium Village, earned credit as their landscape specification included a workmanship clause requiring the contractor's compliance with the Control of Pesticides Regulations, 1986. At Childwall the use of pesticides was prohibited in the specification and therefore the site was not assessed against this criterion. With regard to reducing the need to use pesticides on site, as well as irrigation, the key factors are the use of plants in a more naturalistic, robust manner (as already discussed) and the specification of plants which are suited to the site conditions.

Nursery practices

The plastics commonly used in the manufacture of plant containers, such as polyethylene and polypropylene, are considered non-toxic and recyclable. However, all virgin plastics are derived from the highly polluting petrochemical industry. The detailed checklist criteria therefore included the use of plants from nurseries which are trying to reduce the amount of virgin plastics used in their containers. The designer can take further action, also recognised in the checklist, by limiting the specification of containers to ornamental shrub species (which are usually only available in this condition) whilst specifying trees and native stock as bare-root or hessian root-balled. For both Childwall and Greenwich Millennium Village, it was not possible to confirm if the plant containers were manufactured from recycled or virgin plastics. Two of the schemes that were assessed using the detailed checklist did, however, earn credit against this criterion for using recycled containers, and in one case the containers were collected by the nursery for reuse. In terms of accumulating additional credit by specifying the plant's root conditions, both Childwall and Greenwich Millennium Village succeeded by specifying root-balled, rather than containerised trees.

As well as misuse on site, the use of pesticides in plant nurseries is a pollution concern; the checklist therefore credited the use of plants from nurseries that are pursuing alternative 'integrated pest management' (IPM) approaches. Only one of the eight nurseries used to supply each of the six sites in the detailed study was found not to use biological controls in their propagation and glass houses. This single exception was a nursery which supplied 30% of the plants to one of the sites. As a result, five of the six sites, including Childwall and Greenwich Millennium Village, gained the full two credits whilst the remaining site gained one credit for using 60–80% of plants grown using biological control methods.

Reduced site runoff through sustainable urban drainage schemes (SuDS)

As well as having benefits for site water management, the literature review suggested that fully successful SuDS also have amenity benefits. The landscape assessment therefore credited the use of SuDS for water management purposes, whilst providing further credit where amenity had also been considered.

Only three of the 19 piloted sites used SuDS to reduce site runoff. Childwall used graded quarry tailings as a water-permeable surfacing to form a combined path and infiltration trench along the centre of the scheme. Of the two remaining schemes, one had used soakaways to return the runoff from roads and courtyards into the ground and the other incorporated extensive areas of permeable paving and a bio-swale conveyance system excavated along the boundary of the scheme to receive any residual site runoff. Only this scheme, which also included wetland planting and green roofs, acquired the additional credit for improving amenity. The remaining sites used a combination of bitmac, concrete slabs and block paviours for surfacing, none of which are effective in reducing site runoff.

The Materials Category

Timber sources and treatments

Under the Materials Category, the detailed checklist included criteria which related to the source and treatments of landscape timbers. First, the checklist investigated the use of material from well-managed forests, through the specification of certified timber, or alternatively the use of reclaimed timber. The literature review suggested that certification provided by the Forest Stewardship Council (FSC) is the most credible available. The timber used in the landscape works for both Childwall and Greenwich Millennium Village was all FSC certified and therefore earned credit. Several of the other schemes which had used timber missed out on this credit by not specifying FSC.

The assessment of paints, stains and preservatives was problematic as a range of products were frequently used at a site, each with their own environmental profiles. At Childwall the stain used on the garden fences was a principally water-borne formulation, though containing resource- and energy-intensive (and potentially toxic) mineral solvent and preservative agents. However, the impregnating preservative used was relatively benign water-borne copper salt solution. At Greenwich Millennium Village no impregnating preservatives were used, although the wood stains did include synthetic resin binders (which are derived from the petrochemical industry) and synthetic inorganic mineral pigments (which are based on limited mineral reserves). Both of the sites received half of the available credits. Several of the sites received no credit for their use of pressure-treated timber using chromated copper arsenate (CCA), which has been banned from residential use in North America and is currently under review in Europe.

Reduced-impact metal elements

Clearly reclaimed material is the most environmentally desirable option with regard to metal. However, if this approach has not been taken, there are less harmful specifications which may be regarded as the 'next best' alternative. The best option may be stainless steel, which is manufactured from recycled steel (therefore avoiding the depletion of ore, the very high embodied energy associated with iron smelting and the transport energy used to import iron from as far away as Australia) and does not require a galvanising coating. Where metals had been specified, all the sites had used zinc-galvanised steel, rather than stainless steel products, and consequently no credits were awarded.

Use of reclaimed or recycled stone and aggregate

Natural aggregates have relatively low embodied energy, as potentially does natural stone, depending on the method of extraction. Nevertheless, their extraction can cause noise, dust, loss of habitat and visual amenity, though not toxic pollutants. The substitution of virgin products with a recycled or preferably, where possible, a reclaimed alternative is therefore a more desirable course of action which was credited in the detailed checklist. Childwall and Greenwich Millennium Village were both very effective in accruing credits in this section for their specification of reclaimed aggregates.

At Childwall there was no stone work, but the hardcore used beneath the drives and garden paths was recycled from on-site concrete waste from the demolition of the site's previous buildings and hard standings, and the aggregate laid directly onto formation to form the paths to and around the communal doorstep spaces was reclaimed quarry waste tailings. The only granular material used that was not reclaimed from a pre- or post-consumer waste stream was the aggregate in the ready-mix concrete used to form the foundations of the railing and brick pillar front garden boundaries. The landscape architect had also tried to specify reclaimed concrete beams from the tower blocks for use as trench foundations for the perimeter walls. This did not happen because of the additional time required to isolate and remove the selected beams, which meant that it wasn't cost-effective (there was pressure to demolish and remove the tower blocks as quickly and efficiently as possible).

At Greenwich Millennium Village the aggregates used in the concrete elements were, in part, recycled. The concrete setts and slabs were sourced from a manufacturer who used recycled aggregates. The concrete used to form haunching also incorporated recycled aggregates and the hardcore under the non-adopted roads, paths, drives, communal space and yards was all recycled from crushed waste on site. However, the resin-bound gravel and the loose gravel surfacing used in the communal areas were virgin materials, as was the hardcore beneath adopted roads.

At less successful schemes, although concrete surfacing modules containing recycled aggregate were used, the aggregate used in foundations and haunching was virgin material, as was the crushed and rolled stone used as hardcore fill. The use of reclaimed or recycled concrete, brick, stone and aggregate in the landscape works provided the opportunity to accrue substantial credit in the assessment. However, the checklist also provided credit for the total use of virgin materials which have been extracted, processed and supplied by bodies certified for environmental competence through the International Standards Organisation (ISO) 14001 system or preferably the EC's Eco Management and Auditing Scheme (EMAS). Only one of the schemes which had used virgin materials complied with this standard.

Transport energy

Each site was assessed according to its individual circumstances; the type of transport used to move materials between the sites of extraction, processing and incorporation; and the proximity of alternative materials. For example, it was assumed that due to the broad distribution of nurseries around England, local sourcing of plant materials (i.e. raised and supplied from within the same region as the site) was a realistic target whereas, for example, the more dispersed nature of stainless steel production meant that 'local' was taken as products manufactured in the region of the site, from UK-sourced scrap steel rather than imported feedstock. In order to provide a more accurate picture of the transport energy consumed in relation to each landscape, the distance from the site to the source of constituent raw materials, as well as the final products, was noted. The performance of the six sites using the detailed checklist was again highly variable against these criteria.

Childwall performed very well, as the majority of materials were sourced from within 35 miles of the site. Apart from the use of reclaimed concrete paving and recycled rubble from the site, the reclaimed bricks were sourced from a supplier in St Helens in Cheshire and the clay for them was quarried on Merseyside. The ready-mix concrete was also supplied from St Helens, with the constituent sand and aggregate sourced from local works in Southport and North Wales respectively, though the cement was sourced from Rugby in the West Midlands, some 250 miles from the site. The timber for the fencing was also from a local supplier, who worked timber grown in the UK and Scandinavia. As the vast majority of timber used in UK construction is imported, often from North America and Canada, Scandinavian timber may be seen as the next best thing to UK-grown. All the plants used were sourced from a single nursery in Southport, just 23 miles from the site. Finally, the steel railings were manufactured in Liverpool, but it was not possible to ascertain the original source of the feedstock.

Greenwich Millennium Village also performed well. A good deal of local recycled materials were incorporated into the landscape works, specifically crushed demolition waste used as hardcore and local recycled aggregate and pulverised fuel ash (PFA) used in the concrete to form kerb haunching. However, the loose gravel surfacing incorporated into the doorstep spaces was sourced from North Scotland, some 600 miles from the site, and the aggregates were, in part, from Norway. Although the Norwegian aggregates travelled approximately 750 miles to the site, the majority of the distance was by ship and therefore, per tonne of material, likely to be less transport energy-intensive than the Scottish aggregate, which was transported by road. The planting was sourced from a single nursery, over 100 miles from the site, and some of the timber used in the landscape works was cedar, imported from Canada. Finally, although the metal sculptural pieces and furniture were manufactured locally in Essex, it was not possible to identify the original source of the feedstock.

Hardworks detailing

Many of the schemes in the pilot survey performed badly under this category. There was frequently a poor match between the materials specified and the design form. This often resulted in unnecessary cutting and wastage of materials. At Childwall, however, the use of low-tech surface materials in the communal garden, where crushed waste stone was laid directly onto a compacted formation, was a good example of appropriate detailing (Figure 4.8). The crushed aggregate could easily match the design form and provides appropriate load bearing in this car-free area. It also has the additional benefit of being water permeable.

The detailed landscape checklist also included additional criteria relating to how materials were detailed and their fixing, specifically in relation to aiding reclamation and replacement of materials on decommissioning or damage, and the efficient use of materials.

The reuse of modular walling and surfacing materials can be facilitated by the use of 'soft' lime mortars or sharp sand bedding, rather than 'hard' Ordinary Portland Cement (OPC). Additionally lime mortar has a lower embodied energy than OPC and reabsorbs the CO_2 produced during calcination as it sets (although this is not the case for hydraulic lime mortars with silicate additives). Childwall again performed well under these criteria. The reclaimed concrete slabs and paviours were laid on a sharp sand bed and a hydraulic lime mortar was used to joint the reclaimed brick pillars to the front of the gardens. Geotextile wraps were also used to reduce the required depth of base/sub-base material beneath roads and paving, and to protect

Figure 4.8 Childwall communal garden. Crushed waste stone, gravel or rolled hoggin laid directly onto a compacted formation level provides a cheap, permeable alternative to more labour- and material-intensive solutions like module paving or hot poured surfaces such as bitmac.

the integrity of land drains, extending their working life. Greenwich Millennium Village also performed well. Sharp sand was used to bed concrete slabs in the rear yards, although OPC was used to bed setts and cobbles. At Childwall the use of Allen key fixings (rather than welded joints) for railings, and a close-boarded fencing design where posts, boards, capping and arris rails were bolted or screwed together rather than nailed, would all contribute to aiding efficient maintenance and future reclamation.

Softworks: planting design and establishment

The outline landscape checklist took account of two approaches that reduce the maintenance burden associated with planting. The first was the use of diverse planting that covers the ground quickly with leaves, stems and roots, thus reducing opportunities for unwanted plants, whilst simultaneously reducing the community's susceptibility to disease and infestation. This approach to planting was generally absent for most sites. Typically, a more familiar 'amenity horticulture style' was adopted where beds are planted with blocks of single species, usually hardy, small to medium-sized, ornamental shrubs at regular densities of 3–5 per square metre. The most notable exception was the infrastructure planting at Greenwich Millennium Village, where grasses, perennials, trees and shrubs have been used to create diverse, colourful, multi-layered beds (Figure 4.9), and Childwall, where there was evidence of greater complexity of planting within the private gardens and communal space.

Credit was also available for avoiding the inclusion of small grassed areas which require frequent maintenance, and so ideally should either be planted to provide visual interest and habitat or kept large enough to create an amenity resource for the community. Approximately half of the schemes visited, including Greenwich Millennium Village and Childwall, earned this credit through the use of well-integrated planting and hardworks, particularly around the base of boundaries and behind parking spaces (Figure 4.10).

The detailed checklist assessment enabled an evaluation of the extent to which plant selection was well suited to the site conditions, therefore reducing the inputs of fertilisers, pesticides and water throughout the lifetime of the planting, particularly during establishment. At Childwall the plants were selected with regard to the existing site soils and a drainage survey of the site. At Greenwich Millennium Village there was no existing topsoil on the site and the contaminated nature of the existing land meant that topsoil had to be imported; the plant selection was therefore based on the nature of the imported material, as well as the site's microclimate.

The specified size of the plant material was also investigated. Smaller plant material will tend to establish more successfully and grow at a faster

Figure 4.9 At Greenwich Millennium Village perennials, shrubs and whip planting emerge from a ground cover, and though the scheme is still based to a degree on blocks of one species adjacent to another, the boundaries are beginning to blur. The more informal the composition, the more forgiving it will be of individual plant failures.

rate than large stock. Smaller plants will also require fewer resource inputs in the nursery, and less packaging and container material. At Childwall credit was gained for the specification of at least 80% of the containerised shrub stock as small, 3-litre container-grown plants or smaller. Several of the other sites, including Greenwich Millennium Village, had specified larger, 10- to 20-litre specimens and thus failed against this criterion.

Figure 4.10 Small areas or strips of grass often occur where there are 'spaces left over' in the site layout, for example areas behind car parking spaces. These should be avoided as they require frequent maintenance and are a missed opportunity to provide additional visual interest and habitat.

Although the use of small tree stock is, in theory, more sustainable than planting large trees, the detailed checklist recognised that, due to their vulnerability to vandalism, small trees may not always be appropriate in certain situations. The detailed checklist therefore considered whether the size of trees had been matched with their location. Due to very high resource inputs and establishment problems associated with very large trees, the checklist criteria erred towards the specification of 'as small a tree as is reasonable' in a given situation. Although, as already discussed, new tree planting on these sites was generally very infrequent, ironically a common trait amongst the surveyed sites was the specification of relatively large trees for a given situation, and four of the eligible five sites thus failed against this criterion. This assessment may appear a little harsh; designers want to create immediate visual impact with tree planting and are also aware that vanadalised trees will have a negative impact on house buyers and are also costly to replace.

Softworks preparation and implementation

The detailed checklist also assessed the approach taken towards successful plant establishment, including soil preparation, timing and contractual provision of aftercare. Successful establishment is aided by planting or seeding times that coincide with dormancy and generally favourable climatic conditions. Operations outside these periods require greater resource inputs and increased site attendance and transport of contractors. Childwall and Greenwich Millennium Village both received credit for planting woody vegetation between November and March, during dormancy, and for laying turf in later spring. Several sites lost credit against this criterion because planting had occurred during the summer months.

The conservation of site soils, through careful management of topsoil and the avoidance of compacted subsoil, is also crucial to successful plant establishment. Because of heavy contamination and the residential end-use of the site, the existing soils at Greenwich Millennium Village were removed from site and new material imported. At Childwall the existing topsoil underwent phased removal and storage in cordoned-off mounds (no higher than 1 metre) away from working areas, before being replaced. Furthermore, the earthworks contracts at these two sites were undertaken during spring and summer, thereby avoiding the generally wettest time of year, when reworked topsoil and *in situ* subsoil are most vulnerable to compaction. Heavy machinery was also directed over areas that were not to be planted, thereby avoiding unnecessary and most damaging compaction of subsoil. Childwall gained full credit against these criteria, whilst at Greenwich Millennium Village they were 'not assessed' for the reason outlined above.

Environmental profile of materials

The final criterion under the Materials Category relates to the use of landscape materials with a high relative environmental profile which should be for a minimum of 80% of the landscape surfacing and hard boundaries. Given the standard approach to infrastructure provision on all the schemes, and the poor profile of standard vehicular surfacing materials, none of the pilot sites received credit against this criterion. Childwall did, however, receive an 'A' rating for 70% of its boundary and surfacing of private and shared driveways; but this scheme was too small to include the potential impact of the wider infrastructure.

The Water Category

The outline checklist which was used for the 19 pilot sites assessed against only two criteria: the provision of water butts or a water harvesting system for all units, and the use of bark mulch in planting areas.

Approximately half of the sites (including Greenwich Millennium Village and Childwall) appeared to fully consider the use of features that reduce water consumption on the site. However, all sites failed to provide water harvesting systems for all the housing units and approximately 30% of the sites failed to include any water harvesting at all. The inclusion of water butts in private or communal spaces is a simple and inexpensive way to reduce mains water consumption. Unsurprisingly perhaps, virtually all the sites did, however, include the use of bark mulch, which will help in reducing water lost through evaporation from the soil surface.

The Ecology and Land Use Category

The results for ecology and land use were generally disappointing: half of the pilot sites failed this category and more than a quarter received no credits at all. This would suggest that ecological functioning was broadly not considered in the assessed landscape proposals. It should be noted that, during the investigation of the detailed checklist, it became clear that the landscape proposals for the surveyed sites were prepared prior to the publication of the relevant local biodiversity action plans, and reference to these documents by each of the design teams was therefore not possible.

Conservation of existing landscape features

Conservation of existing vegetation and other features of habitat value is the touchstone of an ecologically functioning constructed landscape. The detailed landscape checklist looked to identify what features had existed on the surveyed sites prior to construction, and what measures were taken to incorporate them into the landscape masterplan. Neither Childwall nor Greenwich Millennium Village included an area of ecological value worth retaining and therefore were not assessed against this criterion. The success of conservation at the other sites was mixed. In some cases established boundary planting and mature trees were retained but there was also evidence of loss of habitat where, for example, the native vegetation along the edge of a stream was removed and replaced with turf. The landscape architect for this site had originally specified wetland planting but this was replaced with mown turf. The reasons for this change were unclear but the landscape architect thought it was possibly to improve ease of maintenance and safety.

Vegetative diversity and connectivity

A number of the larger sites included significant areas of new green space within the layout which should have presented an ideal opportunity to improve the ecological performance of the site. Typically these areas were dominated by closely mown grass, which has limited ecological value, and there was also no attempt to connect them through planting into the housing scheme. Instead, boundaries which could have been formed from planting (which has an 'A' rating in the *Green Guide to Specification*) were typically constructed from hard materials.

The smaller sites were similarly bereft of connecting green features where they had missed an opportunity to utilise hedges, wall or even roof planting to improve diversity of habitat and connectivity. Where new planting had been included, it was frequently small in extent and set within hard surfacing or closely mown lawns. It also tended to be of a single type with little variation in species or structure – predominantly exotic specimen shrubs at standard centres of 500–600 mm, with little or no ground cover and occasional standard or light standard trees. The most notable exceptions were Greenwich Millennium Village, which included an Ecology Park, and Childwall, where less formal plantings of fruiting trees and shrubs, and native shrub mixes have been used in small and fairly isolated areas. The potential of these areas to develop into a habitat resource will depend on how they are managed in future.

Vegetation management

There was generally little evidence of ecologically informed management techniques being used to maintain species and structural diversity at many of the sites. The most notable exception was the Ecology Park at Greenwich Millennium Village which featured meadow management and dead wood piles created from plantation thinnings to increase invertebrate populations. Flexible management regimes can also make an important contribution to improving the habitat value of planting. For example, the simple act of delaying pruning when plants are still laden with berries and fruits can make an important contribution to sustaining wildlife through the winter months.

Conflicting land use

Some sites which did include areas of retained or new planting not only left them unconnected and isolated, but were also laid out so that intense, potentially conflicting land uses were located adjacent to the vegetation. For example, retained trees and hedgerows and new planting were typically squeezed between roads, next to car parks or adjacent to sports pitches and play areas. Whilst planting is a key element of a successful play space and helps to provide a stimulating and educational environment, the vegetation may be subject to frequent trampling and disturbance by children, which will undermine its value as habitat and may be a particular problem where they are the sole areas of planting on the site.

Artificial habitat features

Only two of the pilot sites gained credit for having incorporated artificial habitat features. One of the sites had included bird boxes, whilst the Ecology Park at Greenwich Millennium Village also incorporated bat towers, kingfisher tunnels and tern rafts.

The Health and Well-Being Category

The results from the pilot study and outline checklist suggest that quality of life issues in terms of supporting social sustainability were considered in a significant number of these sites, but not the majority.

Provision of private and communal space

As well as its possible effects on embedded green space cover, the UK Government's policy of increasing housing density has also triggered concerns regarding the resulting provision of private space. Emerging literature suggests that smaller gardens in higher-density residential areas are less likely to support activities that contribute to sustainable urban lifestyles. Furthermore, increased housing density may, in the long term, be associated with poor tree cover.

Part of the problem may be a reduction in the provision of private space in which residents can make their own contribution through tree planting and other sustainable activities supported by the garden. The pilot survey confirmed that increasing density had a significant impact on the provision of private external space and that for schemes with densities in excess of 50 housing units per hectare, it fell below 50 m^2. For some schemes where flats were part of the development, including Greenwich Millennium Village and Childwall, there was no private space provision. Using the outline checklist, all schemes that included flats failed against the assessment criterion of providing a private space for all units.

It has been recognised that in the current climate of increasing housing density, reduction or omission of private space increases the onus on developers to provide well-designed shared residential spaces All the higher-density schemes provided residents with one or more communal doorstep spaces, with the intention that they become surrogate gardens. However, for credit in the assessment, it was not enough that the space was allocated in land use terms alone. For there to be a *de facto* doorstep space worthy of credit, it had to have appropriate visual and functional attributes. The quality of doorstep space on these sites varied considerably, which was also the case with the doorstep spaces provided at some of the lower-density developments.

The communal spaces at Greenwich Millennium Village and Childwall (Figure 4.11) were particularly successful in this respect and featured diverse

Figure 4.11 The communal garden at Childwall has ornamental, as well as functional, planting, lighting and furniture and can be enjoyed by all residents. It is well overlooked and has been designed to encourage a range of community activities such as fruit picking, vegetable growing, recycling and composting, as well as informal socialising.

shrub planting and trees as well as lawns, lighting, seating and good informal surveillance, and as such represented an important community resource. In other sites the doorstep spaces were also well-defined with a strong spatial relationship with at least some of the homes that they served, and variously included seating, gateway features and focal planting. However, the spaces in these schemes were unlikely to provide for children's play and in some cases were so visually sterile and unwelcoming that they provided little evidence of being places for people.

To avoid misleading assessments, the checklist required that at least 60% of all the units within a development had private spaces greater than the appropriate minimum size of $50\,m^2$. However, if the rear gardens backed onto a well-designed communal space (a similar arrangement to that described in the literature as common elsewhere in Europe) a minimum private space provision criterion of $25\,m^2$ was applied. Whilst the assessed sub-area of Greenwich Millennium Village provided well-designed communal space, for which it gained credit, it missed out on providing all the units with a private space and missed providing more than 60% of units with a private space which exceeded the appropriate minimum size of $25\,m^2$ (Figure 4.12).

Garden privacy

To achieve optimal sustainability performance, rear gardens should balance the need for privacy with enabling neighbour interaction, an important aspect of garden use. One simple way of achieving this is to provide a 1.8 or 2 m high privacy screen adjacent to the house, whilst defining the remaining plot boundary with a slightly lower but substantial barrier. This had been achieved through fencing at Greenwich Millennium Village and Childwall which both thus gained credit under this criterion. However, at many of the sites the garden boundary was either too high to provide opportunities for interaction or so insubstantial that it provided no privacy (Figures 4.13, 4.14). Generally speaking, the lack of opportunity for interaction occurred in more 'executive'-style developments, and lack of privacy was an issue in some of the social housing schemes. One site demonstrated the potential advantages of using hedges which the designers felt could either be cut back or allowed to grow, as suits the residents, allowing them to choose the levels of privacy and interaction.

Facilitating children's play in communal spaces

Even when garden sizes are large enough to accommodate young children's play, and the doorstep space is not directly adjacent to all the units it serves,

Figure 4.12 Private gardens at Greenwich Millennium Village backed on to well-designed communal spaces, and therefore the garden size criterion of a minimum of 25 m^2 was applied. Though all the private gardens that were provided met this standard, the flatted units had no private space at all. The scheme therefore gained credit for including communal doorstep spaces, but missed out on credit for providing all the units with a private space, and providing at least 60% of the site's units with private space above the appropriate minimum size.

there are still clearly benefits in providing the opportunity for this activity in communal areas, helping to encourage acquaintance with neighbours and interaction between young children. Of the sites that have included a doorstep area, both Childwall and Greenwich Millennium Village featured small,

147

Figure 4.13 Low, visually permeable boundaries between rear gardens provide no privacy for the residents.

Figure 4.14 Two-metre high 'privacy screens' adjacent to the home, combined with lower fencing for the rest of the plot boundary, provide privacy and the opportunity for interaction. Though closed-board fencing is an excellent means of demarking territory and providing privacy, it may, depending on its location and orientation relative to the wind, cause turbulence in the air flows adjacent to homes.

well-enclosed and well-overlooked doorstep spaces within close proximity to the home (Figure 4.15). None of these spaces included dedicated play equipment, but they did provide a range of landscape structures and elements that could be included in spontaneous play: mounding, sculptures, decks, benches, screens, lawns, paths, lighting and planting. They also provided access to hard smooth surfaces which are not typically available in the garden and can be used for roller blades, bikes and scooters. The provision of traditional play equipment may actually undermine the advantages of doorstep spaces, as they may become a source of unacceptable noise and lead to child/adult conflict.

Figure 4.15 The doorstep spaces at Greenwich Millennium Village are well overlooked and enclosed, and include a number of interesting landscape features for children to explore. The space provides a safe, exciting play resource without the use of play equipment, which can be the source of social problems in such intimately located spaces.

Opportunities for planting and food production

The checklist included credits for including edible plants in either private gardens or communal spaces, providing communal allotment facilities or a suitable growing space within the garden and finally access to composting facilities. Childwall was the only project to plant edibles, which included tarragon, chives, bay, oregano, mint, gooseberry, raspberry, mulberry and loganberry, and an orchard of edible varieties of apple, cherry and plum which were planted in the communal garden. Childwall was also one of only three of the 19 schemes reviewed with the outline checklist to include communal allotment facilities. The majority of the sites did, however, secure credit for including composting facilities which would also gain points under the new Code for Sustainable Homes.

Design cues, labels of care and improving acceptance of ecological plantings

Few of the sites that were assessed incorporated habitat areas that required interpretation or management interventions to make them appear more acceptable. However, the juxtaposition of neat lawns and ornamental

149

planting with informal areas of more spontaneous and functional planting at Childwall and the juxtaposition of minimalist, clean hard structures and willow and alder woodland at Greenwich Millennium Village demonstrated obvious evidence of care and design intention in potentially ecologically valuable landscape areas, and thus earned credit.

Embedded tree cover

The literature suggests that the percentage of a housing area covered by embedded tree canopy, independent of other types of vegetation, has implications for a number of health and well-being issues. More than half of the sites had less than 5% embedded tree canopy cover as provided by the developer (which includes retained and new planting) and thus failed to earn any credit. Approximately one-third of sites gained half a credit for incorporating between 5% and 10% tree cover. This included Childwall, which could not take advantage of mature, established planting on site but which did introduce substantial areas of new tree canopy relative to the site area. Although Greenwich Millennium Village did have significant areas of tree planting which included the communal doorstep spaces, this remained a relatively small percentage of the entire development and therefore did not obtain a credit. Only one site achieved the full credit with a total tree canopy of greater than 10%, which was primarily due to retained mature trees.

What factors encouraged and discouraged residential landscape sustainability?

Of the 19 schemes evaluated using the outline checklist and six schemes that were reassessed using the detailed landscape checklist, only Greenwich Millennium Village and Childwall obtained a 'very good' assessment. With the exception of these two case studies, the evaluation of the landscape frequently did not match the sustainable profile of the housing. Even Greenwich Millennium Village, which achieved top marks under some categories of the landscape checklist, could not replicate its 'excellent' *EcoHomes* assessment. This is perhaps not surprising. The landscape checklist introduces a range of new criteria that are not assessed using *EcoHomes* and were therefore not necessarily a priority for the developer and design team. The following discussion briefly outlines the reasons which may have influenced the sustainable landscape profile of these developments. The discussion draws on information that was gathered from interviews with developers, landscape architects and contractors for each of the six detailed case studies.

These interviews took place following the detailed landscape assessment. They were an opportunity to discuss the final assessment and clarify any areas of ambiguity and, more importantly, to identify what factors influenced the sustainable profile of the development, for good or ill.

Factors which contribute to delivering residential landscape sustainability

Sustainable landscape design brief and the early appointment of a landscape architect

When compared to the other four schemes that were assessed using the detailed checklist, two important factors influenced the successful performances of Greenwich Millennium Village and Childwall: first, the early consideration of landscape sustainability in the design brief, and second, the broad and sustained input of suitably informed, proactive landscape architects. This allowed landscape sustainability to be developed from the initial design stage onwards. Furthermore, the early input of landscape architects gave them the opportunity to enter into a meaningful design dialogue with others, negotiate a suitable landscape budget and develop their brief.

The importance of securing funds at the outset of the project in order to implement the designed landscape cannot be overestimated. Inevitably, unforeseen overspend accumulates throughout projects and, with the landscape works coming at the end of the construction process, this is often accommodated through cuts in the landscape budget. Even Greenwich Millennium Village, and to a lesser extent Childwall, suffered from some adjustment to the landscape budget. For example, at Greenwich Millennium Village, stainless steel, which has a better environmental profile than galvanised steel, was originally specified for the entrance sculptures in the doorstep spaces. However, this was later replaced with galvanised steel as part of a cost-cutting exercise. In those sites where landscape sustainability was not broadly recognised in the brief or where a suitably informed designer was not in place throughout, landscape sustainability was generally poor. This tended to be true for the other four sites, where the focus was solely on meeting an *EcoHomes* rating.

Landscape sustainability was also encouraged through some of the existing practices of developers, designers and contractors. All the landscape architects interviewed included pesticide regulations in their specifications; used site conditions to guide their plant selections and, for example, detailed tree pit preparation to aid plant establishment. However, the initial drivers for these practices are unlikely to be simply a concern for the environment alone. Although landscape softworks may not be covered under the Construction, Design and Management (CDM) regulations, earlier legislation, including regulations relating to control of pesticides and control of substances hazardous to health, means that landscape architects have responsibilities to encourage proper use of chemicals (Control of Pesticides Regulations, 1986; Control of Substances Hazardous to Health Regulations, 2002). Furthermore, with litigation becoming ever more prevalent in the construction industry, efforts to try and ensure good plant establishment are seen as commercially and professionally, as well as environmentally, beneficial.

Factors which may undermine landscape sustainability

The cost and difficulty of sourcing and specifying reclaimed materials

The high cost of reclaimed and other sustainable landscape materials, in terms of both prime cost and time spent sourcing, discouraged landscape sustainability. The majority of recovered demolition and construction waste is recycled, rather than reclaimed. As a result, the demand for reclaimed materials often exceeds supply, reclaimed materials can be expensive and salvage has become a lucrative business. Unsurprisingly, a common symptom of the perceived tension between profit and landscape sustainability was the omission of reclaimed landscape materials. This was mentioned for all the schemes except Childwall which had benefited from a ready, cheap supply of reclaimed materials from the redevelopment's demolition phase.

Where reclaimed materials are not used, the emphasis should be on using relatively benign virgin materials. However, materials such as naturally durable timber were often vetoed on the basis of cost, and specifiers stated that finding the time to access and compile the required advice on green materials and their sources was difficult. The need for sufficient time to source appropriate materials would therefore support their consideration early on in the design process. In a number of cases designers commented that they had substituted less sustainable alternatives because they had not been able to secure sufficient quantities of a reclaimed material and that any further delay in doing so would have implications for the contract schedule.

The influence of social context and tenure

Assumptions regarding the social context and tenure influenced what was considered to be appropriate for the landscape, frequently discouraging landscape sustainability. For example, at a number of the public housing schemes the RSL and design and build contractors assumed that, due to the schemes' social context and public tenure, new planting would be vulnerable to excessive abuse. Furthermore, the funding for these schemes did not provide for plant maintenance by the landlord, nor was it considered appropriate to raise these monies through additional service charges to the residents. Thus frontage planting was seen as an unwanted liability to be passed on directly to the residents or the local authority. As a result, the design and build contractors prioritised plant robustness and low maintenance. Although these are admirable goals, there was often a narrow conception of how to achieve them and mown grass and monoculture shrubs were frequently used.

In some of the private schemes there were similar problems in achieving more sustainable planting designs, although for very different reasons. Generally, the aim of the planting here was to provide ornamentation and generate 'kerb appeal' in order to improve house sales. As a direct consequence, a significant proportion of the plant material was specified in large, resource-intensive sizes to achieve an instant effect, and planting was frequently timed to coincide with the 'final fit out' of completed plots as they went on sale, rather than plant dormancy.

Social context and tenure also influenced the approach to private rear garden planting. At some of the public housing schemes, it was assumed by the developers and designing contractors that the residents would be unwilling to accept maintenance responsibility for garden vegetation. The requirement for Secure by Design certification also discouraged garden hedge planting. For example, at one of the schemes the police architectural liaison officers, who were consulted during certification, had expressed a preference for low wire-mesh fencing, which provides no privacy and has a poor environmental profile. At the private schemes, the principal concern was that providing plants in private rear gardens would impinge on the occupier's opportunities for self-expression, especially where houses were occupied before the first planting season available to the planting contractor.

It should be noted that consultation with residents can help overcome the negative assumptions relating to social context and tenure. Childwall is a public housing scheme in a low-income suburb with significant social problems, but the communal space and private gardens were well equipped with sustainable features, and diversely planted. The majority of the funding for Childwall came from the Liverpool Housing Action Trust (LHAT), who stipulated the residents' involvement in the landscape design. This generated confidence in the developer and his team that their proposals would be accepted and adopted.

Creating space for plants and trees

The extent and structural diversity of planting were frequently undermined by a lack of space, driven by the prioritisation of other elements over vegetation, including house foundations, services and parking spaces. The space required for off-road car parking on the schemes was driven by local planning policy, and some stipulated a relatively high minimum of two spaces per unit, irrespective of housing tenure and type. However, although the RSL developer of one of the schemes considered this unnecessary, the private developers of the family/executive schemes considered it essential if customer expectations were to be met. This finding echoes the outcome of previous work investigating acceptance of reduced parking standards in English housing. This cited work reports that the Government's perceived advocacy of 1.5 spaces per unit has been met with resistance from private housing developers who claimed that this conflicts with customer preference particularly in family and executive schemes (ODPM, 2003a,b).

Although few trees will physically attack foundations (NHBC, 2003; Thompson & Sorvig, 2000), roots can extract moisture and reduce the volume of shrinkable soils (Reynolds, 1979), particularly in areas of low rainfall (NHBC, 2003). In order to receive an NHBC warranty, new housing has to be built with sufficient distance left between trees and foundations, with a view to reducing subsidence risk. The required distances, as set out by the NHBC, depend upon the mature height and water demand of the tree; the shrinkage potential of the soil; local rainfall patterns; and the depth of the foundations (which can be varied). Forbes-Laird (2004), Aldous (1979) and Reynolds (1979) have pointed out that trees are only part of the subsidence problem, with prolonged dry weather being the key factor. Nevertheless, concern about roots and soil shrinkage is affecting how new housing schemes are developed; and this problem is particularly associated with high-density schemes, where limitations on space exacerbate the problem. However, our study found that where housing density increases above 40–50 units per hectare, communal space increases and can sometimes be used by the developer to locate new tree planting. Conversely, some of the lower-density schemes had reduced tree cover because of the omission of front gardens, which were typically paved over to create parking space.

Despite the widespread condemnation of trees for undermining foundations, the case against them may often be overstated (Aldous, 1979; Forbes-Laird, 2004). Certainly, there seemed to be professional tension between the engineers and the landscape architect at one of the sites evaluated using the detailed checklist. The latter charged the NHBC standards with being onerous and the engineers who use them with being conservative. The standards that were contemporaneous with the case sites, as well as the current standards, do nothing to deter this tension, by allowing the 'worst-case scenario' to be assumed (NHBC, 1995, 2003). Engineers can thus assume high-shrinkage soil, low rainfall and the maximum water demand and height for a tree's genus (even though the latter can vary considerably between species) rather than collecting detailed measurements. Furthermore, the National Joint Utilities Group (NJUG), which produces the guidelines on locating utility apparatus in streets, advises that utilities and trees should be kept as far apart as possible (ODPM, 2003b).

Issues related to adoption and maintenance discouraged landscape sustainability

A number of schemes reported that innovative approaches to landscape sustainability that were included in areas of the design intended for adoption by the local highways authority were removed because they did not comply with the conditions for adoption. For example, one of the schemes had included an innovative 'home zone' approach to the street with an unsegregated carriageway which included the provision of a greater number of street trees and shrubs, as well as attractive and innovative surfacing, opportunities for socialising and children's play. The RSL arranged for the home zone to be adopted by the local highways authority. Unfortunately, the conditions of this adoption resulted in the removal of all the key elements from the original concept, including block paving, seating, play areas and trees. Highway adoption was observed to be a barrier to the use of innovative or non-standard materials on several of the sites. As a result, around half of the sites' hard surfacing had to be surfaced with tarmac. Finally, as already noted, on one of the sites which included an existing stream, the adopting water authority vetoed more sustainable planting proposals which were then replaced with mown turf.

Conclusion

This study reveals that even in the absence of assessment tools and guidance, significant strides towards the creation of sustainable residential landscape can be made where there is suitable recognition of its importance and commitment from the outset. It is also clear, however, that in the absence of appropriate guidance and assessment, even where there is a desire to create a more sustainable solution, many schemes are falling short of their potential. This is sometimes attributable to the developer and design team; but it can also be due to issues beyond their control, such as constraints placed on a project by the adopting highway authority.

During this study the feedback we received from developers and designers suggested that an assessment tool, like the Residential Landscape Sustainability Checklist, would have been extremely useful in informing and guiding decision-making with respect to the design and detailing of the landscape. *EcoHomes*, and more recently the new Code for Sustainable Homes, have been extremely influential in promoting sustainable housing design by enabling developers, designers and planning authorities to work towards recognised assessment criteria that will improve the environmental profile of the building. It is hoped that, together with the landscape checklist introduced here, the recently devised Regional Sustainability Checklist for Developments will have a similar impact on improving the sustainability of the residential landscape, by providing planning authorities and developers with assessment tools which give greater attention to landscape issues and how they relate to regional planning and sustainable development policy/objectives.

References

Aldous, T. (1979) Introduction. In: *Trees and Buildings: Complement or Conflict?* T. Aldous (Ed.) London: RIBA Publications.

Control of Pesticides Regulations (1986) SI, 1986/1510.

Control of Substances Hazardous to Health Regulations (2002) SI, 2002/2677.

Forbes-Laird, J. (2004) The root of all evil? *Landscape Design*, May, pp 34–37.

NHBC (1995) *NHBC Standards. Chapter 4.2, Buildings Near Trees.* Amersham: National House Building Council.

NHBC (2003) *NHBC Standards. Chapter 4.2, Buildings Near Trees.* Amersham: National House Building Council.

Office of the Deputy Prime Minister (2003a) *Creating Sustainable Residential Environments: Delivering Planning Policy for Housing: PPG3 Implementation Study.* (online) Available at: www.odpm.gov.uk/stellent/groups/odpm_planning/documents/page/odpm_plan_023007.06.hcsp (accessed 12 March 2004).

Office of the Deputy Prime Minister (2003b) *Better Streets, Better Places: Delivering Sustainable Residential Environments.* (online) Available at: www.odpm.gov.uk/stellent/groups/odpm_planning/documents/page/odpm_plan_023006.hcsp (accessed 12 March 2004).

Reynolds, E.R.C. (1979) Problems of proximity. In: *Trees and Buildings: Complement or Conflict?* T. Aldous (Ed) London: RIBA Publications.

Thompson, J.W. & Sorvig, K. (2000) *Sustainable Landscape Construction: A Guide to Green Building Outdoors.* Washington DC: Island Press.

Appendix

Detailed Residential Landscape Sustainability Checklist

SCHEME DETAILS: . . . .

DATE OF SURVEY: . . . .

1.0 ENERGY CATEGORY

Has the residential landscape been designed to minimise operational energy inputs and emissions of CO_2 to the atmosphere arising from the operation of a home and its services?

1.1 Passive solar gain (3 credits are available)

- The avoidance of potentially overshadowing coniferous planting and landscape structures to the south side of housing units on the site is:

  a) less than 60% of the units (0 credits) ☐   b) 60% to 80% of the units (1 credit) ☐   c) more than 80% of the units (2 credits) ☐   d) N/A ☐

- Do on-site coniferous planting or landscape structures overshadow any homes adjacent to the site?

  a) yes (0 credits) ☐   b) no (1 credit) ☐   c) N/A ☐

Guide to shadow heights at the beginning and end of the heating season. After DTi/Architectural Association (1994)

Latitude 50°–52°; South Wales and South England
flat site: shadow = 3.38 × obstruction height
site tilting 10% towards south: shadow = 2.4 × obstruction height
site tilting 10% towards north: shadow = 5.35 × obstruction height

Latitude >52°; Mid and North Wales, North and Mid England, and Scotland
flat site: shadow = 4.17 × obstruction height
site tilting 10% towards south: shadow = 2.8 × obstruction height
site tilting 10% towards north: shadow = 7.5 × obstruction height

For coniferous trees, the obstruction heights will be based on the mature heights projected for the vegetation in the absence of lopping and thinning.

1.2 Summer shading (3 credits are available)

- The use of landscape vegetation and features to provide shade in high summer for exposed units is:

a) less than 60%
of the units
(0 credits) ☐

b) 60% to 80%
of the units
(1 credit) ☐

c) more than 80%
of the units
(2 credits) ☐

d) N/A ☐

- If the answer above is b) or c), and shade is provided by tree planting, does the species mix of this planting predominantly favour species with late foliation and/or early defoliation times and/or high winter transparency, increasing the period of incident sunlight on walls and roofs in the winter?

a) yes (0 credits) ☐   b) no (1 credit) ☐   c) N/A ☐

Guide to deciduous tree species with late foliation and/or early defoliation times

After Brown & Gillespie (1995)

- Red Maple
- Sugar Maple
- Lime
- Amelanchier
- Beech
- Walnut
- London Plane
- Ash

Guide to deciduous tree species with high bare branch transparency

After BRE (1990a)

- Sycamore
- Silver Maple
- Elm
- Locust
- English Oak

The vegetation considered may be preserved or implemented as part of the site works by the developer. The vegetation could be trees and shrubs, green roofs or climbers/creepers affixed to the external walls of the housing units. The species selection and spacing of the vegetation should avoid potentially excessive shading of houses and open spaces; the assessment will consider the density of tree crowns and frequency of planting centres.

Guide to calculation of heights of new tree planting

Heights used in the calculation should be 60% of those predicted by a reputable nursery. Research has shown that, on average, trees planted within urban situations reach 60% of the size predicted for a nursery tree.

1.3 Wind modification by landscape features (4 credits are available)

- The use of landscape features to mitigate prevailing winds around exposed units has:

a) not been
considered
(0 credits) ☐

b) been partially
considered
(1 credit) ☐

c) been well
considered
(2 credits) ☐

d) N/A ☐

- The use of landscape features to mitigate the chill winds around exposed units has:

  a) not been considered (0 credits) ☐

  b) been partially considered (1 credit) ☐

  c) been well considered (2 credits) ☐

  d) N/A ☐

Guide to landscape design and wind shelter

During the cold season, heat can be conducted to the external skin of the home, where it is then removed by convection. The colder and/or faster the wind against the house, the more effective this process (Brown & Gillespie, 1995). South-westerly winds are the prevailing and fastest flowing in the UK's cold season (BRE, 1990b; Dodd, 1989) whilst winds from the north, north west and north east are the coldest (Barton *et al.*, 1995; BRE, 1990b). Residential landscape design in the UK should consider all these winds (Sustainability Works, 2002). Although wind speeds tend to be slower in built-up areas, such wind will also tend to be more turbulent (BRE, 1990a,b) with a high capacity to carry heat away from a building (Brown & Gillespie, 1995). Landscape boundaries and individual trees and shrubs contribute to the surface roughness and help slow and calm winds (BRE, 1990a), although solid boundaries can increase turbulence (BRE, 1990a). Microclimatic landscape design may also introduce strategic elements into housing which do more than contribute to surface roughness. Windbreaks deflect the flow of air and can be used to protect the edges of a development or can be located at regular intervals throughout a scheme (BRE, 1990a). The optimum permeability for windbreaks is 40–50% void space (Barton *et al.*, 1995; Beazley, 1991; BRE, 1990a; Dodd, 1989) and the most effective zone for sheltering a home is around 7x height of the shelter belt (Barton *et al.*, 1995; Brown & Gillespie, 1995). Climbers creating a layer of still or slow-moving air against the building offer an alternative solution (Dodd, 1989). Though it is desirable to shelter homes from prevailing south-westerlies in winter, these winds are also prevailing in the summer, and as such aid natural ventilation of the home (BRE, 1990a). Relatively open shelter to the south-west will slow the wind, but still allow significant air passage. As an alternative, wall-mounted evergreen climbers on the west elevation of the home will not affect summer wind flow through open windows and doors. Furthermore, through the upturning action of leaves towards the sun, these climbers allow cool air to flow around the outside of the building in the summer. In the winter, these same leaves downturn to the low sun, thus providing the required insulating layer of still air around the home (Johnston & Newton, 1993). Similarly, one of the benefits of a vegetated green roof is insulation of the home during the cold season (Johnston & Newton, 1993; Thompson & Sorvig, 2000).

1.4 External drying space (2 credits are available)

- Has a secure external drying space been provided for all the units?

  a) no (0 credits) ☐   b) yes (2 credits) ☐   c) N/A ☐

Guide to appropriate provision of drying apparatus

After Rao *et al.*, 2000
A minimum of 6 m line for 3+ bed units *or* 3 m for 1 and 2 bed units is required.

Percentage score awarded under the Energy Category carried to collection

Energy references

Barton, H., Davis, G. & Guise, R. (1995) *Sustainable Settlements: A Guide for Planners, Designers and Developers.* Bristol: University of the West of England and the Local Government Board.

Beazley, E. (1991) Sun, shade and shelter near buildings: the forgotten art of planning with microclimate in mind – Part IV. *Landscape Design*, February, pp 46–50.

BRE (1990a) *Climate and Site Development. Part 3: improving microclimate through design.* Digest 350. Garston, Watford: Building Research Establishment.

BRE (1990b) *Climate and Site Development. Part 1: General Climate of the UK.* Digest 350. Garston, Watford: Building Research Establishment.

Brown, R.D. & Gillespie, T.J. (1995) *Microclimatic Landscape Design: Creating Thermal Comfort and Energy Efficiency.* Chichester: John Wiley & Sons.

Department of Trade & Industry/Architectural Association (1994) *Solar Energy and Housing Design: Volume 1, Principles, Objectives and Guidelines.* London: Architectural Association.

Dodd, J. (1989) Greenspace 4: Tempering Cold Winds. *Architects' Journal*, 189(2), pp 61–65.

Johnston, J. & Newton, J. (1993) *Building Green: A Guide to Using Plants on Roofs, Walls and Pavements.* London: London Ecology Unit.

Rao, S., Yates, A., Brownhill, D. & Howard, N. (2000) *EcoHomes: The Environmental Rating for Homes.* Garston, Watford: Building Research Establishment, Centre for Sustainable Construction.

Sustainability Works (2002) *Sustainability Works. The Complete Development Tool for Sustainable Housing.* (online) Available at: www.sustainabilityworks.org.uk.

Thompson, J.W. & Sorvig, K. (2000) *Sustainable Landscape Construction: A Guide to Green Building Outdoors.* Washington DC: Island Press.

2.0 TRANSPORT CATEGORY

Has the residential landscape been designed to include a convenient and convivial transport network?

2.1 Layout of the transport network (7 credits are available)

• Does the pedestrian/cycle network provide direct, convenient access to amenities on/around the site, and link with the existing movement network?

a) no (0 credits) ☐   b) yes (2 credits) ☐   c) N/A ☐

• The perception of safety in relation to the layout of the pedestrian and cycle network is:

a) low (0 credits) ☐   b) moderate (1 credit) ☐   c) high (2 credits) ☐   d) N/A ☐

• Has the road layout been designed to facilitate a 'target maximum mean speed' for vehicles of 20 mph?

a) no (0 credits) ☐   b) yes (2 credits) ☐   c) N/A ☐

• Do the traffic-calming devices used allow for steady vehicle speeds?

a) no (0 credits) ☐   b) yes (1 credit) ☐   c) N/A ☐

Guide to sustainable transport network layout

To provide a convenient pedestrian/cycle network, access to amenities and the existing movement network should be direct, without abrupt junctions/changes in direction (Barton *et al.*, 1995; English Partnerships/Housing Corporation, 2000). Routes should be overlooked by houses (English Partnerships/Housing Corporation, 2000) or kept as short as possible, with the ends intervisible (DoE, 1992). Crossing points must favour pedestrians (Barton *et al.*, 1995; English Partnerships/Housing Corporation, 2000) and traffic should be slowed below 20 mph, by limiting the length of unimpeded road to 40–60 m

(DoE, 1992). The entrance to such areas can be marked (DETR, 1998). Speed humps can slow traffic, but cars may speed between them (Barton *et al.*, 1995). Alternatively, the arrangement of buildings and spaces can calm traffic, without this disadvantage (DTLR/CABE, 2001; English Partnerships/Housing Corporation, 2000).

2.2 Detailed design of the transport network (4 credits are available)

- In terms of its design and management, how successful is the planting along the pedestrian and cycle network, considering microclimate, adsorption of pollution and screening, contributing to perceptions of safety and avoiding nuisance?

| a) | not successful (0 credits) | ☐ | b) | partly successful (1 credit) | ☐ | c) | very successful (2 credits) | ☐ | d) | N/A | ☐ |

(Provide a brief description of the planting around the pedestrian/cycle network in relation to perceptions of safety, nuisance, microclimate and screening in the comment section.)

- In terms of appropriateness of hard detailing and furnishing, how successful is the pedestrian and cycle network?

| a) | not successful (0 credits) | ☐ | b) | partly successful (1 credit) | ☐ | c) | very successful (2 credits) | ☐ | d) | N/A | ☐ |

Guide to sustainable transport network layout

Good lighting is vital to perceived safety on residential routes (CABE, 2005). Pedestrian and cycle routes should be furnished with signage, litter and dog bins (DETR, 2000). Plants can be used to improve the microclimate experienced by pedestrians and cyclists through shade and shelter (Barton *et al.*, 1995). Dunnett & Clayden (2000) have also noted that planting may affect the perceived level of noise from a road, through simply screening the source of the noise (i.e. car's wheels). Furthermore, planting, especially trees, adjacent to roads can improve air quality by filtering noxious exhaust gases such as carbon monoxide and sulphur dioxide, and adsorbing air-borne particulates (Barton *et al.*, 1995; Dunnett & Clayden, 2000). Finally, visual variety and signs of activity are important to perceived safety and conviviality of the movement network (DTLR/CABE, 2001; English Partnerships/Housing Corporation, 2000), both of which can be enhanced through planting and opportunities for residents' own planting adjacent to footways and cycle paths. An assessment of appropriateness of detailing on the pedestrian and cycle network will consider the following (after Barton *et al.*, 1995; DoE, 1992).

Gradients
The pedestrian/cycle network should generally follow site contours. Absolute maxima are 1:12 for pedestrians over very short distances, and 1:14 for cyclists not exceeding 30 m distance. Where greater than 1:12 gradients are unavoidable, it may be a hazard for some ambulant disabled people and if possible, an alternative stepped approach with handrail should be provided.

Widths
A 2-m path is the minimum size to cater for up to 50 dwellings, enabling a single person to pass another with a pram and small child, and allowing for the full range of services to be provided underground. Extra width must be provided for obstructions. Lesser widths can be used along roads serving less than 50 dwellings; a minimum of 1.35 m will allow for electric wheelchairs, and allow pedestrians to pass. A 2-m width can cater for physically unsegregated cycle/pedestrian use in *low cyclist* areas.

For larger numbers of cyclists, the route should be segregated and the overall width should be 3 m (1.5 m each for the cycle path and footpath). At school entrances, and other amenities, all paths should be more than 3 m.

Surfaces

Pedestrians require surface texture to prevent sliding; cyclists prefer very smooth, well-drained pathways without drainage gratings and manhole covers. Also, in high cyclist areas, shared surfaces should be segregated and include clear delineation through a change in materials, clear markings or raised kerbs. Also, the design language used at crossing points must favour pedestrians and cyclists. This may be demonstrated by signage, changes in surfacing materials, planting or lighting. Dropped kerbs may be used, preferably in conjunction with raised platforms across carriageways (English Partnerships/Housing Corporation, 2000).

Many of the measures of sustainable network considerations can be assimilated into an overall concept for shared streets called 'home zones' (Biddulph, 2001). The concept has become well established elsewhere in Europe, and the UK Government has recognised it as a possible way forward in creating safer, more pleasant and ultimately less CO_2 and energy-intensive neighbourhoods (DETR, 2000).

Percentage score under the Transport Category carried to collection

Transport references

Barton, H., Davis, G. & Guise, R. (1995) *Sustainable Settlements: A Guide for Planners, Designers and Developers.* Bristol: University of the West of England and the Local Government Board.

Biddulph, M. (2001) *Home Zones: A Planning and Design Handbook.* Bristol: Policy Press/ Joseph Rowntree Foundation.

CABE (2005) *What Home Buyers Want: Attitudes and Decision Making Among Consumers.* London: Commission for Architecture and the Built Environment.

Department of the Environment (1992) *Design Bulletin 32: Residential Roads and Footpaths, Layout Considerations,* 2nd edn. London: DoE.

Department of Environment, Transport & the Regions (1998) *Places, Streets and Movement: A Companion Guide to Design Bulletin 32: Residential Roads and Footpaths.* London: DETR.

Department of Environment, Transport & the Regions (2000) *Encouraging Walking: Advice to Local Authorities.* London: DETR.

Department for Transport, Local Government & the Regions/CABE (2001) *Better Places to Live by Design: A Companion Guide to PPG 3.* London: DTLR.

Dunnett, N. & Clayden, A. (2000) Resources: the raw materials of landscape. In: *Landscape and Sustainability.* J.F. Benson & M.H. Roe (Eds) London: Spon.

English Partnerships/Housing Corporation (2000) *The Urban Design Compendium.* London: English Partnerships/ Housing Corporation.

3.0 POLLUTION CATEGORY

Do the materials and workmanship specified for the landscape works sever or significantly mitigate potential pollution linkages on site and in the workshop/place of production (excluding CO_2)?

3.1 Contractual obligations (2 credits are available)

* Do the landscape implementation and management specifications provide reference to relevant legislation and codes of practice with relation to the use of chemicals on site?

162   a) no (0 credits) ☐   b) yes (2 credits) ☐   c) N/A ☐

Guidance on contractual obligations

The greatest risk to human and ecosystem health from the use of chemicals in on-site landscape works stems from misuse, i.e. if they are mixed, not diluted, overused, or not applied and handled in accordance with the manufacturers' instructions (Hitchmough, 1994; Simons, 2004; Thompson & Sorvig, 2000). In terms of pollution risk, there seems little evidence against responsible use of modern agrochemicals in the landscape. The approach adopted by most landscape professionals – to use chemicals where they have obvious benefits, but use them responsibly (Kendle *et al.*, 2000) – would seem fundamentally correct. However, in order to remove significant pollution risk in a sustainable landscape project, it is paramount that landscape specifications clearly stipulate that contractors are to be competent and suitably licensed to use the materials specified, and explicitly reference all relevant codes of practice and statutes.

3.2 Timber detailing (4 credits are available)

- Use of chemically untreated naturally durable hardwoods or softwoods/traditionally (non-chemically) treated, non-durable hardwood or softwoods is:

a) less than 60% by volume of the permanent above-ground timber landscape elements (0 credits) ☐	b) 60% to 80% by volume of the permanent above-ground timber landscape elements (1 credit) ☐	c) more than 80% by volume of the permanent above-ground timber landscape elements (2 credits) ☐	d) N/A ☐

Guidance on traditional (non-chemical) treatments for softwoods

Non-chemical, traditional timber treatments for non-durable softwoods that may be undertaken as alternatives to chemical treatments are (after Berge, 2000):

- Self-impregnation of logs
- Boiling timber to clean the cells of fungi
- Burning the outer wood
- Oxidation and exposure to the sun after treatment with elasticity agents.

Guidance on durable hardwoods and softwoods which require no above-ground treatment

After Woolley *et al.* (1997)

- Sweet Chestnut
- Larch
- Yew
- Oak
- Western Red Cedar

- The use of timber detailing that discourages moisture and therefore reduces the likelihood of replacement with treated timber or downstream application of treatments is:

a) less than 60% by volume of the timber landscape elements (0 credits) ☐	b) 60% to 80% by volume of the timber landscape elements (1 credit) ☐	c) more than 80% by volume of the timber landscape elements (2 credits) ☐	d) N/A ☐

Guidance on good timber detailing that encourages longevity

If wood is allowed to become wet and cannot dry out, then even preserved timbers will be vulnerable to fungal and/or insect attack (Woolley *et al.*, 1997). Detailed design which deters moisture uptake is therefore paramount to longevity of exterior timbers, and to reducing the possibility of frequent chemical treatments by home owners. As moisture is most readily absorbed at the end of timbers, i.e. along, rather than across the grain, endgrains must be protected and post ends should not be set in concrete footings which allow ponding (Berge, 2000; Dunnett & Clayden, 2000).

3.3 Reduction of surface runoff (5 credits are available)

- The percentage of the housing area covered by 'embedded green space' – planted/grassed private garden areas, communal doorstep areas, verges, medians, green roofs etc. – is:

  a) low – less than 30% (0 credits) ☐

  b) medium – 30% to 50% (1 credit) ☐

  c) high – more than 50% (2 credits) ☐

Guidance on green space provision and runoff

Through comparing four residential areas in Liverpool, Whitford *et al.* (2001) demonstrated that increased areas of green space within residential areas result in reduced runoff coefficients. The following table demonstrates how the percentage area of green space observed for the four sites in this study have been used as the basis for classifying performance in the landscape checklist.

Site from study by Whitford *et al.* (2001)	Relative runoff	% Green space in residential area (Whitford *et al.*, 2001)	Interpretation in Landscape Checklist, Water Category
1	Low	47%	More than 50% of housing area is 'embedded green space' for maximum credits.
2	Medium	38%	30–50% of housing area is 'embedded green space' for half credits.
3 and 4	High	12–30%	Less than 30% of housing area is 'embedded green space' for no credits.

- Does the development include more extensive areas of unsealed green space, sports pitches, ecology park, neighbourhood park. etc?

  a) no (0 credits) ☐   b) yes (1 credit) ☐   c) N/A ☐

- A sustainable drainage system (SuDS) on the site:

  a) is absent (0 credits)) ☐

  b) considers runoff quantity and quality (1 credit) ☐

  c) considers site amenity as well as runoff quantity and quality (2 credits) ☐

Guidance on reducing site runoff

The major effects of development on hydrology occur through the replacement of vegetation with impermeable surfaces, reducing infiltration into the soil, reducing interception, evaporation/evapotranspiration from vegetative surfaces and thus increasing the surface runoff (Whitford *et al.*, 2001). Together with collecting rainwater for reuse, the most fundamental step in sustainable water management is to minimise the area of impermeable surface on a site (CIRIA, 2000). Nevertheless, as noted by the Scottish Environment Protection Agency (SEPA, 2000), all developments need to be drained to remove excess rainwater. Traditional drainage systems endeavour to remove rainfall from a site as quickly as possible (CIRIA, 2000; Environment Agency, 2003) but this can have a number of impacts, including pollution, flooding and loss of biodiversity and visual amenity. Drainage techniques that avoid these unwanted effects are referred to as sustainable urban drainage systems (SuDS) (Environment Agency, 2003). SuDS should strive to consider quantity and quality of runoff, as well as amenity – water resources, community facilities, education, landscape and habitat value (CIRIA, 2000). In order to deal with residual runoff, source control techniques should first be considered. These include permeable pavements, infiltration trenches and soakaways (CIRIA, 2000). Where these are insufficient to deal with runoff, then the water may require further downstream management. The first step is to deliver any excess runoff to a conveyance system such as swales, filter strips or filter/French drains. The final stage in the water management train, if required, is passive treatment within ponds, basins or wetlands, which receive residual runoff from conveyance systems at either a site or a regional scale.

3.4 Use of reclaimed metal elements (2 credits are available)

- The percentage of metal elements used on the site which are reclaimed is:

a) less than 10% by volume of the metal fencing & structures (0 credits)	b) 10% to 20% by volume of the metal fencing & structures (1 credit)	c) more than 20% by volume of the metal fencing & structures (2 credits)	d) N/A
☐	☐	☐	☐

As outlined in the Materials Category below, one of the principal impacts of newly manufactured metal elements is the production of toxins (such as dioxins). However, the ease of reclaiming metal allows a viable route to having metal structures in the landscape, with all their advantages, whilst avoiding the negative polluting impacts of manufacture and recycling.

> 'Reclaimed materials are probably one of the "greenest" fencing options. Reclamation of materials reduces pressure on virgin resources, has little manufacturing impact, reduces pressure on landfill space, and avoids the energy use and pollution associated with recycling. . . . The only established market for fencing products is for iron and steel fencing . . . there is [also] significant potential for the reclamation of modern steel fencing.'
>
> (Woolley & Kimmins, 2000, p 147)

3.5 Use of recycled plastic elements (excluding nursery containers) (2 credits are available)

- The percentage of plastic elements manufactured from suitable recycled plastic is:

a) less than 60% by volume of the plastic elements (0 credits)	b) 60% to 80% by volume of the plastic elements (1 credit)	c) more than 80% by volume of the plastic elements (2 credits)	d) N/A
☐	☐	☐	☐

Guidance on recycled plastic

Relative to recycling of other materials such as concrete, recycling plastic is a low-energy process and the pollution risk is minimal (Woolley & Kimmins, 2000). There are therefore clear advantages in using recycled plastic over new plastic products, which are derived from the polluting petrochemical industry and have specific problems related to toxin production.

3.6 Use of recycled/reclaimed plastic nursery containers (3 credits are available)

- The specification of the plant material is such that:

a) less than 60% of the containerised plant material is supplied from nurseries which use recycled/ reclaimed plastic pots (0 credits) ☐	b) 60% to 80% of the containerised plant material is supplied from nurseries which use recycled/ reclaimed plastic pots (1 credit) ☐	c) more than 80% of the containerised plant material is supplied from nurseries which use recycled/ reclaimed plastic pots (2 credits) ☐	d) N/A ☐

- Has the specification of container-grown stock been limited to non-native shrubs?

  a) no (0 credits) ☐   b) yes (1 credit) ☐   c) N/A ☐

3.7 Alternative pest controls in the nursery (2 credits are available)

- The use of non-native and native plants that have been grown in nurseries which utilise biolgical pest controls to reduce the intensity of chemical pesticide use is:

a) less than 60% of the plants (0 credits) ☐	b) 60% to 80% of the plants (1 credit) ☐	c) more than 80% of the plants (2 credits) ☐	d) N/A ☐

Guidance on alternative pest controls in the nursery

Pollution of soils, groundwater, surface waters and the air can be caused by the high intensity of horticultural pesticide use, whether under glass or in the field (Dekeyzer, 1996; Molitor, 1998). However, in an approach known as integrated pest management (IPM), biological pest control systems (using beneficial insects, mites and nematodes) combined with optimum hygiene and temperature management can help control pests with much reduced recourse to chemical applications (Dekeyzer, 1996; Dunnett & Clayden, 2000; Dunnett & Hitchmough, 1996; Molitor, 1998).

3.8 Use of reclaimed concrete and brick elements (2 credits are available)

- The percentage of concrete and brick surfacing, foundations and boundary elements that are reclaimed is:

a) less than 10% by volume of the concrete & brick structures (0 credits) ☐	b) 10% to 20% by volume of the concrete & brick structures (1 credit) ☐	c) more than 20% by volume of the concrete & brick structures (2 credits) ☐	d) N/A ☐

Percentage score under the Pollution Category carried to collection

Pollution references

Berge, B. (2000). *Ecology of Building Materials.* London: Architectural Press.

CIRIA (2000) *Sustainable Urban Drainage Systems. A Design Manual for England and Wales.* CIRIA publication C522. London: Construction Industry Research and Information Association.

Dekeyzer, M. (1996) *Factors Influencing the Adoption of Biological Control Technologies in Floriculture Under Glass.* Proceedings of XIII International Symposium on Horticultural Economics. R.G. Brumfield (Ed). pp 67–74.

Dunnett, N. & Clayden, A. (2000) Resources: the raw materials of landscape. In: *Landscape and Sustainability.* J.F. Benson & M.H. Roe (Eds). London: Spon Press.

Dunnett, N. & Hitchmough, J. (1996) Excitement and energy. *Landscape Design*, June, pp 43–46.

Environment Agency (2003) *Sustainable Drainage Systems (SuDS): an Introduction.* Bristol: Environment Agency.

Hitchmough, J.D. (1994) *Urban Landscape Management.* Sydney: Sydney Inkata Press.

Kendle, A.D., Rose, J.E. & Oikawa, J. (2000) *Sustainable landscape management. In: Landscape and Sustainability.* J.F. Benson & M.H. Roe (Eds) London: Spon Press.

Molitor, H.D. (1998) Environmentally sound production in horticulture – the European way. *Journal of the Japanese Society of Horticultural Science*, 67(6), pp 1224–1228.

SEPA (2000) *Sustainable Urban Drainage Systems: Setting the Scene in Scotland.* Stirling: Scottish Environment Protection Agency, Sustainable Urban Drainage Scottish Working Party.

Simons, P. (2004) Can you dig it? In: *Chemical World.* Colour supplement with *The Guardian,* May 22, pp 20–21.

Thompson, J.W. & Sorvig, K. (2000) *Sustainable Landscape Construction: A Guide to Green Building Outdoors.* Washington DC: Island Press.

Whitford, V., Ennos, A.R. & Handley, J.F. (2001) 'City form and natural processes' – indicators for the ecological performance of urban areas and their application to Merseyside, UK. *Landscape and Urban Planning*, 57, pp 91–103.

Woolley, T. & Kimmins, S. (2000) *Green Building Handbook, Volume 2.* London: E. & F.N. Spon.

Woolley, T., Kimmins, S., Harrison, P. & Harrison, R. (1997) *Green Building Handbook.* London: E. & F.N. Spon.

4.0 MATERIALS CATEGORY

Has the residential landscape been designed to use materials that have less impact on the environment over their life cycle?

4.1 Sources of external timber (3 credits are available)

- The use of landscape timber and products which are sourced from suppliers covered by the Forestry Stewardship Council (FSC), or where timber products are manufactured from either pre- or post-consumer waste streams, is:

| a) | less than 60% by volume of the permanent timber landscape elements (0 credits) ☐ | b) | 60% to 80% by volume of the permanent timber landscape elements (1 credit) ☐ | c) | more than 80% by volume of the permanent timber landscape elements (2 credits) ☐ | d) | N/A ☐ |

Guidance on sustainably sourced timber

Only a small proportion of timber production can be described as sustainable, with the majority causing large-scale clear felling, the introduction of fast-growing monoculture and removal of mixed old-growth forests (which cannot be considered renewable in any meaningful sense), as well as a range of further environmental and social impacts (Berge, 2000; Woolley *et al.*, 1997). To be sustainable, timber production must consider the preservation of biological resources of the forest; conserve and manage watershed and soils; recognise local people's rights; and be economically viable (Woolley *et al*, 1997). According to the

167

UK's Association of Environmentally Conscious Builders (AECB), only Forestry Stewardship Council (FSC) certification is credible (AECB, 2003). FSC is an international, independent non-governmental organisation which provides certification to forest owners who require authenticity for their sustainable claims (FSC, 2000). Forests are inspected by FSC-accredited bodies (such as the Soil Association in the UK) against strict environmental, social and economic standards (FSC, 2002). Certification is completed through a chain of custody monitoring system, which tracks the procurement chain (for example, wholesalers, importers, tradesmen) right up to the point at which the timber or derived product becomes available to the end user (FSC, 2002). This ensures that only genuinely FSC-certified material is labelled as such.

4.2 Timber: pre-treatment with paints, stains and preservatives (2 credits are available)

- Are all the paints/stains used on the landscape timbers (except where no treatment/traditional treatment has been used) relatively good environmental performers?

  a) no (0 credits) ☐   b) yes (1 credit) ☐   c) N/A ☐

- Are all the preservatives used on the landscape timbers (except where no treatment/traditional treatment has been used) relatively good environmental performers?

  a) no (0 credits) ☐   b) yes (1 credit) ☐   c) N/A ☐

Guidance on relatively sustainable paints, stains and preservatives

The use of untreated (excepting areas below or indirect contact with the ground) naturally durable hardwoods, sourced from as close to site as possible, is environmentally the best choice for landscape timbers (Woolley & Kimmins, 2000). However, if timber treatments are used, those that include the following constituents have been identified as best environmental performers. For credit, the treatment must have occurred in the factory, which ensures efficacy and minimises pollution risk (Anderson & Howard, 2000).

Solvents
These are used to thin out paints and stains, vaporising from the surface after painting. Most paints and stains use one of two types of solvent: vegetable turpentine, distilled from the sap of coniferous trees or pressed from orange peel, or 'mineral turpentine' (white spirit), distilled from crude oil. Vegetable turpentine is derived from renewable plant sources rather than crude oil and has reduced environmental impacts in relation to primary energy consumption, pollution during production and potential nerve damage caused by vaporising mineral turpentine (Berge, 2000). However, plant-based compounds may be toxic and contribute to photochemical smog (Woolley *et al.*, 1997), hence the inclusion of these substances in the 'materials' rather than the 'pollution' category. Though water-based paints and stains are generally safer for users than solvent-borne paints, having fewer volatile organic compounds (VOCs), they probably use more toxic petrochemicals and therefore cause more pollution during their production (Woolley *et al.*, 1997). However, some specific manufacturers now claim to have created water-miscible paints that use natural methods.
     For credit all the paints and/or stains used on the timber landscape elements will have a vegetable-based, rather than a mineral-based or water-based, solvent (except for specific water-borne specifications that can be shown to have been produced without the use of toxic neutralising agents and preservatives).

Pigments
These can be organic or inorganic. Organic pigments are less durable than their inorganic counterparts (Berge, 2000). There are two types of inorganic pigment: mineral pigment and earth pigment. Most inorganic mineral pigments are now made synthetically and are based on limited or very limited reserves,

and have high associated energy consumption rates and pollution problems, especially cadmium, chrome, zinc, manganese and lead products. Earth pigments can occur ready to use in certain types of earth; they are composed of the decaying products of particular types of stone and have good durability.

For credit all the paints and/or stains used on the timber landscape elements include inorganic earth pigments/naturally derived inorganic mineral pigment rather than synthetic inorganic mineral pigments containing metal salts, or organic pigments with poor durability.

Binders

The principal ingredient of 'natural paints' is linseed oil, which acts as a very stable, durable alternative to synthetic resin binders. Historically, linseed oil has been a traditional paint ingredient, though there is now a modern industry based on considerable investment and research that ensures excellent painting properties. Linseed oil is made by crushing the seeds from the fully renewable crop, flax; it then is blended together with various other natural oils, resins and pigments to produce modern, scientifically tested paints based on natural ingredients (Construction Resources, 2002).

For credit all the paints used on the timber landscape elements use a linseed oil or other natural plant-based binding agent.

Preservatives

Tar-oil preservatives, such as creosote, and oil-borne preservatives such as PCP (pentachlorophenol) have serious associated medical side effects. Solvents vaporise during treatment, and can be released into the wider environment where they are highly mobile and have a high capacity for biological amplification. Creosote can heavily pollute the groundwater and garden (Berge, 2000) and is injurious to many forms of plant life (Woolley *et al.*, 1997). Water-borne salt solutions, particularly those that contain arsenic and chromium, are also potential sources of contamination in a pollution linkage, as they can leach into soils and also have high biological amplification capacities (Berge, 2000). Research suggests that boron is the least harmful of the chemical timber treatments (Woolley *et al.*, 1997). However, it is not suitable for external applications due to its high leaching potential (Thompson & Sorvig, 2000).

For credit all the preservatives used on the timber landscape elements are water borne and include zinc, copper or fluoride (but not boron, chromium or arsenic) compound salts.

4.3 Reduced impact metal elements (2 credits are available)

- Are all the metal elements used in the landscape works (except any that are reclaimed) of a relatively low-impact specification?

    a) no (0 credits) ☐   b) yes (2 credits) ☐   c) N/A ☐

Guidance on reduced impact metal elements

All metals have impacts related to pollution through CO_2 production and toxic by-products of manufacturing processes (Woolley & Kimmins, 2000). Hence the use of 'benign' metal specifications cannot be included in the Pollution Category (reclaimed metal features, which provide the durability, security and visual appeal without the manufacturing impact, are included under the Pollution Category and if used as an alternative will accrue far more credit than any newly manufactured material).

The manufacture of cast iron and steel produce large amounts of CO_2 and produce hormone disrupters – dioxins, heavy metals and acid mists (Woolley & Kimmins, 2000). Similarly zinc used in galvanising has high acid rain and CO_2 production as by-products. Mining of iron ores, zinc and aluminium all have associated impacts related to deforestation through extraction. Stainless steel is an alloy produced from recycled steel, which is not produced from ore anywhere in the world and does not require any protective coatings (Woolley & Kimmins, 2000), but which does use significantly more energy in its production than mild or even galvanised steel (Thompson & Sorvig, 2000).

Occasionally metal chain link or wire is supplied with a polyvinyl chloride (PVC) coating. PVC is produced from vinyl chloride and ethylene dichloride, which are carcinogenic and powerful irritants. Greenpeace is campaigning internationally for an end to industrial chlorine chemistry, including PVC, because of these toxic effects (Thompson & Sorvig, 2000; Woolley & Kimmins, 2000).

The lowest impact (newly manufactured) metal specification is therefore stainless steel, and when used in fencing this should be used as a wire or chain link, without a PVC coating.

4.4 Reduced impact plastic elements (2 credits are available)

- Are all the plastic elements used in the landscape works (except any that are recycled) of a relatively low-impact specification?

  a) no (0 credits) ☐   b) yes (2 credits) ☐   c) N/A ☐

Guidance on reduced-impact plastic elements

Though it has been claimed that toxic chlorine compounds can leach from PVC products (Thompson & Sorvig, 2000) others have claimed that PVC is inert (Woolley & Kimmins, 2000). However, though tightly controlled, because of the use of carcinogenic feeder stock (the vinyl chloride monomer and ethylene dichloride) and the possibility of dioxin release, the manufacture of PVC potentially poses considerable health risks and PVC is not recyclable to any significant degree (Thompson & Sorvig, 2000; Woolley & Kimmins, 2000).

PVC should not be used. Alternative plastics to PVC, which are recyclable and relatively non-toxic, include high-density polyethylene (HDPE).

It should be noted that most plastics, whether produced from non-toxic materials or not, derive from the polluting petrochemical industry.

> *'Drilling muds and waste-water* [from drilling for oil] *can contain heavy metals, caustic soda, barium sulphate, and organics that increase BOD; non-toxic sediments are also a water pollution issue. Benzene and other carcinogens, as well as VOCs* [volatile organic compounds] *SO and NO* [sulphur and nitrogen oxides which combine with water vapour to produce sulphuric and nitric acids] CO_2 *and CO are associated with oil drilling or processing. Oil-related accidents are among the most serious sources of environmental damage. Pipelines and access roads can disrupt habitat if not carefully designed and maintained.'*
>
> (Thompson & Sorvig, 2000, p 298)

4.5 Reduced-impact stone, cement and aggregates (8 credits available)

- The percentage of stone surfacing, features or boundaries which are reclaimed from pre- or post-consumer waste streams is:

  a) less than 10%   b) 10% to 20%   c) more than 20%   d) N/A
      by volume   by volume   by volume
      (0 credits) ☐   (1 credit) ☐   (2 credits) ☐   ☐

- The percentage of concrete surfacing, boundaries, haunching, bedding and foundations (other than that which is reclaimed) that incorporate recycled aggregates is:

  a) less than 60%   b) 60% to 80%   c) more than 80%   d) N/A
      by volume   by volume   by volume
      (0 credits) ☐   (1 credit) ☐   (2 credits) ☐   ☐

- The percentage of aggregates used as infill, and base and surface courses which are recycled from demolition waste or reclaimed from pre- or post-consumer waste streams is:

a) less than 60%   b) 60% to 80%   c) more than 80%   d) N/A

by volume   by volume   by volume

(0 credits) ☐   (1 credit) ☐   (2 credits) ☐   ☐

- Is all of the virgin stone, brick, concrete, cement and aggregates used on the site of a low-impact specification, sourced from UK operators with ISO 14001 accreditation?

a) no (0 credits) ☐   b) yes (1 credit) ☐   c) N/A ☐

OR

- Are all of the virgin stone, brick, concrete, cement and aggregates used on the site of a low-impact specification, from UK operators with EMAS accreditation?

a) no (0 credits) ☐   b) yes (2 credits) ☐   c) N/A ☐

Where there is a mix of masonry materials, some from ISO-accredited operators and some accredited by EMAS, used on site, the EMAS materials can replace ISO 14001 but not vice verse. For 1 credit, 100% of the masonry materials must be accredited by one of these systems, e.g. if 60% of the masonry used is ISO 14001 accredited, the remainder must be EMAS accredited. For both available marks, 100% must be EMAS accredited.

Guidance on sources of stone and aggregates

The main impacts relating to stone and aggregate are the effects of mining, specifically in terms of noise, dust, visual intrusion and loss of amenity, and transport energy for such dense materials (DETR, 2000). The general lack of toxic pollutants related to the winning and processing of these materials is the reason why they are not considered in the Pollution Category. 'Recycled aggregates' includes the substitution of coarse quarried deposits with crushed building rubble and other demolition waste, as well as substituting finer quarried aggregates with lightweight alternatives derived from industrial by-products such as clinker and pulverised fuel ash.

Environmental management systems
ISO 14001, published by the Internation Organisation for Standardisation, establishes a co-ordinated framework of controls to manage environmental protection in an organisation including environmental performance evaluation, life cycle assessment and environmental auditing. To receive accredited status, an organisation must make commitments to legal compliance, pollution prevention and continual improvement. Status is conferred through certification by an external expert body.

The EC Eco-Management and Audit Scheme (EMAS) requires a verified environmental statement that describes raw materials, energy usage, emissions, discharges, wastes and efficiency in recycling, and performance is continuously reviewed.

> *'If ... any trade association is to recommend members to adopt a specifc environmental management standard, Friends of the Earth believes that is should be the EC Eco-Management and Audit Scheme (EMAS). EMAS provides a more credible overall system because unlike ISO 14001 it requires legal compliance as the entry level for certification, places performance improvement explicitly at its core, requires employee involvement and, perhaps most importantly, includes measures requiring public reporting on environmental impact and performance.'*

(Friends of the Earth, 2001, p 8)

4.6 Use of 'local' materials (11 credits are available)

- To what extent has the geographical source of timber been considered in the landscape, with a view to lowering the overall embodied energy of the works?

  a) poorly
  considered
  (0 credits) ☐

  b) partially
  considered
  (2 credits) ☐

  c) well
  considered
  (3 credits) ☐

  d) N/A ☐

- To what extent has the geographical source of plants been considered in the landscape, with a view to lowering the overall embodied energy of the works?

  a) poorly
  considered
  (0 credits) ☐

  b) partially
  considered
  (1 credit) ☐

  c) well
  considered
  (2 credits) ☐

  d) N/A ☐

- To what extent has the geographical source of dense stone, bricks, concrete, cement and aggregates been considered in the landscape, with a view to lowering the overall embodied energy of the works?

  a) poorly
  considered
  (0 credits) ☐

  b) partially
  considered
  (2 credits) ☐

  c) well
  considered
  (3 credits) ☐

  d) N/A ☐

- To what extent has the geographical source of highly processed materials been considered in the landscape, with a view to lowering the overall embodied energy of the works?

  a) poorly
  considered
  (0 credits) ☐

  b) partially
  considered
  (2 credits) ☐

  c) well
  considered
  (3 credits) ☐

  d) N/A ☐

Guidance on 'local' materials

One of the principles of green building generally, and sustainable landscape construction specifically, is to use locally sourced materials (Dunnett & Clayden, 2000; Woolley et al., 1997). Though the embodied energy of construction materials may be calculated on the basis of extraction and processing required in their production (Morel et al., 2001), more usually it also takes transportation into account (Woolley et al., 1997) and therefore local sourcing of materials is seen as one potential route to reduce embodied energy (Howard, 2000). In terms of energy and pollution, the ideal material would be one that has low processing energy, i.e. reclaimed materials or unprocessed natural materials such as timber, and natural stone and aggregates, sourced as close to the development site as possible. For higher-density materials such as aggregates and stone, which are potentially low/moderate energy products if they do not have to travel far, transportation by road can increase the embodied energy by an average of 0.0056 GJ per tonne per mile (Woolley et al., 1997). Furthermore, the environmental effects of mineral extraction can be a source of impacts along the transport routes to sites of use and processing, as well as at the site of extraction. A recent report by the BRE/DTI advocates the use of local construction materials (BRE/DTI, 2003).

It is not possible to supply a universal definition of 'local' materials. For development within or close to major conurbations, it may be possible to source the majority of the materials from within, say, 50 miles of the site. This may not be possible for a development in a more remote area; should we relax the limits for such developments? A BRE report from 2000 highlighted the fact that development pressures and abundance of local minerals are not equally distributed throughout the UK; the South East has particularly heavy pressures on its mineral resources and as a result demand can only be met by extended travel distances for mineral resources (Howard, 2000). The definition of 'local' must also take account of the varying amounts of transport energy used, depending on the mode of transport employed. Recent research and guidance from the United States and Canada have suggested that the energy required to carry a tonne of construction materials by rail or ship is far less than that required to carry a tonne by road for the equivalent distance (Caceres & Richards, 2003; Thompson & Sorvig, 2000; VTPI, 2002).

4.7 Landscape hardworks detailing (11 credits are available)

- Have paving modules been used on site in such a way as to avoid excessive cutting?

  a) no (0 credits) ☐   b) yes (2 credits) ☐   c) N/A ☐

- Have design gradients been used in the design of hard surfacing?

  a) no (0 credits) ☐   b) yes (2 credits) ☐   c) N/A ☐

Guidance on design gradients

> '*This requires the designer to ensure that the design specification is functionally appropriate for the design context. For example, the extent of hard surfacing and materials used should support but not surpass the required level of use.*'
>
> (Dunnett & Clayden, 2000, p 196)

- The use of hydraulic lime mortars with natural or added clay or pozzolanic material in joints and bedding, rather than cement mortars, is:

a) less than 60% by area of the mortared boundaries and surfacing (0 credits)	b) 60% to 80% by area of the mortared boundaries and surfacing (1 credit)	c) more than 80% by area of the mortared boundaries and surfacing (2 credits)	d) N/A
☐	☐	☐	☐

OR

- The use of pure, non-hydraulic lime mortars in joints and bedding, rather than cement mortars, is:

a) less than 60% by area of the mortared boundaries and surfacing (0 credits)	b) 60% to 80% by area of the mortared boundaries and surfacing (2 credits)	c) more than 80% by area of the mortared boundaries and surfacing (3 credits)	d) N/A
☐	☐	☐	☐

Where there is a mix of non-hydraulic lime mortars (NHL) and hydraulic lime (HL) mortars used on site, NHL can replace HL but not vice versa. For example, if 50% of the mortar used is NHL and 40% is HL, 2 credits can be awarded. If only 10% of the mortar is NHL and only 50% is HL, then only 1 credit can be awarded.

Guidance on the benefits of lime mortars

Until the early 20th century, all landscape and garden features used lime mortars. All lime mortars are softer and less brittle than cement mortars, yet are highly durable. On demolition, the softer lime mortar is much easier to remove when reclaiming bricks, slabs, stones or sets, and whilst the production of lime cement involves firing at high temperatures, with associated high energy demands, it is less than for cement kilns (Woolley *et al.*, 1997).

The production of all cements requires the raw limestone or chalk to be burnt in the process of 'calcination', and this process produces large amounts of CO_2 (Berge, 2000; Woolley *et al.*, 1997).

$$CaCO_3 + energy \rightarrow CaO + CO_2 \text{ (calcination)}$$

For the production of non-hydraulic lime mortar calcination is followed by the process of 'slaking', which produces calcium hydroxide. This can then be mixed with sand and water to form mortar putty which reacts and sets in the air (Berge, 2000).

$$CaO + H_2O \rightarrow Ca(OH)_2 \text{ (slaking)}$$
$$Ca(OH)_2 + CO_2 \rightarrow CaCO_3 + H_2O \text{ (setting)}$$

As can be seen from the above, non-hydraulic lime absorbs CO_2 as it sets, offsetting to some extent that produced during calcination (Woolley *et al.*, 1997). In contrast, hydraulic lime mortars and Ordinary Portland Cement (OPC), which are based on mixtures of lime and various amounts of silicate, require water to set during relatively complex reactions. However, these reactions do not absorb the CO_2 produced in calcination at all, in the case of OPC, or to a much lesser degree in the case of hydraulic lime (Woolley *et al.*, 1997).

Production of OPC also releases heavy metals, fluoric compounds and carbon monoxide into the atmosphere (Woolley *et al.*, 1997). This citation also makes reference to concerns regarding the use of hazardous wastes as fuels in the cement industry.

Lime mortar production can also release carbon monoxide and fluoric compounds into the atmosphere, and hence its use cannot be included in the Pollution Category.

- The use of fixings and details to enable reclamation and opportunities for progressive replacement of landscape structures (other than mortared walls/block surfacing) is:

  a) absent (0 credits) ☐   b) limited (1 credit) ☐   c) extensive (2 credits) ☐   d) N/A ☐

Guidance on fixings and details to enable reclamation and opportunities for progressive replacement

The use of fixings that allow failed modules or parts of a structure to be removed and replaced without the replacement of the whole structure is more efficient in terms of waste production. Examples might include the use of bolts and screws rather than nails in timber structures, and the use of allen key fixings rather than welded joints in metal structures.

> *'Screws and bolts can be retained and re-used ur recycled. Use of screw and bolt connections also means that materials they join together can be easily dismantled and re-used.'*
>
> (Berge, 2000, p 389)

- Have geotextiles been used around all soakaways and land drains and between the formation level and sub-bases of all pavements and roads?

  a) no (0 credits) ☐   b) yes (2 credits) ☐   c) N/A ☐

Guidance on further hardworks detailing issues

When used in combination with any layers of granular fill, geotextiles conserve the integrity of the layers by hindering the movement of particles between them, and stop soils from washing into the interstices between particles, reducing permeability. When used between the formation layer of a pavement and the granular base layer, a geotextile prevents the movement of the pavement into a soft or not well-compacted subgrade. Whilst this can be seen as insurance against essentially poor workmanship, the geotextile also strengthens the pavement and reduces the depth of base required. A geotextile between the formation and the base/ sub-base can reduce the depth of this granular course by up to a third (Dunnett & Clayden, 2000).

4.8 Landscape softworks (23 credits are available)

- In order to promote establishment, is the specification of all plant species based on site conditions, including soil character, drainage and microclimate?

  a) no (0 credits) ☐   b) yes (4 credits) ☐   c) N/A ☐

- The use of plantings in reduced maintenance communities that incorporate comprehensive ground cover, species diversity and use of plants in compatible assemblages (not including the highway corridor) is:

  a) less than 60% of newly planted area (0 credits) ☐   b) 60% to 80% of newly planted area (2 credits) ☐   c) more than 80% of newly planted area (4 credits) ☐   d) N/A ☐

- Has planting (outside of the highway corridor) been specified such that plant size, habit and character are appropriate to context, avoiding excessive cutting back and pruning?

  a) no (0 credits) ☐   b) yes (1 credit) ☐   c) N/A ☐

- Are soft treatment of medians, roundabouts, splitters and verges in the highway corridor low maintenance?

  a) no (0 credits) ☐   b) yes (2 credits) ☐   c) N/A ☐

- Have small grassed areas with no amenity value (outside the highway corridor) been avoided?

  a) no (0 credits) ☐   b) yes (2 credits) ☐   c) N/A ☐

Guidance on low-maintenance planting design

Standard planting styles are based on simple compositions, e.g. mown turf and low-diversity shrub mass (Dunnett & Clayden, 2000; Dunnett & Hitchmough, 2004). These are likely to rely on considerable resource inputs (Dunnett & Clayden, 2000). Although any designed landscape which includes vegetation can never be 'no maintenance' (Thompson & Sorvig, 2000), the style of the planting can reduce this burden. The resource inputs for all plantings is greatest during the 'establishment phase' – the time between planting and the fusing of a plant community canopy – and therefore it is advantageous to minimise this period (Hitchmough, 1994). Planting style and habit of individual plant selections can play a part in this. Mono-cultures can establish and fuse quickly, but have serious drawbacks in terms of potential maintenance requirements. Whilst diversity in planting is generally agreed to provide resistance to pests and disease (Dunnett & Clayden, 2000), infestations are likely to be more severe in monoculture plantings (Ard, 1999). By way of contrast, it has been suggested that diverse nature-like planting designs, which are dynamic and accommodate self-regeneration and nutrient cycling, will minimise maintenance requirements (Ard, 1999; Dunnett & Clayden, 2000; Dunnett & Hitchmough, 1996). Once these diverse communities become established, they form a matrix of roots, stems, foliage and flowers which provides protection for its members and resists invasion from outsiders (Thompson, 1997), although such informality is also more able to accommodate the dynamism of plant failures and self-sowing where it does occur (Ard, 1999). Although requiring significant maintenance, closely mown turf is ideal for residential areas where sitting out or informal play is to be accommodated (Beer, 1983). However, patches of grass which are too small to accommodate these activities are relatively expensive to maintain (Beer, 1983; Hitchmough, 1994), are potentially unsightly and their upkeep is not offset by social benefits.

- The specification of tree sizes which balance resource inputs with context is:

| a) | less than 60% of newly planted trees (0 credits) ☐ | b) | 60% to 80% of newly planted trees (1 credit) ☐ | c) | more than 80% of newly planted trees (2 credits) ☐ | d) | N/A ☐ |

Guidance on tree sizes which balance resource inputs with the threat of vandalism

Specification of tree sizes which balance resource inputs and the threat of vandalism in 'high-risk' areas

- Between standard and heavy standard size.

Specification of tree sizes which balance resource inputs and the threat of vandalism in 'low-risk' areas

- Light standard size or smaller, including *seedlings, transplants, whips, feathereds, half standards and extra-light standards.*

Whether an area of landscape works is at 'high risk' or 'low risk' is a reflection of the vulnerability to vandalism. Where the works are 'high risk' both during construction and following handover, steps must be taken to protect that landscape for its own sake, protect the investment of the client and avoid the duplication of environmental impacts through replacement works and materials.

   Though from a resource point of view smaller tree stock is more sustainable – they require less energy and resource input in the nursery, and are more likely to adapt to site conditions than larger trees (Dunnett & Hitchmough, 1996) – they are more vulnerable to vandalism. In 'high-risk' circumstances, steps that increase the initial environmental impact of the specification must be weighed against the potentially greater impact on environmental and social sustainability caused by the compounded impact of replacement and making good works, or even the abandonment of the tree planting. An on-line tree planting guide published by the Tree Council in the UK suggests that semi-mature trees may be required where there is risk of vandalism (Tree Council, 2003) and this is echoed by the similar guidance produced by ENFO, Ireland's public information service on environmental matters, which advocates heavy standard trees in such conditions (ENFO, 2003).

- The percentage of containerised shrub stock in containers of 3 litres or less is:

| a) | less than 60% of the plants (0 credits) ☐ | b) | 60% to 80% of the plants (1 credit) ☐ | c) | more than 80% of the plants (2 credits) ☐ | d) | N/A ☐ |

- The use of plants from nurseries which have a policy of not using peat in growing media where possible, and reduced peat formulations elsewhere, is:

| a) | less than 60% of the plants (0 credits) | ☐ | b) | 60% to 80% of the plants (1 credit) | ☐ | c) | more than 80% of the plants (2 credits) | ☐ | d) | N/A | ☐ |

Guide to certified, peat-free composts

Peat is the dominant raw material for horticultural growing media in Europe (Molitor, 1998). However, the use of horticultural peat is a major threat to the UK's remaining lowland raised peat bogs (Rollins, 2003; Wildlife Trusts, no date) of which only 6000 ha remain (Jowett, 2005).

Unfortunately, peat-free media have suffered from a poor reputation with regard to the quality of associated plant growth (Jowett, 2005). However, in the UK, the Composting Association (TCA) together with the the Waste and Resource Action Programme (WRAP) have now developed Publicly Available Specification 100 (PAS 100) for composted materials. Launched in November 2002 and published by the British Standards Institute, the specification provides minimum requirements for input materials, process of composting and, crucially, the quality of the compost. Media which meet this specification are also entitled to TCA accreditation and can be used as an alternative to peat (The Composting Association/The Waste Resources Action Programme, no date). Accreditation provides a quality assurance for the horticultural industry which may have been lacking in the past. However, total substitution of peat with alternative recycled materials (even those achieving the new standard) is not yet viable for some plants (Jowett, 2005). For example, ericaceous shrubs require lower pH in the growing medium, and may not establish in the currently available peat alternatives (Holmes *et al.*, 2000). However, there are viable peat alternatives, such as green compost and forestry by-products, for many of the sectors of commercial horticulture and where total substitution is not yet viable, there could be reductions in peat use through the use of peat-free dilutants (Holmes *et al.*, 2000).

- The use of plants that have been grown in nurseries which undertake energy usage and waste management audits is:

| a) | less than 60% of the plants (0 credits) | ☐ | b) | 60% to 80% of the plants (1 credit) | ☐ | c) | more than 80% of the plants (2 credits) | ☐ | d) | N/A | ☐ |

- The use of plants that have been grown in nurseries which collect rainwater for irrigation and/or reuse irrigation water is:

| a) | less than 60% of the plants (0 credits) | ☐ | b) | 60% to 80% of the plants (1 credit) | ☐ | c) | more than 80% of the plants (2 credits) | ☐ | d) | N/A | ☐ |

Guidance on sustainable horticultural issues and certification

In addition to the use of peat-free composts, sustainable horticultural techniques that will be considered for accreditation include: waste management; packaging policies; energy audits; the use and reuse of rainwater for irrigation and reuse of non-rainwater irrigation (Dunnett & Clayden, 2000; Dunnett & Hitchmough, 1996; Molitor, 1998).

Certification for the use of all or some of these techniques is currently provided by the MPS – the Floriculture Environmental Project, a Dutch company that undertakes 'green' assessment and certification of horticultural growers (Jenkins, 2001) – and the ADAS-audited British Ornamental Pot Producers accreditation scheme (BOPP) which has recently been expanded to growers of hardy nursery stock

(Sawyer, 2003). Though intended as a general certification scheme for organic husbandry, a small number of UK nurseries have met the accreditation standards of the Soil Association in the UK (Soil Association, 2002a); this standard covers benign pest control, peat-free composts, water management and recycling of waste (Soil Association, 2002b).

4.9 Landscape implementation (16 credits are available)

- Is plant failure on the site greater than 10%?

    a) yes (0 credits) ☐   b) no (2 credits) ☐   c) N/A ☐

- Were all the soft landscape works undertaken in the appropriate seasons: October to May for decidous planting, early or late spring for coniferous planting, late spring or late summer for grassing?

    a) no (0 credits) ☐   b) yes (2 credits) ☐   c) N/A ☐

- Were site soils protected during the construction works, including cordoning off *in situ* soils where appropriate, and advice on topsoil stripping, storage and spreading included within the earthworks contract?

    a) no (0 credits) ☐   b) yes (2 credits) ☐   c) N/A ☐

- Was the earthworks contract programmed to avoid the traditionally wet times of the year, reducing the risk of soil compaction and loss of structure?

    a) no (0 credits) ☐   b) yes (2 credits) ☐   c) N/A ☐

- Was tree pit excavation specified to consider drainage, to help avoid waterlogging?

    a) no (0 credits) ☐   b) yes (2 credits) ☐   c) N/A ☐

- Does the landscape softworks specification refer to proper site storage and handling of plants?

    a) no (0 credits) ☐   b) yes (2 credits) ☐   c) N/A ☐

- Is the implementation contractor also party to a maintenance contract for the softworks, ensuring that he is responsible for softworks defects that occur following practical completion of the contract?

    a) no (0 credits) ☐   b) yes (2 credits) ☐   c) N/A ☐

- Has the development has been registered for the Greenleaf Standard, helping to ensure ongoing commitment to plant health and maintenance?

    a) no (0 credits) ☐   b) yes (2 credits) ☐   c) N/A ☐

Guidance on landscape softworks implementation and plant health

For accreditation, the landscape specification should include reference to the JCLI Plant Handling Code, the landscape industry standard devised by the JCLI and the CPSE (Council for Plant Supply and Establishment).

According to the JCLI Standard Form of Conditions of Contract (2000 revision), if the contractor is responsible for maintenance following practical completion of the works, then they are also responsible for making good any defects that occur during the stipulated defects liability period. On the other hand, if the employer takes responsibility for the upkeep of the works after practical completion, the contractor is relieved of responsibility for any defects that occur after this time. The JCLI's position on the latter situation is:

> 'This is not generally recommended because of the lack of a plant guarantee and due to the difficulty in assessing plant failures at practical completion particularly when practical completion follows just after planting in the dormant season.'

(JCLI, 1998, p 3)

The Greenleaf Standard, which recognises quality in new housing landscapes, is managed by the New Homes Marketing Board and is partly assessed by new homes warranty providers NHBC and Zurich. A development is registered for the award at its inception, though the scheme does not become eligible for a Greenleaf Award until three years after completion, the time judged to be sufficient to assess how a landscape scheme is maturing. In the interim, the developer must display Greenleaf flags on site, communicating their commitment and alerting visitors and residents to the developer's pledge. If at any time it is felt that the developer is not seeing through his commitment, any individual or group can alert the New Homes Marketing Board to this, who will then undertake an independent audit. If the developer is found to be failing in their commitment, the scheme can be struck off and the right to use the award in marketing of that or any other scheme will be withdrawn.

The Greenleaf Standard Pledge includes:

- Succesful incorporation of existing trees, hedgerows, rivers, ponds and other natural features into the new development
- Effectively using new landscaping to enhance the scheme
- Ensuring maintenance of the new works is provided to minimise or eliminate the presence of litter, poorly cared-for planting, and dead and dying vegetation.

4.10 Environmental impact of materials: *Green Guide to Housing Specification* (2 credits are available)

- According to environmental profiles within the BRE's *Green Guide to Housing Specification*, the area of landscape surfacing and hard boundaries within the housing area that achieve an A rating is:

  a)   less than 80% (0 credits) ☐   b)   greater than 80% (2 credits) ☐

Guidance on the *Green Guide to Housing Specification*

The A rating reflects a superior relative environmental profile for the given element according to the BRE Life Cycle Assessment procedure (see Anderson & Howard, 2000).

'A-rated' hard boundaries

- Drystone walling
- Galvanised steel post and wire
- Galvanised wire chainlink fence with steel posts
- Perforated concrete blockwork wall
- Plastic-coated chainlink fence with steel posts

- Pre-treated timber closed-board fencing
- Pre-treated timber palisade or picket fencing
- Pre-treated timber post and panel fencing
- Pre-treated timber post and rail fence
- Pre-treated post-and-trellis fencing

'A-rated' surfacing

- Wood chips over sub-base
- Glass aggregate from waste over sub-base
- Gravel over sub-base

- Bark mulch
- Glass aggregate from waste as mulch
- Low-maintenance planting

- Pretreated softwood timber decking on concrete foundations
- River pebbles

Percentage score under the Materials Category carried to collection

Materials references

AECB (Association of Environmentally Conscious Builders) (2003) *The Big Timber Debate.* (online) Available at: www.aecb.net (accessed 1 June 2003).

Anderson, J. & Howard, N. (2000) *The Green Guide to Housing Specification. An Environmental Profiling System for Building Materials and Components Used in Housing.* Garston, Watford: Building Research Establishment, Centre for Sustainable Construction.

Ard, J. (IPM Associates Inc.) (1999) *Fundamentals of a Low Maintenance, Integrated Pest Management Approach to Landscape Design.* (online) Available at: www.enf.org/~ipma/des-cnsd.html (accessed 19 May 2004).

Beer, A.R. (1983) *The Landscape Architect and Housing Areas.* University of Sheffield, Department of Landscape. Paper LA 11.

Berge, B. (2000) *Ecology of Building Materials.* London: Architectural Press.

BRE/DTI (2003) *Construction Site Transport. The Next Big Thing.* Garston, Watford: Building Research Establishment.

Caceres, J. & Richards, D. (David Suzuki Foundation) (2003) *Greenhouse Gas Reduction Opportunities for the Freight Transport Sector.* (online) Available at: www.davidsuzuki.org (accessed 8 October 2003).

Composting Association/Waste Resources Action Programme (no date) *Introduction to BSI PAS 100. Summary of the BSI Specification for Composted Materials.* Banbury: Waste Resources Action Programme.

Construction Resources (2002) *Britain's First Ecological Builders' Merchant and Building Centre.* (online) Available at: www.constructionresources.com (accessed 1 October 2002).

Department of the Environment, Transport & the Regions (2000) *Mineral Planning Guidance Note 11: Controlling and Mitigating the Environment Effects of Mineral Extraction in England, Consultation Paper.* (online) Available at: www.planning.odpm.gov.uk/consult/mpg11/ draft/01.htm (accessed 16 June 2003).

Dunnett, N. & Clayden, A. (2000) Resources: the raw materials of landscape. In: *Landscape and Sustainability.* J.F. Benson & M.H. Roe (Eds) London: Spon.

Dunnett, N. & Hitchmough, J. (1996) Excitement and energy. *Landscape Design*, June, pp 43–46.

Dunnett, N. & Hitchmough, J. (2004) More than nature. *Landscape Design*, April, pp 28–30.

ENFO (2003) *Tree Planting.* (online) Available at: www.enfo.ie/leaflets/as12.htm (accessed 29 September 2003).

Friends of the Earth (2001) *Raw Deal. The QPA's Response to the Case for an Aggregate Tax. Consultation Response.* (online) Available at: www.foe.co.uk/resource/consultation_responses /raw_deal.html (accessed 16 June 2003).

FSC (2000) *FSC Principles & Criteria for Forest Stewardship. Document 1.2 Revised February 2000.* Powys: Forest Stewardship Council UK Working Group.

FSC (2002) *Forest Stewardship Council UK Working Group. Annual Report, March 2001–February 2002.* Powys: Forest Stewardship Council UK Working Group.

Hitchmough, J.D. (1994) *Urban Landscape Management.* Sydney: Sydney Inkata Press.

Holmes, S., Lightfoot-Brown, S. & Bragg, N. (2000) *Peat Alternatives. A Review of Performance, Future Availability and Sustainability for Commercial Plant Production in the UK.* (online) Available at: www.adas.co.uk/horticulture/ GOVREPORTS/PTALTREV.htm (accessed 29 November 2001).

Howard, N. (2000) *Sustainable Construction: The Data.* BRE Report CR258/99. Garston, Watford: Building Research Establishment, Centre for Sustainable Construction.

JCLI (1998) *JLI Practice Note No. 5 Explanatory Notes Regarding the JCLI Agreement for Landscape Works. December 1998.* London: The Landscape Institute.

Jenkins, A. (2001) Proving green credentials pays dividends. *Horticulture Week.* November 15, p 11.

Jowett, C. (2005) For peat's sake. *Landscape Design*, February, pp 10–14.

Molitor, H.D. (1998) Environmentally sound production in horticulture – the European way. *Journal of the Japanese Society of Horticultural Science*, 67(6), pp 1224–1228.

Morel, J.C., Mesbah, A., Oggero, M. & Walker, P. (2001) *Building houses with local materials: means to drastically reduce the environmental impact of construction.* Building & Environment, 36, pp 1119–1126.

Rollins, J. (2003) Precious peat. *Natural World*, Spring, pp 35–37.

Sawyer, G. (2003) EU standards to cover all growers. *Horticulture Week*, February 6, p 6.

Soil Association (2002a) *UK Organic Producers, Listed by County and Last Name*. Bristol: Soil Association.

Soil Association (2002b) *Soil Association standards for Organic Farming and Production. Revision 14, 2002/2003*. Bristol: Soil Association.

Thompson, J.W. & Sorvig, K. (2000) *Sustainable Landscape Construction: A Guide to Green Building Outdoors*. Washington DC: Island Press.

Thompson, P. (1997) *The Self Sustaining Garden*. London: B.T. Batsford Ltd.

Tree Council (2003) *Tree Planting Guide*. (online) Available at: www.treecouncil.org.uk/info/ packng2.html (accessed 29 September 2003).

Victoria Transport Policy Institute (VTPI) (2002) *Freight Transport Management. Increasing Commercial Vehicle Transport Efficiency*. (online) Available at: www.vtpi.org/tdm/tdm16.html (accessed 8 October 2003).

Wildlife Trusts (no date) *For Peat's Sake*. Public consultation leaflet. Newark: The Wildlife Trusts.

Woolley, T. & Kimmins, S. (2000) *Green Building Handbook, Volume 2*. London: E. & F.N. Spon.

Woolley, T., Kimmins, S., Harrison, P. & Harrison, R. (1997) *Green Building Handbook*. London: E. & F.N. Spon.

5.0 WATER CATEGORY

Does the residential landscape include water harvesting measures and help reduce water consumption on the site?

5.1 Alternative sources of water (2 credits are available)

• Have water butts or another collection device been provided for all the housing units?

   a) no (0 credits) ☐   b) yes (2 credits) ☐

5.2 Mulching (2 credits are available)

• Have all the planting beds received a covering of mulch?

   a) no (0 credits) ☐   b) yes (2 credits) ☐

Guidance on reduced domestic water consumption

The UK's water consumption has risen by 70% over the last 30 years (Rao *et al.*, 2000). In many regions water is abstracted unsustainably and aquifers are being steadily depleted (Howard, 2000). Unfortunately, climate change modelling predicts that this will be exacerbated by drier summers followed by infrequent but high-intensity rainfall in winter, which runs off rather than percolates into the ground (Howard, 2000). Domestic users should be prioritised in efforts to promote a water-efficient society (Howard, 2000). Using mid-1990s figures, it was estimated that up to 3% of the domestic water consumed by each person, each day in the UK can be attributed to irrigating the garden (Barton *et al.*, 1995). Garden water butts can be connected to the downpipes which transport water from the roof of the house down to the drainage system (CIRIA, 2000). This 'grey water' can then be used to irrigate the garden or for other 'low-grade' uses rather than potable 'white water' from the mains supply. Water butts are a very simple form of water harvesting but other, more sophisticated, systems can be used which store rainwater in the rear garden, before pumping it back into the house for toilet flushing (Barton *et al.*, 1995). Furthermore, water lost from planting areas by soil surface evaporation can be dramatically reduced through the application of a 50 mm depth of bark mulch dressing (Thompson & Sorvig, 2000).

Percentage score under the Water Category carried to collection

Water references

Barton, H., Davis, G. & Guise, R. (1995) *Sustainable Settlements: A Guide for Planners, Designers and Developers*. Bristol: University of the West of England and the Local Government Board.

CIRIA (2000) *Sustainable Urban Drainage Systems. A Design Manual for England and Wales.* CIRIA publication C522. London: Construction Industry Research and Information Association.

Howard, N. (2000) *Sustainable Construction: The Data.* BRE Report CR258/99. Garston, Watford: Building Research Establishment, Centre for Sustainable Construction.

Rao, S., Yates, A., Brownhill, D. & Howard, N. (2000) *EcoHomes: The Environmental Rating for Homes.* Garston, Watford: Building Research Establishment, Centre for Sustainable Construction.

Thompson, J.W. & Sorvig, K. (2000) *Sustainable Landscape Construction: A Guide to Green Building Outdoors.* Washington DC: Island Press.

6.0 LAND USE AND ECOLOGY

Has the residential landscape been designed to conserve or enhance the biological diversity of the site, by protecting and creating habitats and increasing species populations?

6.1 Conservation of existing habitat features (2 credits are available)

- The conservation of landscape features of habitat value or potential value in the masterplan, and strategies for their protection from the construction works, are:

  a) poor (0 credits) ☐   b) fair (1 credit) ☐   c) good (2 credits) ☐   d) N/A ☐

6.2 Enhancing the ecological value of the site through capital works (7 credits are available)

- The use of retained vegetation, new planting or a combination of the two in relation to considering habitat potential, diversity and ecotones is:

  a) poor (0 credits) ☐   b) fair (1 credit) ☐   c) good (2 credits) ☐   d) N/A ☐

- Have artificial habitat features, such as bat boxes and bird boxes, been used?

  a) no (0 credits) ☐   b) yes (1 credit) ☐

Guidance on protecting and enhancing the ecological value of the site

Dunnett & Clayden (2000) introduce a three-stage protocol for site habitat and ecosystem conservation.

- Identify and plan for what already exists; a fundamental objective should be the enrichment of existing ecological capital.
- Restore existing habitats which may be degraded.
- Identify future potential. Create new habitats where land offers potential opportunities. Restore appropriate connections between habitats.

An initial survey of a site's pre-development characteristics should guide new planting proposals but also provide a picture of the site's ecological capital in terms of existing habitat features (Dunnett & Clayden, 2000; Dunnett & Hitchmough, 1996; Thompson & Sorvig, 2000). Once an inventory of these features has been made, steps must be taken to integrate them into the design proposal and management plan, and physically protect them during the construction process. In terms of species biodiversity within a habitat, heterogeneity in relation to vertical and age structure and number of plant species present are key (Jensen *et al.*, 2000). For example, Dunnett & Hitchmough (2004) and Hitchmough *et al.* (2004) have suggested that biodiversity in urban green space is driven by the number of plant species and vegetation layers present. Through a study of Sheffield gardens, Thompson (2004) has identified that tree canopy layers are especially important for supporting invertebrate diversity. Diversity of habitat on a single site can be maximised through the use of extraneous material arising from the construction phase, such as the use of building rubble and subsoil as planting media, and the use of dead or uprooted vegetation to form habitat features (Ruff, 1982). By locating different habitats adjacent to one another, transitional 'ecotones' are created which are especially diverse and may be of high value for wildlife (Gilbert & Anderson, 1998; Ruff, 1982). On the other hand, habitats should be located away from potentially disruptive land uses such as roads and play areas (Collinge, 1996; Jensen *et al.*, 2000). The extent of habitats should be maximised (Barton *et al.*, 1995; Goldstein *et al.*, 1983) as should the degree of irregularity and convolution of their edges which is positively correlated with biodiversity and also nutrient, material and organism exchange between a habitat and its neighbour (Collinge, 1996; Dramstad *et al.*, 1996; Gilbert & Anderson, 1998).

- Has an invasive plant policy been adopted, including removal of existing problematic species, and ensuring planting proposals do not threaten existing habitats on or around the site, through potentially invasive native and non-native species?

  a) no (0 credits) ☐   b) yes (2 credits) ☐

Guidance on invasive plant policy

An invasive plant policy should include strategies for aggresively invasive species present on site prior to construction. Surveys should be undertaken by a qualified consultant ecologist or landscape architect and strategies for treatment and removal should be agreed with the Environment Agency. Failure to do so can lead to prosecution; in 1981, the Wildlife and Countryside Act made it illegal to spread Japanese knotweed, Japanese seaweed, giant kelp and giant hogweed by either direct planting or mismanagement. Excavated soil from areas infested by Japanese knotweed must be disposed of at a licensed landfill site and not reused in construction. When disposing of contaminated soil it is essential that the landfill operator is made aware of the presence of Japanese knotweed, and that the soil is not used for restoration works at the tip site. The Environmental Protection Act 1990 places a duty of care on all waste producers to ensure that any wastes are disposed of safely and that a written description of the wastes, and any specific harmful properties, is provided to the site operator. Other, less obviously aggressive, species can become problematic if they threaten the integrity of existing habitats on and around the site. The planting design for a site should therefore err on the side of caution and avoid using potentially aggressive species adjacent to existing areas of habitat value. Non-native species seen as a priority risk have recently been identified in the DEFRA report *The Non-native Species Review Group Report,* which has received the backing of the RHS and the Garden Centre Association (Seddon, 2003).

- With regard to the use of native plants,on a rural or an ecologically sensitive site, the use of stock that has provenance from within the same region of the site is:

  a) less than 60% of the plants (0 credits) ☐   b) 60% to 80% of the plants (1 credit) ☐   c) more than 80% of the plants (2 credits) ☐   d) N/A ☐

OR

- With regard to the use of native plants on a site with little nature conservation value, is all of the stock provenance from within the UK?

  a) no (0 credits) ☐   b) yes (2 credits) ☐   c) N/A ☐

Guidance on plant provenance

> *'The more local one wishes to specify, the more difficult it is to obtain the right material. As a general rule, for most planting of native species, native origin (i.e. from the UK) can be specified with confidence if no local origin material is available. Again, as with the use of native species, decisions should be based upon the context of the site. There is little point in adhering blindly to the principles of local provenance on, for example, disturbed urban sites with little nature conservation value. Conversely with a sensitive rural site, specification of local provenance should be a standard consideration.'*

(Dunnett & Clayden, 2000, pp 190–191)

6.3 Connectivity of green features across the site (4 credits are available)

- The connectivity of green features on the site is:

  a) poor (0 credits) ☐   b) fair (1 credit) ☐   c) good (2 credits) ☐   d) N/A ☐

The isolation and resulting vulnerability of habitats can be addressed through landscape connectivity, particularly in the forms of wildlife corridors and stepping stones (Dramstad *et al.*, 1996; Spellerberg & Gaywood, 1993). Connectivity between vegetation patches within and around a site is a key principle of landscape ecology and ecological design (Dunnett & Clayden, 2000). Several authors have reported on the importance of connectivity at the site scale and the use of fine-scale connecting features such as lines of trees, fences and hedgerows (Barton *et al.*, 1995; Dramstad *et al.*, 1996; Goldstein *et al.*, 1983; Johnston & Newton, 1993). Fine linear features may also provide an additional habitat resource in their own right (Spellerberg & Gaywood, 1993).

- To improve amenity, has the green network been integrated with the pedestrian and cycle network?

  a) no (0 credits) ☐   b) yes (2 credits) ☐   c) N/A ☐

6.4 Areas of potential habitat value and compatible adjacent land uses (2 credits are available)

- Does the site layout minimise conflict between areas of potential habitat value and harsh or intense land uses?

  a) no (0 credits) ☐   b) yes (2 credits) ☐   c) N/A ☐

6.5 Enhancing the ecological value of the site through management works (2 credits are available)

- To what extent will ecologically informed management techniques be used on the site?

  a) none (0 credits) ☐   b) limited (1 credit) ☐   c) extensive (2 credits) ☐   d) N/A ☐

Guidance on enhancing the ecological value of the site through management works

Just as planting proposals should look to enhance biodiversity through consideration of vertical and age structure, so can management plans. Management proposals should look to encourage succession and vertical structure through thinning and brashing, allowing light and seed to reach the ground. Old and dead wood that is not causing a potential nuisance or hazard should be left *in situ*, or removed and placed on the ground within a range of moisture and light conditions. The management plan should look to encourage traditional techniques, where appropriate, and can include coppicing in woodlands, hay-making in meadows, hedge-laying and reed-cutting and pollarding in wetlands and adjacent to water bodies. Finally, management plans require in-built flexibility. A management regime may patently fail to produce the habitat intended. It is therefore vital that the development is subject to periodic monitoring by a consultant ecologist, and that the plans can be amended according to their professional recommendations.

Percentage score under the Land Use and Ecology Category carried to collection

Land Use and Ecology references

Barton, H., Davis, G. & Guise, R. (1995) *Sustainable Settlements: A Guide for Planners, Designers and Developers.* Bristol: University of the West of England and the Local Government Board.

Collinge, S.K. (1996) Ecological consequences of habitat fragmentation: implications for landscape architecture and planning. *Landscape and Urban Planning*, 36, pp 59–77.

Dramstad, W.E., Olson, J.D. & Forman, R.T.T. (1996) *Landscape Ecology Principles in Landscape Architecture and Land-Use Planning.* Washington DC: Harvard University Graduate School of Design/Island Press/American Society of Landscape Architects.

Dunnett, N. & Clayden, A. (2000) Resources: the raw materials of landscape. In: *Landscape and Sustainability.* J.F. Benson & M.H. Roe (Eds) London: Spon.

Dunnett, N. & Hitchmough, J. (1996) Excitement and energy. *Landscape Design*, June, pp 43–46.

Dunnett, N. & Hitchmough, J. (2004) More than nature. *Landscape Design*, April, pp 28–30.

Gilbert, O. & Anderson, P. (1998) *Habitat Creation and Repair.* Oxford: Oxford University Press.

Goldstein, E.L., Meir, G. & DeGraff, R.M. (1983) Wildlife and greenspace planning in medium scale residential developments. *Urban Ecology*, 7, pp 201–214.

Hitchmough, J.D., Dunnett, N. & Jorgensen, A. (2004) Enriching urban spaces. *Green Places*, April, pp 30–32.

Jensen, M.B., Persson, B., Guldager, S., Reeh, U. & Nilsson, K. (2000) Green structure and sustainability – developing a tool for local planning. *Landscape and Urban Planning*, 52, pp 117–133.

Johnston, J. & Newton, J. (1993) *Building Green: A Guide to Using Plants on Roofs, Walls and Pavements.* London: London Ecology Unit.

Ruff, A. (1982) An ecological approach to landscape design. In: *An Ecological Approach to Urban Landscape Design.* A. Ruff & Tregay, R. (Eds) Department of Town & Country Planning, University of Manchester. Occasional Paper, No. 8. pp 4–12.

Seddon, E. (2003) Report aims to help win war against alien plants. *Horticulture Week*, April 3, p 4.

Spellerberg, I. & Gaywood, M. (1993) Linear landscape features. *Landscape Design*, September, pp 19–21.

Thompson, J.W. & Sorvig, K. (2000) *Sustainable Landscape Construction: A Guide to Green Building Outdoors.* Washington DC: Island Press.

Thompson, K. (2004) BUGS in the borders. *The Garden*, May, pp 346–349.

7.0 HEALTH AND WELL-BEING

Have materials and network layouts within the residential landscape been designed to contribute to the quality of life of the residents and encourage them to produce their own fresh food and recycle nutrients?

7.1 Provision of private and communal spaces (8 credits are available)

• Has a private external space been provided for all units?

   a) no (0 credits) ☐   b) yes (2 credits) ☐

• Has recognisable 'doorstep' communal space(s) been provided within the assessed housing or immediately adjacent?

   a) no (0 credits) ☐   b) yes (2 credits) ☐

- If the answer to the above is No, or if it is Yes but some of the units are removed from the doorstep space that serves them, then an appropriate minimum private garden area is $50\,m^2$.

    If the answer to the above is Yes and all of the units are spatially related to the doorstep space that serves them, then an appropriate minimum private garden area is $25\,m^2$.

- The provision of private spaces with an appropriate area is:

    a) less than 60%
       of the units
       (0 credits) ☐

    b) 60% to 80%
       of the units
       (1 credit) ☐

    c) more than 80%
       of the units
       (2 credits) ☐

    d) N/A ☐

- Have communal doorstep area(s) been designed to successfully incorporate children's play?

    a) no (0 credits) ☐

    b) yes
       (2 credits) ☐

    c) N/A ☐

Guidance on private and communal space provision

Private garden space is highly valued in the UK. In a 2004 survey across the full range of life-stage groups and types of dwellings in England, over three-quarters of respondents preferred to have a private garden space rather than a shared communal space (CABE, 2005). This echoes the findings of an earlier survey by the Scottish Executive where, generally, residents expressed a preference for private space, where they can be self-expressive, over communal space (SE, 2002). Dunnett & Qasim (2002) reviewed a number of studies on the value of private gardens and noted a range of reported social benefits in addition to opportunities for self-expression: safe children's play; health, therapeutic and restorative benefits; and neighbourly interaction and community building. According to Maslow's hierarchy of human needs, as presented by Preece (1991, p 107), gardens thus contribute to meeting the full range of human needs, from the basic requirement of security for the family, through to higher needs of friendship, esteem and self-actualisation.

In contemporary English society, garden size is important and inadequate space is a common motive for moving home (CABE, 2005). Modern housing is often criticised by the public for providing too little garden space (CABE, 2005). To provide sufficient space for children's play, a minimum garden area standard of 20 m^2 has been suggested by Beer (1983), although 40 m^2 minimum has been suggested for gardens which need to reconcile play and other activities such as sitting out, clothes drying, storage and composting (Barton *et al.*, 1995). Findings from studies based in Sheffield suggest that gardens of all sizes are capable of supporting a range of wildlife (Thompson, 2004) and those below 50 m^2 can accommodate vegetable growing, bird boxes and ponds (Dunnett & Qasim, 2002). However, gardens measuring less than 50 m^2 may not be conducive to tree planting by residents (Dunnett & Qasim, 2002). A minimum garden standard of 50 m^2 would therefore appear to provide adequate space for children's play if required – although large families with more than three children may require at least 75 m^2 (Cook, 1968) – as well as provide sufficient space for residents to contribute to a site's tree cover.

The influential standards currently adopted by Essex County Council allow much reduced private space provision of just 25 m^2 in some circumstances (Essex County Council, 1997). The innovative BedZED project in South London has demonstrated that careful building design can provide 25 m^2 of personal space for all flat-dwellers, through the use of roof terraces. Such features can be detailed to be safe for use by families with children (CABE, 2005). However, the Essex standards require such small private space provision to be complemented by adjacent, high-quality communal space. Communal spaces cannot provide the benefits related to personal control (Dunnett & Qasim, 2002) and, as discussed above, are not seen by the public as acceptable substitutes for private space. However, it has been suggested that communal spaces within housing areas provide opportunities for interaction between residents (Frith &

Harrison, 2004; Gilchrist, 2000; Williams, 2005), helping the formation of social contacts (Williams, 2005). Furthermore, residents' ability to see and hear others in 'doorstep' public spaces near their home greatly influences their sense of community (Williams, 2005). It has also been suggested that the inclusion of communal spaces within housing discourages crime and antisocial behaviour (DETR, 2000; McKay, 1998 cited in CABE Space, 2004). This is somewhat at odds with the statement made by Frith & Harrison (2004) that public housing providers dislike communal spaces because of potential antisocial behaviour, and concerns that such spaces can lack the security required for safe children's play (CABE, 2005). There appear to have been few studies exploring residents' attitudes towards, and experiences of, communal residential spaces that might provide clues as to how potential problems can be avoided. However, two recent studies of North American neighbourhoods suggest that the provision and design of communal residential spaces do have implications for residents' sense of community and their willingness to participate in social interaction. Joongsub & Kaplan (2004) found that in two contrasting neighbourhoods in Maryland, provision of public green space was seen as important (relevant to other physical features) in encouraging a sense of community. However, residents within the neighbourhood with doorstep communal spaces reported substantially greater sense of community and gave green space a higher ranking in terms of importance in fostering their sense of community (Joongsub & Kaplan, 2004). In a further study of two contrasting neighbourhoods in California, Williams (2005) found that diverse spaces which provide for a number of uses and enjoy good surveillance were found to experience more social interaction than those which were homogenous in design and had poor surveillance opportunities. These findings echo the communal space design rules and guidance provided by Quayle & Driessen van der Lieck (1997), Barton et al. (1995) and Beer (1983): communal spaces which are small, clearly identified with adjacent housing, easily accessible and richly designed to provide for a range of activities are preferred by residents, and are more likely to foster community sentiment, compared with large, more remote and more homogenous areas. Richly designed communal spaces can accommodate a range of activities; for example, allotment gardening, recycling and children's play (Barton et al., 1995; Dunnett & Qasim, 2002; Hopkins, 2000; Williams, 2005). With regard to children's play, Beer (1983) suggests that doorstep communal spaces are key given the propensity for children of all ages (up to the age of 15) to play in shared space near the home. Gathering of young people in communal spaces near the home can be seen as threatening, but this is often unjust (Gilchrist, 2000). Nevertheless, play equipment may cause conflict and is best avoided. Low-key play opportunities offered by a variety of surfacing, boundaries, level changes and planting can provide stimulating experiential places for very young children, but also places for older children, parents and the elderly to socialise (Beer, 1983). Furthermore, fundamental concerns relating to security, particularly in relation to children's play, and provision of appropriate maintenance within communal spaces need to be addressed before a shared space can be effective (CABE, 2005).

7.2 The residential landscape and health and well-being (12 credits are available)

- Has privacy been successfully incorporated into the design of private external areas?

    a) no (0 credits) ☐   b) yes (2 credits) ☐   c) N/A ☐

Guidance on privacy in private spaces

Where private spaces are provided with little more than post and wire boundaries, residents may not be able or wish to change this, and as a result the space will lack privacy and users will feel uncomfortable and 'watched' (Beer, 1983). Such insubstantial treatments can also result in a garden which is less usable as play space (due to security concerns) and, if the residents choose not to maintain their garden in a manner deemed acceptable by neighbours, can have a negative impact on the visual quality of the area (Beer, 1983). However, tall screening around the whole of the space can also cause problems as people, children and adults alike, appreciate the opportunity to make friends over the fence, and it has been shown that friendship/acquaintance networks are a strong influence on the way in which people settle into their new home (Beer, 1983) and help promote physical and mental health (Gilchrist, 2000).

- Has food-bearing vegetation been provided within the private gardens or communal space(s) by the developer?

  a) no (0 credits) ☐   b) yes (2 credits) ☐   c) N/A ☐

- Have residents been provided with the opportunity to grow their own food in either communal allotment spaces or private gardens (this will require an unplanted area with a minimum 300 mm depth of topsoil)?

  a) no (0 credits) ☐   b) yes (2 credits) ☐   c) N/A ☐

Guidance on urban food production

> 'The basic premise (of the food-producing neighbourhood) *is simple. It is that it is an essential component of any settlement which is striving for sustainability that it should be able to produce as much of its food needs as it can.*'

(Hopkins, 2000, p 199)

One-fifth of UK citizens suffer from food poverty, exacerbated by the out-of-town locations of many cheaper food stores. Further environmental impacts of the food industry are also highly significant, with each phase consuming considerable amounts of energy. The industry relies on fossil fuels and is a major contributor to global warming, and modern agriculture has had a devastating effect on global biodiversity (Hopkins, 2000). Yet back gardens can be highly productive areas of land, which are relatively easy to manage, easy to water and pleasurable to work in (Hopkins, 2000). In high-density developments, allotments can be provided in lieu of larger gardens, or any garden at all. Direct contact with landscape through provision of harvestable food can help encourage personal well-being (Boyes-McLauchlan, 1990).

- Have either communal or individual compost bins been provided for all residents?

  a) no (0 credits) ☐   b) yes (2 credits) ☐   c) N/A ☐

Guidance on composting

Gardens can also provide opportunities for composting (Dunnett & Qasim, 2002) which can enrich the garden soil and contribute to successful plant husbandry, whilst vastly reducing the amount of landfill waste produced by residents (Hopkins, 2000). Garden planting undertaken by residents not only achieves aesthetic and creative goals, but also provides a great deal of diverse, multi-layered plantings which drive invertebrate biodiversity (Thompson, 2004).

- Have design cues and other design interventions been used to improve the acceptance of areas of potential habitat value?

  a) no (0 credits) ☐   b) yes (2 credits) ☐   c) N/A ☐

Guidance on design cues and other design interventions to improve acceptance of vegetation

The relationship between landscape preference and ecological quality is unclear (Williams & Cary, 2002). However, what can be drawn from existing preference studies is that more naturalistic and diverse vegetation can be made more acceptable through a degree of design intervention and management control. One such approach is the use of 'design cues' – visible indicators that show a landscape to be intentional and cared for (Nassauer, 1988). Though care, perception of which is a primary determinant of landscape attractiveness (Nassauer, 1988), is usually associated with keeping landscapes neat and tidy, signage and interpretation can communicate the care being shown to 'messy' plantings by explaining the ecological function of the vegetation, and that the look of the planting is intentional and not due to neglect (Nassauer, 1988). Design cues are important devices in the widening of the public's perception of what cared-for landscapes look like. The literature introduces a number of 'design cues' and other design and management interventions that can demonstrate care for, and broaden the aesthetic appeal of, ecologically informed planting, and which could be used to integrate planting of habitat value into a residential setting.

- Rather than remove unsightly elements such as dead trees, and hide potentially offensive management activities such as clearing, involve and inform the public about the benefits through newsletters, signage and interpretation (Gobster, 1994; Rhode & Kendle, 1994).
- Neatly mown strips or neat post and rail fencing around woodland edges and alongside paths through woodland (Gobster, 1994).
- Neatly mown strips and areas of turf alongside meadows (Nassauer, 1993).
- Use traditional planting design rules of colour composition, massing and structure, and attractive foliage to accentuate the appeal of both exotic and native species, particularly near paths and other focal areas (Henderson *et al.*, 1998; Nassauer, 1993; Schulhof, 1989).
- Juxtapose naturalistic plantings with more formal planting treatments such as a limited number of clipped hedges and shrubs (Henderson *et al.*, 1998).

As noted by Schulhof (1989), such measures have an implicit element of stylisation and compromise ecological accuracy to suit public taste. Gobster (1994) has also described these 'compromised' habitats as garden-like and symbolic of an ecosystem, rather than fully functioning, but nevertheless notes that they still have high species diversity and conservation value. Furthermore, as pointed out by Dunnett & Hitchmough (2004), public acceptance of more ecologically rich vegetation, particularly near the home, is crucial to its success.

- The percentage of embedded tree cover provided by the developer (based on predicted canopy spread for new planting, and observed canopy spread for existing retained trees), contributing to the health and well-being of residents is:

a) less than 5% (0 credits) ☐ b) 5–10% (1 credit) ☐ c) more than 10% (2 credits) ☐

The coverage of trees on a housing site, independent of other types of vegetation, also has implications for the health and well-being of the residents. Smardon (1988) summarises the sociological and community benefits of residential trees as: increased opportunities for play; pleasant noises such as creaking branches and birdsong; helping the formation of cognitive mental maps; and the symbolic presence of nature. Taylor *et al.* (1998) have shown that increased tree cover within the shared residential open spaces of an American urban residential area related to increases in the creativity of children's play and increases in the access that these children had to an adult (defined as an adult being within view) within these spaces. Furthermore, Schroeder & Cannon (1987) have shown that the visual quality of residential streets increases with the number and size of trees (and therefore percentage canopy cover) within front yards and the street. Schroeder & Ruffolo (1996) measured attitudes towards residential street trees by questioning the residents of the streets. Though this study was able to demonstrate that living with residential tree planting is not without its annoyances (leaf litter and other debris, and suckering), the perceived benefits of the trees, in particular their visual qualities, were seen to outweigh the negatives and again, a preference for larger, mature-looking trees was noted. There appears to have been little comparable work in the UK, but research by Hitchmough & Bonugli (1997) analysed the attitudes towards street trees in four treeless streets in Ayr, Scotland. This study suggests that tree planting by house-builders may be most successful; that is, the environmental, social and psychological benefits of trees can be experienced with reduced risk of annoyance, when trees are located away from obvious areas of conflict, such as adjacent to driveways, are overlooked by residents and are specified at a size which is sufficiently robust for its context.

Percentage score under the Health and Well-being Category carried to collection

Health and Well-being references

Barton, H., Davis, G. & Guise, R. (1995) *Sustainable Settlements: A Guide for Planners, Designers and Developers.* Bristol: University of the West of England and the Local Government Board.

Beer, A.R. (1983) *The Landscape Architect and Housing Areas.* University of Sheffield, Department of Landscape. Paper LA 11.

Boyes-McLauchlan, M. (1990) Edible landscapes. *Landscape Design*, October, pp 53–54.

CABE (2005) *What Home Buyers Want: Attitudes and Decision Making Among Consumers.* London: Commission for Architecture and the Built Environment.

CABE Space (2004) *The Value of Public Space.* London: Commission for Architecture and the Built Environment.

Cook, J. (1968) Gardens on housing estates: a survey of user attitudes and behaviour on seven layouts. *Town Planning Review*, 39, pp 217–234.

Department of the Environment, Transport & the Regions (2000) *Regeneration Research Summary: Millennium Villages and Sustainable Communities Final Report* (Number 30) London: DETR.

Dunnett, N. & Hitchmough, J. (2004) More than nature. *Landscape Design*, April, pp 28–30.

Dunnett, N. & Qasim, M. (2002) *Private Gardens, Urban Density and City Form.* Unpublished conference paper. Department of Landscape, University of Sheffield.

Essex County Council (1997) *The Essex Design Guide.* Chelmsford: Essex County Council and Essex Planning Officers Association.

Frith, M. & Harrison, S. (2004) Decent homes, decent spaces. In: *Decent Homes, Decent Spaces: Improving the Green Spaces for Social Housing.* M. Frith & S. Harrison (Eds) London: Neighbourhoods Green, pp 1–5.

Gilchrist, A. (2000) Design for living: the challenge of sustainable communities. In: *Sustainable Communities: The Potential for Eco-Neighbourhoods.* H. Barton (Ed.) London: Earthscan.

Gobster, P.H. (1994) The urban savanna. reuniting ecological preference and function. *Restoration Management Notes*, 12(1), pp 64–71.

Henderson, S.P.B., Perkins, N.H. & Nelischer, M. (1998) Residential lawn alternatives: a study of their distribution, form and structure. *Landscape and Urban Planning*, 42, pp 135–145.

Hitchmough, J.D. & Bonugli, A.M. (1997) Attitudes of residents of a medium sized town in South West Scotland to street trees. *Landscape Research*, 22(3), pp 327–337.

Hopkins, R. (2000) The food producing neighbourhood. In: *Sustainable Communities: The Potential for Eco-Neighbourhoods.* H. Barton (Ed.) London: Earthscan.

Joongsub, K. & Kaplan, R. (2004) Physical and psychological factors in sense of community: new urbanist Kentlands and nearby Orchard Village. *Environment and Behaviour*, 36(3), pp 313–340.

Nassauer, J.I. (1988) The aesthetics of horticulture: neatness as a form of care. *HortScience*, 23(6), pp 973–977.

Nassauer, J.I. (1993) The ecological function and the perception of suburban residential landscapes. In: *Managing Urban and High-Use Recreational Settings.* P.H. Gobster (Ed) St Paul, Minnesota: USDA Forestry Service, North Central Forest Experiment Station, pp 55–65.

Preece, R.A. (1991) *Designs on the Landscape.* London: Belhaven Press.

Quayle, M. & Driessen van der Lieck, T.C. (1997) Growing community: a case for hybrid landscapes. *Landscape and Urban Planning*, 39, pp 99–107.

Rhode, C.L.E. & Kendle, A.D. (1994) *Human Well-Being, Natural Landscapes and Wildlife in Urban Areas. A Review.* English Nature Science Report No 22. Reading: English Nature.

Schroeder, H.W. & Cannon, W.N. (1987) Visual quality of residential streets: both street and yard trees make a difference. *Journal of Arboriculture*, 13(10), pp 236–238.

Schroeder, H.W. & Ruffolo, S.R. (1996) Householder evaluations of street trees in a Chicago suburb. *Journal of Arboriculture*, 22(1), pp 35–43.

Schulhof, R. (1989) Public perceptions of native vegetation. *Restoration and Management Notes*, 7(2), pp 69–72.

Scottish Executive (2002) *Scottish Planning Policy Note 1: The Planning System.* Edinburgh: Scottish Executive.

Smardon, R.C. (1988) Perception and aesthetics of the urban environment: review of the role of vegetation. *Landscape and Urban Planning*, 15, pp 85–106.

Taylor, A.F., Wiley, A. & Kuo, F.E. (1998) Growing up in the inner city: green spaces as places to grow. *Environment and Behaviour*, 30(1), pp 3–27.

Thompson, K. (2004) BUGS in the borders. *The Garden*, May, pp 346–349.

Williams, J. (2005) Designing neighbourhoods for social interaction: the case for cohousing. *Journal of Urban Design*, 10(2), pp 195–227.

Williams, K. & Cary, J. (2002) Landscape preferences, ecological quality, and biodiversity protection. *Environment and Behaviour*, 34(2), pp 257–274.

8.0 COLLECTION

Enter the percentage score achieved for each category and apply the weighting factor to give the weighted category score. Note: combine the performances in the Energy and Transport Categories to calculate a combined percentage score and then a combined weighted category score.

	% SCORE	WEIGHTING FACTOR	WEIGHTED CATEGORY SCORE
1.0 ENERGY CATEGORY		× 0.31	
2.0 TRANSPORT CATEGORY			
3.0 POLLUTION CATEGORY		× 0.16	
4.0 MATERIALS CATEGORY		× 0.16	
5.0 WATER CATEGORY		× 0.05	
6.0 LAND USE & ECOLOGY CATEGORY		× 0.16	
7.0 HEALTH & WELL-BEING CATEGORY		× 0.16	

Now add together all six of the weighted category scores to give an overall score out of 100 – the final percentage score. This can then be compared to the rating benchmarks below, so that an appropriate rating, from Fail to Excellent, can be applied.

FAIL = <36% ☐

PASS = 36% ☐

GOOD = 48% ☐

VERY GOOD = 60% ☐

EXCELLENT = 70% ☐

Index